the concert
register of
herbert von karajan
philharmonic
autocrat
compiled by
john hunt

Philharmonic Autocrat 2
Published by John Hunt.
© 2001 John Hunt
reprinted 2009
ISBN 978-1-901395-09-9

notes on illustrations
with maria callas/*page 104*
with sviatoslav richter/*page 216*

Sole distributors:
Travis & Emery,
17 Cecil Court,
London, WC2N 4EZ,
United Kingdom.
(+44) 20 7 459 2129.
sales@travis-and-emery.com

philharmonic autocrat 2
corrections

*page 24/*9 july 1935
footnote should read "schäferspiel
and prélude were ballet performances"

*page 207/*17 june 1964
"kuchts" should read "kuchta"

*page 301/*31 may 1978
mozart symphony 5 should read
symphony 35

*page 338/*30-31 december 1986
and 1 january 1987
soloist's name battle should be added

acknowledgement
these publications have been made possible by contributions or advance subscriptions from

Stefano Angeloni	Stathis Arfanis
Yoshihiro Asada	E.C. Blake
Charles Brooke	Gordon Buffard
George Burr	Edward Chibas*
George Cobby	Robert Dandois
Dennis Davis	F. De Vilder
Richard Dennis	John Derry
Hans-Peter Ebner*	Henry Fogel*
Andrew Fox	Nobuo Fukumoto
Peter Fülöp	Brian Godfrey
Jean-Pierre Goossens	N. Goulty
Johann Gratz	A.C. Greenburgh
Michael Harris	Tadashi Hasegawa*
Naoya Hirabayashi	Don Hodgman
Martin Holland	Chris Hunt
Bodo Igesz	Rodney Kempster
Detlef Kissmann	Bent Klovborg
John Larsen	Douglas MacIntosh
Elisabeth Legge-Schwarzkopf*	Norman MacDougall
John Mallinson*	Neil Mantle
Carlo Marinelli	Philip Moores
Bruce Morrison	W. Moyle
Alessandro Nava	Alan Newcombe
Hugh Palmer*	Jim Parsons*
Laurence Pateman	James Pearson
Johann Christian Petersen	Linda Perkins
Yves Saillard	Ingo Schwarz
Robin Scott	Tom Scragg*
Yoshihiko Suzuki*	H.A. Van Dijk
Urs Weber*	Nigel Wood
G. Wright	

*indicates life subscriber

AACHEN
STÄDTISCHE  KONZERTE
IM STÄDTISCHEN KONZERTHAUS COMPHAUSBADSTRASSE

Donnerstag, den 27. April 1939, 20 Uhr:

10. Städtisches Konzert

Leiter: Generalmusikdirektor Herbert von Karajan

Solisten: **Helene Fahrni** (Sopran)
Günther Baum (Baß)
Chor: **Der Städtische Gesangverein**
(Chorvorbereitung: Städtischer Chordirektor Wilhelm Pitz)
Orchester: **Das Städtische Orchester**
Orgel: **Dr. Hans Klotz**

Johannes Brahms:
(1833—1897)

Ein deutsches Requiem

für Soli, Chor, Orchester und Orgel (Werk 45)

Philharmonic autocrat 2

This edition, listing for the first time virtually all the public conducting appearances of the twentieth century's most significant classical music figure, is intended as a companion volume to **Philharmonic autocrat 1**, *the discography which was published in the year 2000. Together they replace "Philharmonic autocrat" of 1993 (discography and concert register) and the even earlier discography "From Adam to Webern".*

The main impetus for an update was the fact that when Richard Osborne's biography of Herbert von Karajan appeared in 1999, itself the most significant assessment of the conductor's life and work to have been published so far, Chatto and Windus saw fit not to include the discography which every serious record collector would immediately look for. The two volumes which I present therefore aim to fill that gap and to provide the necesary statistics to supplement Richard's text.

Richard Osborne is of course only one of many researchers and enthusiasts to whom I am indebted for data, be it new information or corrections to the previous editions. First and foremost, those avid archivists – both sadly no longer with us – Gisela Tamsen and Anneliese Eggebrecht must be thanked (I was lucky enough to spend several working sessions with Frau Eggebrecht on sorting Karajan archive material before it was passed to the Karajan Centrum in Vienna to form the basis of their extensive website). And, in alphabetical order, the following friends and colleagues:- Stathis Arfanis, Richard Chlupaty, Lyn Clemo, Gérard Colin, Sigrit Fleiss, Philip Goodman, Michael Gray, Syd Gray, Bill Holland, Roderick Krüsemann, David Lampon, Bruce Morrison, James Pearson, Rosemarie Ripperger, Robin Scott, Angelo Scottini, Malcolm Walker and Nicola Zaccaria.

My first attempt at a listing of Karajan's appearances came up with perhaps 75% of his concert programmes and operas. In the intervening eight years it has been possible, with further careful research, to increase that percentage so that I can now safely say that a good 95% of those performances have been traced. The astounding total of 3540 appearances does include a handful of student performances as a pianist and one or two

EUROPAHAUS, SAARLANDSTR.
GEGENÜBER ANHALTER BAHNHOF

SINFONIEKONZERT
DER STAATSKAPELLE

Sonntag, den 5. Dezember 1943, 10½ Uhr · Außer Abonnement
Montag, den 6. Dezember 1943, 15 Uhr · Außer Abonnement

JOSEPH HAYDN Sinfonie D-dur (Londoner Nr. 2)
- Allegro
- Andante
- Menuett
- Finale

RICHARD WAGNER Vorspiel und Liebestod aus „Tristan und Isolde"

P A U S E

MAX BRUCH Violinkonzert Nr. 1 g-moll, op. 26
- Vorspiel
- Adagio
- Finale

Solist: **SIGFRIED BORRIES**

CARL MARIA VON WEBER Ouvertüre zu „Oberon"

Leitung: **HERBERT VON KARAJAN**

Beim Klingelzeichen zu Beginn des Konzerts werden die Eingänge zum Konzertsaal geschlossen. Vor Beendigung des angefangenen Musikstückes kann niemand mehr Einlaß erlangen.

Beim Einsetzen des Voralarms oder der Luftwarnung, nicht erst beim Alarm selbst, muß das Konzert laut polizeilicher Anordnung sofort beendet werden. Als Zeichen werden während des Spiels alle Saaltüren geöffnet. Die Zuhörer suchen nicht die Luftschutzräume auf, sondern begeben sich auf den Nachhauseweg.

Verantwortlich für den Inhalt: Julius Kapp, Staatsoper · Verlag: Max Beck Verlag, Leipzig · Druck: Erich Thieme, Berlin-Niederschöneweide

concert announcement for a programme which was eventually cancelled (see page 62)

events which may have been of a private nature. I am also aware that a few opera dates may still be missing in the Aachen period from 1935-1942, and would be most happy to hear from readers who can fill in these or any other gaps. And it should be borne in mind that some of the immediate post-war concerts with the various Italian radio orchestras (RAI), researched for me by Angelo Scottini, were studio performances recorded for broadcast at a later date.

The two-column layout is virtually self-explanatory: first column gives city and date of performance, below which orchestra, chorus and vocal or instrumental soloists are named, and second column then lists the works played. In the case of operas, singers of the principal roles are also given in this second column, as are any other comments considered relevant to the performance, such as first appearance with particular orchestras or special circumstances surrounding the event. Special appendices have been added at the end of the book listing operas and choral works, those two categories in which Karajan achieved particular success. Further appendices list the most important instrumental and vocal soloists with whom he worked, from which it can be seen that virtually no significant names of performers active in the period 1930-1990 are missing, except of course for the inevitable triumvirate Horowitz-Rubinstein-Heifetz.

It is assumed that most readers of a volume like this will already be familiar with the broad arc of Karajan's conducting work: apprentice years in provincial Ulm, the Aachen period as youngest Generalmusikdirektor in Germany, the early Berlin period with its associations of which political (and other) commentators have made so much, post-war work with the Vienna Symphony, Vienna Philharmonic, Philharmonia, La Scala and Vienna Staatsoper, and the Berlin Philharmonic and Salzburg Festival years concurrent with his own creation, the Salzburg Easter Festival.

An almost recognisable style of programme building can be observed developing over the years. From around 1960 the standard concert layout of overture, concerto and symphony can be seen to be giving way to something more sophisticated: a major work might be prefaced or more often followed by a second half of lighter proportion (shorter pieces by

GESELLSCHAFT DER MUSIKFREUNDE IN WIEN

BEETHOVEN-ZYKLUS
4. KONZERT

HERBERT VON KARAJAN

Konzertdirektor der Gesellschaft der Musikfreunde in Wien

WIENER FESTWOCHEN
Freitag, 12. Juni 1970

Debussy and Ravel, for example). By the late 1970s one notices Karajan's favourite layout of just two contrasting or complementary pieces: particular predilections were the pairing of a Mozart divertimento or symphony with a large-scale Richard Strauss or other big nineteenth or twentieth century work; or perhaps Stravinsky's Apollo with a Brahms or Beethoven symphony.

It is interesting how pure statistics can help to debunk false assumptions or broad generalisations. Contrary to what we might be told, Karajan conducted a fair amount of twentieth-century music: at the time of his death the Berlin Philharmonic Orchestra listed in one of its tributes no less than thirteen scores of which he had given the world or Berlin premieres: composers' names included Shostakovich, Stravinsky, Henze and Messiaen. Or at the Vienna Staatsoper 1957-1964, where the conductor was accused of pushing aside the established ensemble members in favour of expensive international singers: actual cast lists constantly include names like Anton Dermota, Paul Schöffler, Hilde Rössl-Majdan, Wilma Lipp, Irmgard Seefried and so on!

John Hunt 2001
fax in UK 020 8540 1774
fax from outside UK 0044 20 8540 1774

performances as pianist during childhood and student years

salzburg   mozart rondo k485
27 january 1917

salzburg   mozart fantasia k397
26 january 1918

salzburg   beethoven rondo in c
22 june 1918

salzburg   mozart rondo k382
26 january 1919
mozarteum orchestra
paumgartner

salzburg   liszt three consolations
14 april 1920

salzburg   mozart unspecified piano concerto
9 april 1922
mozarteum orchestra
paumgartner

salzburg   brahms piano sonata 3
6 february 1924

salzburg   liszt piano concerto 1
5 march 1925
mozarteum orchestra
paumgartner

salzburg   franck violin sonata/vladigerov two pieces
17 december 1925   for violin and piano
schmalwieser, violin

salzburg   liszt hungarian rhapsody 12
24 march 1926

salzburg   liszt piano concerto 1
12 may 1926
mozarteum orchestra
müller

performances as pianist during childhood and student years/concluded
salzburg   vladigerov piano concerto 1
25 june 1926
mozarteum orchestra
paumgartner

musical assistant to performances conducted by schalk
salzburg   beethoven fidelio
20, 24 and 28   *lehmann/helletsgruber/kalenberg/gallos/*
august 1928   *mayr/jerger/markhoff*
vienna philharmonic
vienna opera chorus

vienna   rossini guillaume tell overture
17 december 1928   *first conducting appearance*
conservatoire orchestra

salzburg   tchaikovsky symphony 5/mozart piano
22 january 1929   concerto 23/strauss don juan
mozarteum orchestra   *first fully professional conducting appearance*
pessl

ulm   mozart le nozze di figaro
2, 4, 10, 12 and 15   *barthe/rappel/atlasz/monthy/buhlmann*
march 1929
ulm orchestra
and chorus

ulm   *mozart programme*
17 march 1929   eine kleine nachtmusik/arias with piano
matinee performance   accompaniment/piano concerto 20 in 2-piano
ulm orchestra   arrangement without orchestra/kegelstatt trio
members
barthe
monthy
schulmann and
karajan, pianos

ulm   mozart le nozze di figaro
17, 25 and 31   *cast as above*
march 1929
ulm orchestra
and chorus

salzburg
19 april 1929
mozarteum orchestra

strauss salome
wühler-hallauer/karvasy/schmid/forto

salzburg
27 june 1929
mozarteum orchestra
and chorus

lortzing der waffenschmied
günter/schacht/görlich/lubinski/
scheibenbogen; concluding performance
of an opera course at mozarteum conservatory

ulm
9, 14, 18, 20, 22
and 26 october 1929
ulm orchestra
and chorus

verdi rigoletto
barthe/köstler/trojan-regar/carli/monthy

ulm
24 november and
3, 7, 12, 16, 20, 22
and 28 december 1929
ulm orchestra
and chorus

flotow martha
barthe/köstler/trojan-regar/domke/carli

ulm
8 february and
4 and 7 march 1930
ulm orchestra
and chorus

mascagni cavalleria rusticana
flaschner/rappel/köstler/schmid/monthy;
double bill shared with another conductor

ulm
11, 14 and 20
march 1930
ulm orchestra
and chorus

mozart don giovanni
barthe/flaschner/rappel/peltzer/monthy/
domke/schlechter/carli

ulm
18, 21, 23 and 27
march 1930
ulm orchestra
and chorus

weinberger schwanda der dudelsackpfeifer
barthe/köstler/trojan-regar/monthy/carli

Salzburger Stadttheater

KONSERVATORIUM MOZARTEUM IN SALZBURG

Schluß-Aufführung der Opernschule
Herr Prof. **Groß**

DONNERSTAG den 27. JUNI 1929, abends ½8 Uhr,

Der Waffenschmied
Komische Oper in 3 Akten von Albert Lortzing

Musikalische Leitung: HERIBERT KARAJAN

Hans Stadinger, berühmter Waffenschmied und Tierarzt	Ferdinand Görlich
Marie, seine Tochter	Mizzi Güntner
Graf von Liebenau, als Geselle Konrad verkleidet	Josef Scheibenbogen
Georg, sein Knappe	Hans Lubinski
Irmentraut, Wirtschafterin im Hause Stadingers	Else Schacht
Brenner, Gastwirt, Stadingers Schwager	Josef Wagner
Ritter Adelhof	Roman Sporer a. G.
Ein Geselle	Hans Krätz

Die große Pause wird durch rote Lichtzeichen an der Bühnenrampe angezeigt.
Büfett im ersten Stock.

Preise der Plätze:

Orchester-Fauteuils, 1. bis 3. Reihe . . . S 4.—	Logensitze im I. Rang, II. Reihe . . . S 3.—
Parkett-Fauteuils, 4. bis 6. Reihe . . . S 3.—	Theaterlogen . . . S 5.—
Parkett-Fauteuils, 7. bis 8. Reihe . . . S 2.50	II. Rang Balkonsitz, I. Reihe . . . S 3.—
Parkett-Fauteuils, 9. bis 12. Reihe . . . S 2.20	II. Rang Sperrsitz, II. Reihe . . . S 2.—
Parkett-Fauteuils, 13. bis 15. Reihe . . . S 2.—	II. Rang Balkonsitz, I. Reihe Nr. 1—13 S 1.50
Stehparterre . . . S —.80	II. Rang Sperrsitz, III. Reihe . . . S 1.50
Logen im I. Rang Nr. 1—6 . . . S 10.—	II. Rang Sperrsitz, II. Reihe Nr. 1—11 S 1.—
Logen im I. Rang Nr. 7—11 . . . S 12.—	II. Rang Sperrsitz, IV. und V. Reihe . . . S 1.—
Logensitze im I. Rang, I. Reihe . . . S 4.—	II. Rang Stehplatz . . . S —.60

Anfang 7½ Uhr   **Kassa-Eröffnung 7 Uhr**   **Ende gegen 10 Uhr**

Karten an der Abendkassa und im Vorverkauf an der Tageskassa am Mittwoch den 26. Juni 1929 von 9½ Uhr vormittags bis 12½ Uhr mittags und von 4 Uhr nachmittags bis 6 Uhr abends.

salzburg 6 june 1930 *mozarteum orchestra and chorus*	mascagni cavalleria rusticana/strauss josephslegende ballet *gahagan/schacht/holzleitner/gofriller/balaban*
salzburg 23 june 1930 *stadttheater orchestra and chorus*	puccini tosca *gahagan/gofriller/gross*
vienna 22 july 1930 *vienna symphony*	open-air concert of popular works *first public appearance in vienna*
salzburg 19 august 1930	participation in gartenkonzert at schloss leopoldskron
ulm 30 september, 3, 9, 12, 13 and 20 october and 1 and 15 november 1930 *ulm orchestra and chorus*	rossini il barbiere di siviglia *zöbisch/geyer/junge/katona/bodenstein*
ulm 7, 9, 11 and 27 november 1930 *ulm orchestra and chorus*	bizet carmen *benda-wrana/kiesling/junge/w.lorenz*
ulm 25, 28 and 30 december 1930 and 2 january 1931 *ulm orchestra and chorus*	puccini la boheme *kiesling/zöbisch/golday/schlechter/steinbach*
ulm 31 december 1930 *ulm orchestra members*	bunter abend *karajan provided piano accompaniment for operetta and popular songs*

ulm
22, 26 and 30
january and
2 february 1931
*ulm orchestra
and chorus*

donizetti don pasquale
zöbisch/junge/bodenstein/katona

ulm
1 march 1931
ulm orchestra

orchestral concert
conducting shared with otto schulmann

ulm
5, 10 and 20
march 1931
*ulm orchestra
and chorus*

d'albert tiefland
*bauer/zöbisch/golday/katona/steinbach;
further performance of the opera conducted by
karajan in klagenfurt on 16 april 1931 but it is
not clear whether this was a guest performance
by the ulm company or given with local forces*

salzburg
22 july 1931
*mozarteum orchestra
lawton*

wagner meistersinger overture/schumann
piano concerto/tchaikovsky piano concerto 1/
strauss till eulenspiegel

ulm
29 september and
2, 7, 8 and 14
october 1931
*ulm orchestra
and chorus*

puccini madama butterfly
crespy/bauer/martino/löffler

ulm
30 october and
1 and 3 november 1931
*ulm orchestra
and chorus*

verdi il trovatore
sunko-saller/klose/martino/löffler/hein

ulm
11 november 1931
ulm orchestra

beethoven symphony 3/weber euryanthe
overture/strauss tod und verklärung

special performances 20-27 november 1931 to mark 150th anniversary of founding of ulm stadttheater

ulm 20 november 1931 *ulm orchestra* *and chorus*	**wagner die meistersinger von nürnberg** *kiesling/bauer/wörle/beyer/monthy/papst/* *hein*
ulm 22 november 1931 *ulm orchestra* *and chorus*	**puccini madama butterfly** *cast as for 29 september 1931*
ulm 23 november 1931	**orchestral concert** *programme as for 11 november 1931*
ulm 26 november 1931 *ulm orchestra* *and chorus*	**verdi il trovatore** *cast as for 30 october 1931*
ulm 5, 13 and 19 december 1931 *ulm orchestra* *and chorus*	**verdi il trovatore** *cast as for 30 october 1931*
ulm 25 december 1931 *ulm orchestra* *and chorus*	**schwanda der dudelsackpfeifer** *bauer/kiesling/papst/monthy*
ulm 28 january, 1 and 20 february and 9 march 1932 *ulm orchestra* *and chorus*	**beethoven fidelio** *sunko-saller/christof/silten/beyer/papst/* *monthy*
ulm 21 february 1932 *ulm orchestra members* *schmalwieser, violin* *karajan, piano*	**chamber concert** *programme included franck violin sonata*

ulm
15, 18, 21 and 23
march 1932
*ulm orchestra
and chorus*

strauss der rosenkavalier
*sunko-saller/christof/bauer/martino/
papst/monthy*

ulm
20, 23 and 25
october and
4, 7, 20 and 24
november 1932
*ulm orchestra
and chorus*

lortzing undine
*bürkner/winkler/walter/beyer/messer/
sahler*

ulm
25 and 30
december 1932,
3, 5, 8, 16 and 25
january and
13 february 1933
*ulm orchestra
and chorus*

wagner tannhäuser
*bürkner/kittel/redlich/walter/friedrich/
messer/hirche*

ulm
12, 15, 21, 23 and
24 january and
12 february 1933
*ulm orchestra
and chorus*

nicolai die lustigen weiber von windsor
redlich/kittel/friedrich/sahler/messer

ulm
22 february 1933
*ulm orchestra
karajan, piano*

mozart piano concerto 20/debussy prélude a
l'apres-midi/tchaikovsky symphony 6

ulm
28 february 1933

lustiger abend
*karajan provided piano accompaniment for
operetta and popular songs*

ulm
17, 21, 23 and
25 march 1933
*ulm orchestra
and chorus*

verdi la traviata
kittel/friedrich/messer

salzburg paumgartner music for goethe's faust part one
17, 21, 25 and 31 *first official appearance at salzburg festival*
august 1933
mozarteum orchestra

ulm lortzing der wildschütz
8, 10, 12, 16 and 20 *boy/halbeck/otto/sahler*
october 1933
*ulm orchestra
and chorus*

ulm handel giulio cesare
24 october, *boy/halbeck/otto/höfermayer*
2 and 22 november
and 2, 4 and 16
december 1933
*ulm orchestra
and chorus*

ulm *richard strauss programme*
26 november 1933 don juan/allerseelen/die heiligen drei könige/
ulm orchestra ein heldenleben
halbeck

ulm wagner lohengrin
25 and 28 *halbeck/boy/otto/höfermayer/hirche*
december 1933,
2, 5, 10, 20 and
28 january,
7 and 21 february
and 11 march 1934
*ulm orchestra
and chorus*

ulm strauss arabella
9, 15 and 20 *halbeck/eckert/müller/siemsen/
february 1934 höfermayer/sahler*
*ulm orchestra
and chorus*

ulm
21, 23, 26, 29
and 31 march 1934
*ulm orchestra
and chorus*

mozart le nozze di figaro
*halbeck/sörensen/eckert/höfermayer/hirche;
final appearances as chief conductor in ulm*

salzburg
21 august 1934
vienna philharmonic

open-air ballet performance
debussy prélude a l'apres-midi/ravel la valse/
debussy fantaisie pour piano et orchestre
*first appearance with vienna philharmonic;
not part of the salzburg festival*

aachen
18 and 24
september 1934
*stadttheater
orchestra and chorus*

beethoven fidelio
*johnn-fehrmann/kreutzfeldt/rosving/kuhn/
martini/eccarius; first appearances in aachen*

aachen
23 october 1934
*stadttheater
orchestra*

wagner die walküre
*johnn-fehrmann/hauswald/besalla/rosving/
martini/kuhn*

aachen
30 november and
10 december 1934
*stadttheater
orchestra and chorus*

mozart die zauberflöte
hauswald/kreutzfeldt/fidesser/kuhn/martini

aachen
8 december 1934
*stadttheater
orchestra
bleier*

weber euryanthe overture/tchaikovsky violin
concerto/brahms symphony 1

aachen
5 january 1935
stadttheater
orchestra and chorus

strauss der rosenkavalier
krasa-jank/kreutzfeldt/besalla/erthal/eccarius

karlsruhe
31 january 1935
*badische staatskapelle
and chorus*

wagner tannhäuser
sunko-saller/reich-dörlich/strack/seiler

aachen
22 and 26
february 1935
stadttheater
orchestra and chorus

wagner tannhäuser
*krasa-jank/johnn-fehrmann/rosving/reuland/
kuhn/martini*

karlsruhe
12 march 1935
*badische staatskapelle
and chorus*

mozart le nozze di figaro

aachen
26 may 1935
stadttheater
orchestra

wagner siegfried
*schlüter/besalla/kreutzfeldt/grahl/fober/
martini/kuhn/kuhlmann*

aachen
25 june 1935
stadttheater
orchestra and chorus

handel giulio cesare
*krasa-jank/besalla/noort/martini/kuhn;
open-air performance*

aachen
29 june 1935
stadttheater
orchestra and chorus

open-air concert
works included trunk feier der neuen front
conducting shared with wilhelm pitz

aachen
9 july 1935
stadttheater
orchestra

rokoko-abend
mozart bastien und bastienne/mozart ein
schäferspiel/debussy prélude a l'apres-midi
schäferspiel and pré

aachen wagner die meistersinger von nürnberg
20 and 23 dippel/hertzberg/rosving/reuland/martini/
september 1935 kuhn/illert
stadttheater
orchestra and chorus

aachen beethoven programme
9 and 10 egmont overture/piano concerto 5/symphony 5
october 1935
stadttheater
orchestra
gieseking

aachen lieder recital by karl erb
16 october 1935 *karajan acted as piano accompanist*

aachen weber oberon overture/beethoven violin
26 october 1935 concerto/brahms symphony 2
stadttheater
orchestra
d.grümmer

aachen strauss die frau ohne schatten
1 november 1935 dippel/wühler/besalla/rosving/martini
stadttheater
orchestra and chorus

aachen verdi messa da requiem
20 and 21 *viorica ursuleac was originally announced as*
november 1935 *soprano soloist for these performances*
stadttheater
orchestra and chorus
heidersbach
rünger
rosvaenge
willy

aachen
23 november 1935
stadttheater
orchestra

wagner programme with soloists of aachen company
excerpts from rienzi/lohengein/meistersinger/
tristan/tannhäuser/walküre; siegfried idyll

aachen
7 december 1935
stadttheater orchestra
gräwe

jerger partita/höller hymnen für orchester/
beethoven piano concerto 3/haydn symphony 104

aachen
11 and 12
december 1935
stadttheater orchestra
kulenkampff

debussy la mer/brahms violin concerto/
tchaikovsky symphony 6

krefeld
16 december 1935
*aachen stadttheater
orchestra, telmanyi*

bach violin concerto in e/r.mengelberg violin concerto/brahms symphony 1

aachen
21 december 1935
stadttheater orchestra

programme included
van hoof erinnerungsouvertüre/gilson das meer

aachen
31 december 1935
*stadttheater
orchestra and chorus*

j.strauss die fledermaus
cast included holgerlloef

cologne
1935-1936
*cologne radio
orchestra and chorus*

bizet carmen
verdi rigoletto
concert performances for radio; casts included peter anders

aachen
4 january 1936
stadttheater orchestra

handel concerto grosso op 6 no 12/tchaikovsky symphony 5
programme also included wedig piano concerto conducted by the composer and with thelen-diehl as soloist

aachen
10 and 13
january 1936
*stadttheater
orchestra and chorus*

wagner lohengrin
dippel/besalla/noort/kuhn/martini

aachen
15 and 16
january 1936
*stadttheater
orchestra and chorus
merz-tunner, witt*

bach nun ist die kraft/kodaly psalmus hungaricus/philipp sinfonische friedensmesse

aachen
1 february 1936
stadttheater
orchestra
oldenburg

j. strauss programme
zigeunerbaron overture/kaiserwalzer/leichtes blut/dorfschwalben aus österreich/g'schichten aus dem wienerwald/fledermaus overture/ künstlerleben/annen polka/frühlingsstimmen/ perpetuum mobile/an der schönen blauen donau

ulm
3 february 1936
ulm orchestra
d.grümmer

weber oberon overture/bruch violin concerto/ tchaikovsky symphony 5

düren
4 february 1936
aachen stadttheater
orchestra and chorus

d'albert tiefland
fritz/wühler/kossler/treskow/kuhn; guest performance by aachen stadttheater

aachen
4 and 5
march 1936
stadttheater
orchestra
cassado

brahms symphony 3/dvorak cello concerto/ strauss tod und verklärung

aachen
14 march 1936
stadttheater
orchestra

programme included
trapp concerto for orchestra

aachen
4 april 1936
stadttheater orchestra
hermann

mozart programme
eine kleine nachtmusik/flute concerto 2/ symphony 41

aachen
22 and 23
april 1936
stadttheater
orchestra and chorus
fahrni
pitzinger
marten
drissen

bach mass in b minor

brussels
26 april 1936
aachen stadttheater
orchestra and chorus
soloists as above

bach mass in b minor
first appearance outside german-speaking countries

aachen
3 may 1936
stadttheater
orchestra and chorus

wagner tristan und isolde
wühler/wollgarten/grahl/frese/kuhn

aachen
13 may 1936
stadttheater orchestra

concert of contemporary music
wunsch fest auf monbijou/frommel suite for small orchestra/waertisch rondo for large orchestra/pepping partita/atterberg älven

aachen
14 may 1936
stadttheater orchestra

concert of contemporary music
pepping partita/g.schumann gestern abend war vetter michel da/palmgren piano concerto/ ravel la valse

cologne						orchestral concert
15 may 1936
cologne orchestra
backhaus

aachen						puccini tosca
28 june 1936					*wühler/helm/kronenberg*
stadttheater orchestra
and chorus

aachen						verdi aida
18 september 1936				*wühler/besalla/noort/höfermayer/kuhn/*
stadttheater orchestra			*kuhlmann; irmgard seefried also made her*
and chorus					*professional stage début in this performance*
						in the small role of priestess

aachen						siegl festliche ouvertüre/rehberg piano concerto/
25 september 1936				beethoven symphony 6
stadttheater
orchestra
rehberg

aachen						weber euryanthe overture/schumann piano
7 and 8						concerto/beethoven symphony 3
october 1936
stadttheater
orchestra
cortot

aachen
14 october 1936
stadttheater
orchestra and chorus

mozart don giovanni
wühler/panzer/küst/meyer-welfing/illert/
höfermayer/kuhn

aachen
24 october 1936
staddtheater
orchestra
dreier von schönberg

maler orchesterspiel (first performance)/
mozart piano concerto 27/bruckner
symphony 4

aachen
9 november 1936
stadttheater
orchestra

wagner das rheingold
hertzog/besalla/diller/meyer-welfing/kuhn/
kuhlmann/reuland

aachen
18 and 19
november 1936
stadttheater
orchestra and chorus
ginster, nissen

brahms ein deutsches requiem

aachen
2 december 1936
stadttheater
orchestra and chorus

wagner götterdämmerung
rünger/panzer/besalla/helm/höfermayer/
kuhn/illert

aachen
8 and 9
december 1936
stadttheater orchestra
francescatti

respighi fontane di roma/paganini violin
concerto 1/brahms symphony 4

ulm
14 december 1936
ulm orchestra
karajan, piano

mozart programme
eine kleine nachtmusik/rondo k382/
symphony 41

aachen
19 december 1936
stadttheater
orchestra
aeschbacher

ebel symphonic overture (first performance)/
beethoven piano concerto 3/tchaikovsky
symphony 6

aachen
6 january 1937
stadttheater
orchestra members

geminiani concerto op 3 no 2/bach suite 2/
bach double concerto bwv 1043/dittersdorf
harpsichord concerto/mozart symphony 33

aachen
10 january 1937
stadttheater
orchestra and chorus

wagner tristan und isolde
rünger/henderichs/helm/höfermayer/kuhn

aachen
12 and 13
january 1937
stadttheater orchestra
and chorus
fahrni
marten
baum

haydn die schöpfung

gothenburg
4 february 1937
gothenburg symphony

mozart symphony 41/beethoven symphony 3

gothenburg
7 february 1937
gothenburg symphony
mitchell

handel concerto op 6 no 12/bruch violin
concerto/wagner siegfried idyll/wagner
meistersinger overture

aachen
6 march 1937
stadttheater orchestra
lenzen

höller symphonic fantasy on frescobaldi (first
performance)/franck variations symphoniques/
dvorak symphony 9

aachen
12 march 1937
stadttheater orchestra

wagner meistersinger overture/bruckner symphony 4

aachen
17 and 18
march 1937
*stadttheater
orchestra and chorus
merz-tunner
pitzinger
erb
willy
esser*

bach matthäus-passion

aachen
13 and 14
april 1937
*stadttheater orchestra
fischer*

beethoven coriolan overture/mozart piano concerto 9/bruckner symphony 5

aachen
24 april 1937
stadttheater orchestra
küsshauer

schubert symphony 8/hilber piano concerto
(first performance)/strauss till eulenspiegel

aachen
25 april 1937
stadttheater
orchestra and chorus

verdi un ballo in maschera
wühler/besalla/meyer-welfing/höfermayer

vienna
1 may 1937
vienna philharmonic
vienna opera chorus

wagner tristan und isolde
a.konetzni/szantho/kalenberg/dermota/
kipnis/destal/duhan; first appearance at
vienna staatsoper

brussels
9 may 1937
aachen stadttheater
orchestra and chorus
ginster
fischer
marten
hotter
höfermayer

brahms ein deutsches requiem/bruckner
te deum

aachen 18 september 1937 *stadttheater* *orchestra and chorus*	wagner der fliegende holländer *halten/hertzog/noort/kuhn/höfermayer*
aachen 25 september 1937 *stadttheater* *orchestra* *ehlert* *nelting*	jerger symphonic variations/bruch violin concerto/casella scarlattiana/schumann symphony 3
aachen 6 and 7 october 1937 *stadttheater orchestra* *aeschbacher*	liszt piano concerto 2/stravinsky firebird/ schubert symphony 9
aachen 9 october 1937 *stadttheater orchestra* *h. and r.scholz*	delius brigg fair/göhler passacaglia and fugue (first performance)/mozart concerto for two pianos/beethoven symphony 7
aachen 16 october 1937 *stadttheater* *orchestra and chorus*	wagner der fliegende holländer *halten/hertzog/jank/kuhn/höfermayer*
aachen 3 november 1937 *stadttheater* *orchestra and chorus*	mozart cosi fan tutte *wellhagen/besalla/küst/meyer-welfing/* *eccarius/höfermayer*

aachen
17 and 18
november 1937
stadttheater
orchestra and chorus
horn-stoll
fischer
witt
drissen

beethoven missa solemnis

first complete ring cycle
aachen
21 november 1937
stadttheater orchestra

wagner das rheingold
hertzog/besalla/höfermayer/reuland/kuhn/
worringen/illert

aachen
24 november 1937
stadttheater orchestra

wagner die walküre
schlüter/holten/besalla/beetz/bockelmann/
kuhn

aachen
26 november 1937
stadttheater orchestra

wagner siegfried
schlüter/besalla/küst/helm/reuland/
lindlar/illert/kuhn

aachen
28 november 1937
stadttheater
orchestra and chorus

wagner götterdämmerung
rünger/besalla/dippel/helm/höfermayer/
kuhn/illert

aachen
4 december 1937
stadttheater orchestra
mazzacurati

unger four landscapes from faust (first performance)/boccherini cello concerto/ravel boléro/tchaikovsky symphony 5

aachen
15 and 16
december 1937
stadttheater orchestra
kulenkampff
de machula

brahms double concerto/bruckner symphony 8

aachen berlioz symphonie fantastique/beethoven piano
5 and 6 concerto 4/ravel daphnis et chloé second suite
january 1938
stadttheater orchestra
backhaus

maastricht d'albert tiefland
11 january 1938 *holten/helm/illert/höfermayer; guest performance*
utrecht orchestra *by aachen stadttheater; performance also repeated*
aachen stadttheater *in utrecht and scheveningen*
chorus

aachen verdi otello
14 january 1938 *wellhagen/beetz/meyer-welfing/höfermayer*
stadttheater
orchestra and chorus

aachen maler flämisches rondo (first performance)/
15 january 1938 spohr violin concerto 7/röhrig festliches
stadttheater orchestra vorspiel (first performance)/brahms symphony 1
zernick

amsterdam haydn symphony 104/beethoven violin concerto/
23 january 1938 brahms symphony 1
concertgebouw
orchestra
roodenburg

stockholm wagner meistersinger overture/smetana moldau/
29 january 1938 ravel la valse/berlioz danses des sylphes and
stockholm radio marche hongroise
orchestra

stockholm mozart symphony 33/dvorak symphony 9
1 february 1938
stockholm radio
orchestra

stockholm sibelius symphony 6/ulfrstad piano concerto
7 february 1938
stockholm radio
orchestra
aavatsmark

aachen
12 february 1938
*stadttheater orchestra
schmitz*

cherubini anacréon overture/trenker violin concerto/haydn symphony 103/respighi pini di roma

brussels
20 february 1938
*aachen stadttheater orchestra and chorus
fahrni, fischer,
w.ludwig, baum,
naideweier*

bach matthäus-passion

aachen
february 1938
stadttheater orchestra

wagner die walküre
cast included bockelmann

salzburg
3 march 1938
mozarteum orchestra

mozart symphony 33/smetana moldau/ brahms symphony 1

düren
17 march 1938
aachen stadttheater orchestra

haydn symphony 103/ravel daphnis et chloé second suite/beethoven symphony 8

aachen
19 march 1938
*stadttheater orchestra
hoffman*

sczuka merry overture (first performance)/ brahms piano concerto 2/beethoven symphony 8

aachen
30 and 31 march 1938
*stadttheater orchestra and chorus
rokyta, börner,
erb, willy,
höfermayer*

bach matthäus-passion

aachen
2 april 1938
stadttheater orchestra

rossini italiana in algeri overture/debussy ibéria/brahms symphony 4

berlin 8 april 1938 *berlin philharmonic*	mozart symphony 33/ravel daphnis et chloé second suite/brahms symphony 4 *first appearance in berlin and with the* *berlin philharmonic orchestra*	39

aachen
15 april 1938
stadttheater
orchestra and chorus

beethoven fidelio
besalla/küst/noort/reuland/kuhn/
eccarius/höfermayer

aachen
27 and 28
april 1938
stadttheater
orchestra and chorus
fahrni, hochreiter,
knoll, watzke

beethoven symphony 9

aachen
23 september 1938
stadttheater
orchestra and chorus

wagner lohengrin
scheibenhofer/besalla/helm/kuhn/bard

aachen
24 september 1938
stadttheater orchestra
kolberg

rasch toccata (first performance)/beethoven
violin concerto/beethoven symphony 5

berlin
27 september 1938
berlin philharmonic
tröster

sibelius symphony 6/haydn cello concerto
in d/beethoven symphony 5

berlin
30 september 1938
staatskapelle
and chorus

beethoven fidelio
rünger/spletter/völker/zimmermann/
manowarda/grossmann/prohaska;
first appearance at berlin staatsoper

aachen
4 october 1938
stadttheater
orchestra and chorus

verdi il trovatore
scheibenhofer/wollgarten/fassnacht/
bard/illert

aachen
5 and 6
october 1938
stadttheater orchestra
kolessa

pfitzner käthchen von heilbronn overture/
schumann piano concerto/dukas l'apprenti
sorcier/beethoven symphony 7

aachen
15 october 1938
stadttheater orchestra
langnese

suder chamber symphony (first performance)/
rachmaninov piano concerto 2/schumann
symphony 4

berlin
21 october 1938
staatskapelle
and chorus

wagner tristan und isolde
rünger/klose/seibel/grossmann/manowarda

aachen
2 and 3
november 1938
stadttheater orchestra
ney

mozart piano concerto 21/beethoven piano
concerto 5/liszt piano concerto 1

berlin
9 november 1938
staatskapelle
and chorus

wagner tristan und isolde
fuchs/klose/pistor/prohaska/manowarda

aachen
16 and 17
november 1938
stadttheater
orchestra and chorus
ginster
w.ludwig
ravelli

haydn die jahreszeiten

berlin
november 1938
reichssender
orchestra

mozart symphony 35/beethoven piano
concerto 5/strauss tod und verklärung

aachen
30 november 1938
stadttheater
orchestra and chorus

mozart die entführung aus dem serail
jacobi/küst/schmid-berikoven/reuland/
illert

aachen
3 december 1938
stadttheater orchestra
gesangsverein
karajan and
willems, pianos

haydn symphony 83/brahms liebesliederwalzer/ franck symphony in d minor

aachen
7 and 8
december 1938
staddtheater
orchestra and chorus
briem
klaembt
meyer-welfing
höfermayer

bruckner programme
symphony 9/te deum

berlin
18, 23 and 26
december 1938
and 1, 17 and 22
january 1939
staatskapelle
and chorus

mozart die zauberflöte
lemnitz/berger/rosvaenge/krenn/manowarda/
bockelmann; first performances of a new
production

aachen
3 january 1939
stadttheater
orchestra and chorus

puccini tosca
scheibenhofen/bard/schmid-berikoven

aachen
4 and 5
january 1939
stadttheater orchestra
mainardi

strauss don quixote/casella notturno and tarantella for cello and orchestra/tchaikovsky symphony 5

aacchen
7 january 1939
stadttheater orchestra

oboussier suite for small orchestra/strauss don juan/tchaikovsky symphony 5

brussels
15 january 1939
*aachen stadttheater
orchestra and chorus*

beethoven missa solemnis

berlin
19 january 1939
*staatskapelle
and chorus*

beethoven fidelio
*rünger/spletter/völker/zimmermann/
manowarda/grossmann/prohaska*

berlin
28 january and
3, 7 and 15
february 1939
*staatskapelle
and chorus*

wagner-régeny die bürger von calais
*m.fuchs/lemnitz/wittrisch/rödin/hofmann/
e.fuchs; world premiere performances*

berlin
5, 16 and 23
february 1939
*staatskapelle
and chorus*

mozart die zauberflöte

berlin
24 february 1939
*staatskapelle
and chorus*

beethoven fidelio

liege
28 february 1939
*aachen stadttheater
orchestra*

wagner die walküre
*schrader/gaden/karen/seibert/treskov/s.nilsson
guest performance by aachen stadttheater*

aachen
8 and 9
march 1939
*stadttheater orchestra
kulenkampff*

sibelius en saga/tchaikovsky violin concerto/
brahms symphony 2
*kulenkampff deputised for kempff, who was
to have played mozart piano concerto 20*

berlin
11 march 1939
*staatskapelle
and chorus*

mozart die zauberflöte

stockholm
14 march 1939
*stockholm radio
orchestra*

tchaikovsky symphony 6/ravel daphnis et chloé second suite

stockholm
15 march 1939
*stockholm
philharmonic
fischer*

rosenberg last judgement prelude/brahms piano concerto 2/tchaikovsky symphony 4

stockholm
16 march 1939
*stockholm radio
orchestra*

haydn symphony 94/j.strauss zigeunerbaron overture, kaiserwalzer and perpetuum mobile

berlin
19 march 1939
*staatskapelle
and chorus*

wagner tristan und isolde
rünger/klose/seibert/grossmann/manowarda

berlin
20 march 1939
*staatskapelle
and chorus*

wagner-régeny die bürger von calais
cast as for 28 january 1939

aachen
25 march 1939
*stadttheater orchestra
d.grümmer
petermann*

sibelius symphony 1/mozart sinfonia concertante for violin and viola/liszt les préludes

aachen
28 and 29
march 1939
*stadttheater
orchestra and chorus
horn-stoll
hochreiter
erb
willy
wolks*

bach matthäus-passion

berlin
14 april 1939
berlin philharmonic

haydn symphony 103/debussy la mer/
tchaikovsky symphony 6

berlin
15 and 28
april 1939
*staatskapelle
and chorus*

mozart die zauberflöte

berlin
17 april 1939
*staatskapelle
and chorus*

wagner-régeny die bürger von calais

berlin
20 april 1939
*staatskapelle
and chorus*

beethoven fidelio

aachen
26 and 27
april 1939
*stadttheater
orchestra and chorus
fahrni
baum*

brahms ein deutsches requiem

aachen
29 april 1939
*stadttheater orchestra
hoffman*

pfitzner käthchen von heilbronn overture/
mozart piano concerto 26/brahms
symphony 2

berlin
8 may 1939
*aachen stadttheater
orchestra and chorus
fahrni
schmitt-walter*

brahms ein deutsches requiem

aachen 9 may 1939 *stadttheater* *orchestra and chorus*	strauss friedenstag *scheibenhofer/bard/illert/schmid-berikoven*
düren 10 may 1939 *aachen stadttheater* *orchestra* *fassbender*	**pfitzner käthchen von heilbronn overture/** **haydn cello concerto in d/brahms symphony 2**
berlin 15 may and 3 june 1939 *staatskapelle* *and chorus*	beethoven fidelio
berlin 16 may 1939 *staatskapelle* *and chorus*	mozart die zauberflöte
berlin 2 and 9 june 1939 *staatskapelle* *and chorus*	**wagner die meistersinger von nürnberg** *heidersbach/berglund/svanholm/klein/* *bockelmann/manowarda/e.fuchs*
aachen 7 june 1939 *stadttheater* *orchestra and chorus*	**wagner die meistersinger von nürnberg** **festwiese (closing scene)** *beckhaus/aldenhoff/bard/marbod/illert* *open-air performance*
athens 13 june 1939 *odeon orchestra*	**haydn symphony 103/smetana moldau/** **brahms symphony 4**
aachen 24 september 1939 *stadttheater* *orchestra and chorus*	wagner tannhäuser *scheibenhofer/küst/herbert/wijgers/mund/* *kaufmann*

berlin
1 and 21
october and
5 november 1939
*staatskapelle
and chorus*

beethoven fidelio

berlin
15 october and
9 november 1939
*staatskapelle
and chorus*

wagner tristan und isolde

aachen
1 november 1939
*stadttheater
orchestra and chorus*

verdi un ballo in maschera
*scheibenhofer/küst/herbert/bard/
schmid-berikoven*

berlin
11 november and
25 december 1939
*staatskapelle
and chorus*

wagner die meistersinger von nürnberg

aachen
19 november 1939
*stadttheater
orchestra and chorus
klotz*

beethoven leonore 3 overture/handel organ concerto in f/nuffel three psalms for organ, chorus and orchestra
programme also included bach toccata and fugue in d minor for solo organ

aachen
22 and 23
november 1939
*stadttheater
orchestra and chorus
briem
fischer
sturm
watzke*

beethoven symphony 9

aachen beethoven symphony 9
26 november 1939
stadttheater
orchestra and chorus
küst
herbert
wijgers
bard

berlin beethoven fidelio
1 december 1939
staatskapelle
and chorus

aachen scriabin poeme de l'extase/dvorak violin
13 and 14 concerto/tchaikovsky symphony 4
december 1939
stadttheater orchestra
prihoda

aachen jerger salzburger hof- und barockmusik/
17 december 1939 mozart violin concerto 5/tchaikovsky
stadttheater orchestra symphony 4
d.grümmer

berlin beethoven fidelio
2 and 15
january 1940
staatskapelle
and chorus

aachen haydn symphony 101/mozart piano concerto
7 january 1940 15/strauss tod und verklärung
stadttheater orchestra
gebhardt

aachen haydn die schöpfung
9 january 1940
stadttheater
orchestra and chorus
horn-stoll
marten
baum

berlin
17 january and
4 february 1940
*staatskapelle
and chorus*

mozart die zauberflöte

berlin
18 february and
14 march 1940
*staatskapelle
and chorus*

strauss elektra
*rünger/klose/scheppan/argyris/prohaska
first performances of a new production to mark
the composer's seventy-fifth birthday*

berlin
10 march 1940
*staatskapelle
and chorus*

wagner tristan und isolde

aachen
17 march 1940
*stadttheater
orchestra and chorus
briem
hennecke
w.ludwig
hüsch
bard*

bach matthäus-passion

aachen
22, 24 and 26
march 1940
*stadttheater
orchestra and chorus*

wagner parsifal
*henderichs/wijgers/tappolet/bard/illert/
kaufmann
cast also included elisabeth grümmer in her
professional singing debut as a flower maiden*

aachen
28 march 1940
*stadttheater orchestra
kempff*

blacher konzertante musik/mozart piano
concerto 20/dvorak symphony 9

berlin
30 march 1940
*staatskapelle
and chorus*

mozart die zauberflöte

berlin
2 and 28
april 1940
*staatskapelle
and chorus*

strauss elektra

berlin
4 april 1940
*staatskapelle
and chorus*

beethoven fidelio

berlin
6 april 1940
*staatskapelle
and chorus*

wagner die meistersinger von nürnberg

mannheim
15 april 1940
*nationalorchester
mannheim
mainardi*

handel concerto grosso op 6 no 12/haydn cello concerto in d/tchaikovsky symphony 4

aachen
19 april 1940
*stadttheater
orchestra and chorus*

bizet carmen
rohs/scheibenhofer/wijgers/bard

aachen
25 april 1940
*stadttheater
orchestra and chorus
schilling
fischer
marten
schirp*

pfitzner von deutscher seele

milan
9 may 1940
*la scala orchestra
martinenghi*

cherubini anacréon overture/strauss don quixote/brahms symphony 1
first appearance in italy; this replaced a performance of matthäus-passion originally scheduled

milan
12 may 1940
la scala orchestra

beethoven leonore 3 overture/mozart symphony 35/tchaikovsky symphony 4

berlin
31 may and
11 june 1940
staatskapelle and chorus

strauss elektra

berlin
14 june 1940
staatskapelle and chorus

wagner die meistersinger von nürnberg

aachen
21 september 1940
stadttheater orchestra and chorus

wagner die meistersinger von nürnberg
schiffer/kinzel/wijgers/kempf/bard/waibel/worringen

aachen
29 september 1940
stadttheater orchestra

strauss also sprach zarathustra/tchaikovsky symphony 5

aachen
3 and 4
october 1940
stadttheater orchestra mainardi

haydn cello concerto in d/bruckner symphony 8

berlin
6 october 1940
staatskapelle and chorus

beethoven fidelio

berlin
13 october 1940
staatskapelle and chorus

strauss elektra

berlin
20 and 21
october 1940
staatskapelle

cherubini anacréon overture/strauss also sprach zarathustra/brahms symphony 1
first appearance as chief conductor of the berlin staatskapelle concerts

aachen
24 and 25
october 1940
stadttheater orchestra
bustabo

borck symphonic prelude (first performance)/ bruch violin concerto/beethoven symphony 7

berlin
1 and 28
november 1940
staatskapelle
and chorus

strauss elektra

berlin
7 november and
4 december 1940
staatskapelle
and chorus

beethoven fidelio

berlin
10 and 11
november 1940
staatskapelle
kulenkampff

handel concerto grosso op 6 no 12/dvorak violin concerto/tchaikovsky symphony 4

aachen
15 november 1940
stadttheater
orchestra and chorus

d'albert tiefland
seefried/vogel/bard/worringen/waibel

aachen
21 and 22
november 1940
stadttheater
orchestra and chorus
horn-stoll
fischer
marten
baum

bach mass in b minor

aachen
24 november 1940
stadttheater orchestra

locatelli concerto grosso 10/respighi pini di roma/
beethoven symphony 7

berlin
1 december 1940
staatskapelle

j.strauss kaiserwalzer
*forces request concert for radio; other
participants included dal monte and rosvaenge*

berlin
8 and 9
december 1940
*staatskapelle
michelangeli*

borck symphonic prelude/grieg piano concerto/
beethoven symphony 7

aachen
12 and 13
december 1940
*stadttheater orchestra
gebhardt*

haydn symphony 104/rachmaninov piano
concerto 2/franck symphony in d minor

paris
17, 18 and 19
december 1940
*aachen stadttheater
orchestra and chorus
briem
hennecks/fischer
w.ludwig
driessen/schirp*

bach mass in b minor
first appearance in france

berlin
29 december 1940
and 3 january 1941
*staatskapelle
and chorus*

mozart die zauberflöte

berlin
5 and 6
january 1941
staatskapelle

franck symphony in d minor/haydn symphony 95/
respighi pini di roma

aachen   orff carmina burana
16 and 17
january 1941
stadttheater
orchestra and chorus
beilke
daus
schmitt-walter

aachen   orff carmina burana
19 january 1941
stadttheater
orchestra and chorus
wolski
daus
läuter

berlin   locatelli concerto grosso 10/rachmaninov
9 and 10   piano concerto 3/mozart divertimento 15/
february 1941   strauss tod und verklärung
staatskapelle
gieseking

berlin   wagner die meistersinger von nürnberg
13 february 1941
staatskapelle
and chorus

rome   locatelli concerto grosso 10/weber durch die
7 march 1941   wälder from der freischütz/pfitzner an die
berlin staatskapelle   nacht/strauss tod und verklärung/beethoven
völker   symphony 7

rome   wagner die meistersinger von nürnberg
9 march 1941   müller/tegethoff/lorenz/arnold/bockelmann/
berlin staatskapelle   hofmann/hüsch/e.fuchs; *guest performance*
and chorus   *by berlin staatsoper*

florence   locatelli concerto grosso 10/brahms symphony 4/
16 march 1941   smetana moldau/wagner meistersinger overture
berlin staatskapelle

aachen
11 april 1941
stadttheater
orchestra and chorus

wagner parsifal
henderichs/wijgers/bard/tappolet/illert/
kaufmann

budapest
23 april 1941
berlin staatskapelle

mozart symphony 35/strauss tod und
verklärung/beethoven symphony 7

budapest
april 1941
berlin staatskapelle
and chorus

strauss elektra
guest performance by berlin staatsoper

aachen
28 and 29
april 1941
stadttheater
orchestra and chorus
scheppan, klose,
w.ludwig, greindl,
bard, läuter

bach matthäus-passion

berlin
3 and 4
may 1941
staatskapelle

gluck alceste overture/bruckner symphony 8

aachen
7 may 1941
stadttheater
orchestra and chorus

verdi falstaff
grümmer/seefried/schroeder/kinzel/bard/
schmid-berikoven/läuter

paris
22 and 25
may 1941
berlin staatskapelle
and chorus

wagner tristan und isolde
lubin/klose/lorenz/prohaska; guest
performances by berlin staatsoper

paris
24 may 1941
berlin staatskapelle

mozart symphony 35/strauss tod und
verklärung/beethoven symphony 7
wagner meistersinger overture played as encore

florence cherubini anacréon overture/mozart symphony
30 and 31 35/strauss till eulenspiegel/beethoven
may 1941 symphony 7
maggio musicale
orchestra

aachen strauss der rosenkavalier
13 september 1941 *emmerich-conrads/graf/rohs/läuter/*
stadttheater *worringen*
orchestra and chorus

aachen
21 september 1941
stadttheater orchestra

aachen kraak symphonic prelude/franck variations
2 and 3 symphoniques pour piano et orchestre/
october 1941 bruckner symphony 7
stadttheater orchestra
hansen

berlin wagner die meistersinger von nürnberg
5 october 1941
staatskapelle
and chorus

berlin strauss elektra
7 october 1941
staatskapelle
and chorus

berlin kraak symphonic prelude/franck variations
12 and 13 symphoniques pour piano et orchestre/
october 1941 bruckner symphony 7
staatskapelle
hansen

berlin wagner tristan und isolde
15 october 1941
staatskapelle
and chorus

milan
25 and 26
october 1941
la scala orchestra

locatelli concerto grosso 10/schumann symphony 4/beethoven symphony 5

berlin
2 november 1941
*staatskapelle
and chorus*

wagner tristan und isolde

berlin
5 and 21
november 1941
*staatskapelle
and chorus*

mozart die zauberflöte

berlin
9 and 10
november 1941
*staatskapelle
mainardi*

rasch toccata/schubert symphony 8/strauss don quixote

berlin
13 november 1941
*staatskapelle
and chorus*

strauss elektra

berlin
16 november 1941
*staatskapelle
and chorus*

wagner die meistersinger von nürnberg

berlin
23 and 24
november 1941
*staatskapelle
fischer*

mozart programme
symphony 40/piano concerto 20/symphony 41

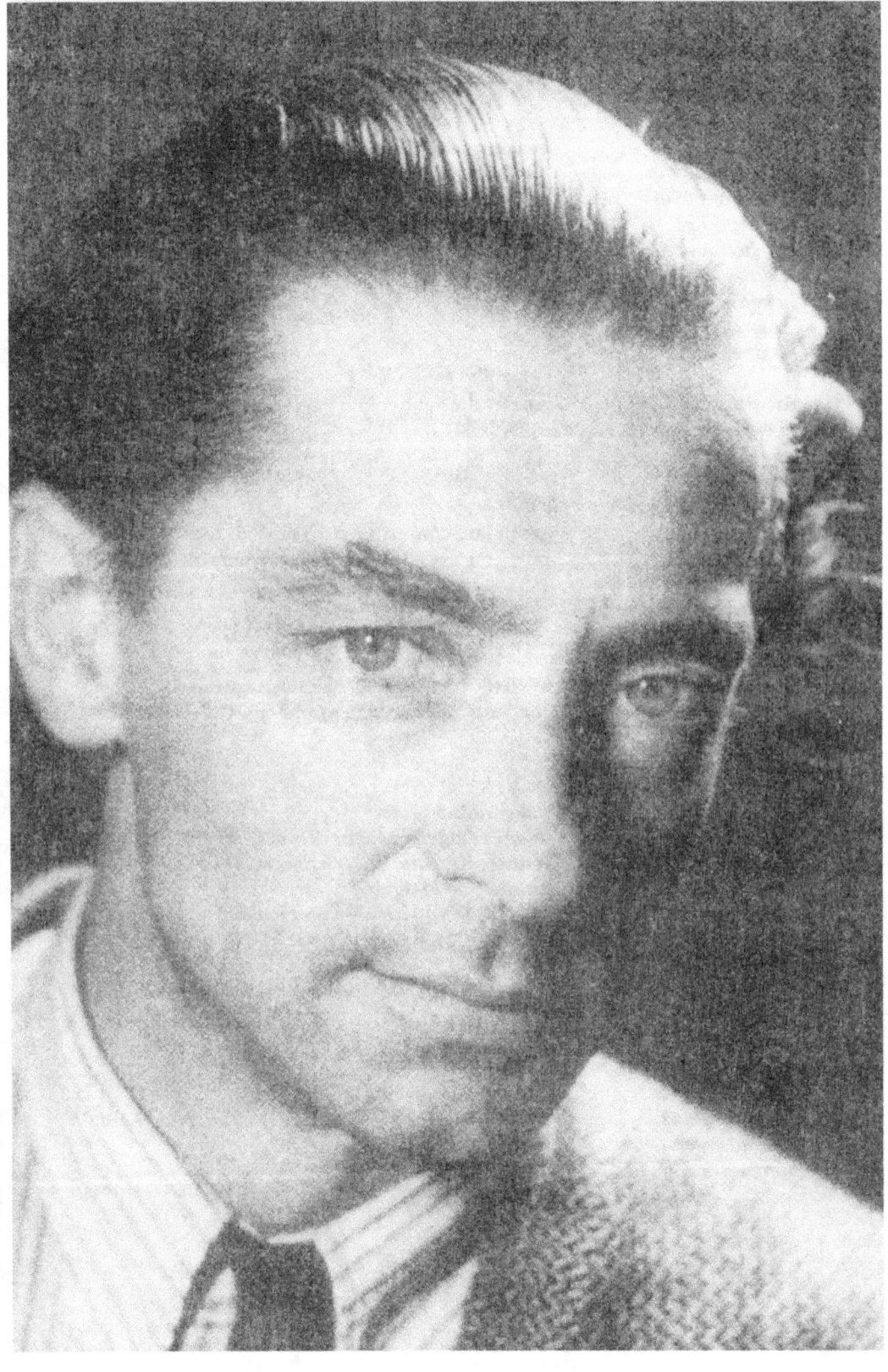

aachen mozart mass in c minor/verdi te deum
27 and 30 *additional performance of this programme*
november 1941 *scheduled for 28 november was postponed until*
stadttheater *15 february 1942*
orchestra and chorus
horn-stoll
seefried
marten
waibel

berlin mozart die zauberflöte
6 december 1941
staatskapelle
and chorus

aachen geminiani concerto grosso op 3 no 2/dvorak
11 and 12 cello concerto/beethoven symphony 3
december 1941
stadttheater orchestra
hoelscher

aachen mozart symphony 40/beethoven piano
14 december 1941 concerto 3/schumann symphony 4
stadttheater orchestra
schuchter

berlin orff carmina burana
20 and 22 *lemnitz/zimmermann/domgraf-fassbänder/*
december 1941 *rödin/neumann; first performances of a new*
staatskapelle *production in double bill with the werner egk*
and chorus *ballet joan von zarissa conducted by the composer*

berlin mozart die zauberflöte
25 december 1941 *lemnitz/berger/anders/neumann/manowarda/*
staatskapelle *bockelmann*
and chorus

aachen mozart don giovanni
1 january 1942 *emmerich-conrads/seefried/graf/buchow/bard/*
stadttheater *worringen/waibel*
orchestra and chorus

berlin orff carmina burana
2, 14, 20 and 26
january 1942
staatskapelle
and chorus

aachen beethoven missa solemnis
8 and 9
january 1942
stadttheater
orchestra and chorus
briem
klose
w.ludwig
drissen

berlin mozart die zauberflöte
15 january 1942
staatskapelle
and chorus

berlin beethoven missa solemnis
18 and 19
january 1942
staatskapelle
aachen stadttheater
chorus
briem
klose
w.ludwig
drissen

berlin wagner die meistersinger von nürnberg
22 january 1942
staatskapelle
and chorus

berlin wagner tristan und isolde
1 february 1942
staatskapelle
and chorus

berlin
6 and 19
february 1942
*staatskapelle
and chorus*

orff carmina burana
final appearances with company of berlin staatsoper

berlin
8 and 9
february 1942
*staatskapelle
de vito*

sibelius symphony 1/bruch violin concerto/
liszt les préludes

aachen
12 and 13
february 1942
*stadttheater orchestra
de vito*

schumann manfred overture/bruch violin concerto/brahms symphony 2

aachen
15 february 1942
*stadttheater
orchestra and chorus
horn-stoll
seefried
marten
waibel*

mozart mass in c minor/verdi te deum
performance postponed from 28 november 1941

berlin
22 and 23
february 1942
staatskapelle

geminiani concerto grosso op 3 no 2/vinski enigma/brahms symphony 3

aachen
21 and 22
april 1942
*stadttheater
orchestra and chorus
briem
hochreiter
marten
bard
greindl*

bach matthäus-passion
*final appearances as generalmusikdirektor
in aachen*

florence
13, 17 and 20
may 1942
*maggio musicale
orchestra and chorus*

mozart don giovanni
*caniglia/favero/danco/albanese/stabile/tajo/
pasero*

florence
2 june 1942
*maggio musicale
orchestra and chorus
briem
rohs
marten
watzke*

beethoven programme
egmont overture/symphony 9

berlin
18 and 19
october 1942
*staatskapelle
erdmann*

beethoven programme
coriolan overture/piano concerto 3/symphony 3

milan
1 november 1942
la scala orchestra

handel concerto grosso op 6 no 12/dvorak symphony 9/strauss don juan/verdi forza del destino overture

berlin
29 and 30
november 1942
*staatskapelle
hansen
gebhardt
kiss
karajan*

bach concerto for 4 pianos/bruckner symphony 5

berlin
27, 28 and 29
december 1942
*berlin philharmonic
beilke*

johann strauss programme
zigeunerbaron overture/kaiserwalzer/
pizzicato polka/g'schichten aus dem
wienerwald/leichtes blut/künstlerleben/
fledermaus overture/frühlingsstimmen/
perpetuum mobile/an der schönen blauen
donau

62

berlin
24 and 25
january 1943
staatskapelle

berger legende vom prinzen eugen/dvorak symphony 9/kodaly hary janos suite/verdi forza del destino overture

berlin
14 and 15
february 1943
staatskapelle
borries

strauss don juan/mozart violin concerto 4/schumann symphony 4

copenhagen
22 february 1943
royal danish
orchestra

mozart symphony 35/strauss don juan/beethoven symphony 7

milan
13 march 1943
la scala orchestra
and chorus
martelli and
karajan, pianos

bach suite 3/haydn symphony 45/brahms liebeslieder-walzer/mozart symphony 33

berlin
18 and 19
april 1943
staatskapelle
hoelscher

sibelius symphony 4/haydn cello concerto in d/smetana moldau and vysherad

berlin
9 and 10
may 1943
staatskapelle

bach brandenburg concerto 2/haydn symphony 103/reger mozart variations/wagner tannhäuser overture

berlin
7 and 8
november 1943
staatskapelle

bach suite 3/mozart sinfonia concertante for wind/beethoven symphony 5

berlin staatskapelle concerts announced for 5 and 6 december 1943 and for 2 and 3 january 1944 were cancelled, probably due to risk of air raids, although for the january 1944 concerts it was announced that both conductor and soloist were indisposed

berlin   mozart piano concerto 23/bruckner symphony 9
13 and 14
march 1944
staatskapelle
then-bergh

berlin   einem concerto for orchestra (first performance)/
3 and 4   schubert symphony 9
april 1944
staatskapelle

paris   handel concerto grosso op 6 no 12/debussy la
19 april 1944   mer/beethoven symphony 5
paris radio   *according to richard osborne a work by roussel*
orchestra   *was also performed at this concert*

paris   ravel boléro/schumann symphony 4/strauss
4 may 1944   don juan/bach brandenburg concerto 2
paris radio
orchestra

berlin   *richard strauss eightieth birthday celebration*
14 and 15   couperin suite/die heiligen drei könige/
may 1944   allerseelen/ein heldenleben
staatskapelle
berger

berlin   bruckner symphony 8, first three movements
26 and 28   *magnetophon recording for radio transmission*
june 1944
staatskapelle

linz   bruckner symphony 8
23 july 1944
linz-bruckner-
reichsorchester

berlin   bruckner symphony 8, final movement
19 september 1944   *magnetophon recording for radio transmission;*
staatskapelle   *this movement recorded in experimental stereo*

berlin bruckner symphony 8
4, 5 and 8
october 1944
staatskapelle

berlin weber euryanthe overture/schumann piano
1 and 2 concerto/brahms symphony 4
november 1944
staatskapelle
gieseking

berlin *chamber concert*
3 november 1944 thuille sextet for woodwind, horn and piano
staatskapelle *other works not involving karajan*
chamber ensemble
karajan, piano

berlin beethoven coriolan overture/mozart
4 and 5 maurerische trauermusik/beethoven
december 1944 symphony 6
staatskapelle

linz bach die kunst der fuge
14 december 1944
linz-bruckner-
reichsorchester

berlin beethoven symphony 3
december 1944 *magnetophon recording for radio transmission*
staatskapelle

berlin weber der freischütz overture/schumann
18 and 19 symphony 4/mozart symphony 35/strauss
february 1945 till eulenspiegel
staatskapelle *final appearance with berlin staatskapelle*

trieste haydn symphony 104/strauss tod und verklärung/
27 september 1945 beethoven symphony 5
teatro verdi
orchestra

Staatsoper

Im Beethovensaal

Sonntag, den 18. Februar 1945, 15,30 Uhr

Preußische Staatskapelle

Konzert

Leitung: Herbert von Karajan

Carl Maria v. Weber: Ouvertüre zu „Der Freischütz"
Robert Schumann: Sinfonie Nr. 4 d-moll

Pause

Wolfgang Amadeus Mozart: Haffner-Sinfonie Köch.-Verz. 385
Richard Strauß: Till Eulenspiegels lustige Streiche

Kartenverkauf nur am Tage selbst ab 13,30 Uhr

trieste
29 september 1945
teatro verdi
orchestra

tchaikovsky symphony 6/strauss tod und verklärung/sibelius finlandia

trieste
6 and 7
october 1945
teatro verdi
orchestra

locatelli concerto grosso op 4 no 10/wagner siegfried idyll/brahms symphony 1

vienna
12 and 13
january 1946
vienna philharmonic

haydn symphony 104/strauss don juan/ brahms symphony 1

further vienna philharmonic concerts scheduled for 18 and 19 january and 2 march 1946 cancelled at short notice by russian occupying powers in vienna

musical assistant to performances conducted by prohaska and swarowsky

salzburg
august 1946
vienna philharmonic
vienna opera chorus

strauss der rosenkavalier
konetzni/cunitz/schwaiger/dermota/krenn/ hann/schmidt
mozart le nozze di figaro
cebotari/seefried/mayerhofer/höfermayer/ kunz

vienna
25 and 26
october 1947
vienna philharmonic

bruckner symphony 8

trieste
22 november 1947
teatro verdi
orchestra

beethoven programme
symphony 2/symphony 3

trieste
24 november 1947
teatro verdi
orchestra

beethoven symphony 3/sibelius swan of tuonela/strauss till eulenspiegel

venice
30 november 1947
la fenice orchestra

locatelli concerto grosso op 4 no 10/schumann symphony 4/strauss metamorphosen (first performance in italy)/tchaikovsky romeo and juliet

vienna
20 and 21
december 1947
vienna philharmonic
wiener singverein
schwarzkopf
höngen
patzak
hotter

beethoven symphony 9

vienna
10 and 11
january 1948
vienna philharmonic

locatelli concerto grosso op 4 no 10/mozart symphony 33/tchaikovsky symphony 5

vienna
14 and 15
february 1948
vienna philharmonic

vaughan williams tallis fantasia/prokofiev symphony 1/brahms symphony 4

vienna
21 and 22
february 1948
vienna symphony

reger mozart variations/sibelius symphony 7/sibelius finlandia

vienna
28 and 29
february 1948
vienna philharmonic
wiener singverein
welitsch/loose
höngen
w.ludwig
weber

verdi messa da requiem

PHILHARMONISCHE KONZERTE
106. BESTANDSJAHR 1947/48

Sonntag, den 11. Jänner 1948, 11 Uhr vormittags
im Großen Musikvereins-Saal

4. Abonnement-Konzert

Öffentliche Generalprobe: Samstag, den 10. Jänner 1948, 15 Uhr

Dirigent:

HERBERT von KARAJAN

PROGRAMM:

P. A. Locatelli .... Concerto da camera
        1. Adagio
        2. Allegro
        3. Minuetto con variazioni

W. A. Mozart .... Symphonie B-Dur (K.-V. 319)
        1. Allegro assai
        2. Andante moderato
        3. Minuetto
        4. Finale: Allegro assai

P. I. Tschaikowsky ... Symphonie Nr. 5, e-moll, op. 64
        1. Andante — Allegro con anima
        2. Andante cantabile, con alcuna licenza
        3. Valse: Allegro moderato
        4. Finale: Andante maestoso

Klavier: Bösendorfer

---

5. Abonnement-Konzert

Sonntag, den 25. Jänner 1948, 11 Uhr, im Großen Musikvereins-Saal
Öffentliche Generalprobe: Samstag, den 24. Jänner 1948, 15 Uhr

Dirigent: Dr. Volkmar Andreae

Schoeck .... Suite für Streicher
Beethoven .... II. Leonoren-Ouvertüre
Bruckner .... IV. Symphonie (Originalfassung)

PHILHARMONISCHE KONZERTE
106. BESTANDSJAHR 1947/48

Palmsonntag, den 21. März 1948, 11 Uhr vormittags
im Großen Musikvereins-Saal

Außerordentliches Konzert

Öffentliche Generalprobe: Samstag, den 20. März 1948, 15 Uhr

Dirigent:

HERBERT von KARAJAN

Richard Wagner:

„PARSIFAL"

III. Akt, konzertante Aufführung

Mitwirkende:

Horst Taubmann (Tenor)
Kammersänger Paul Schöffler (Bariton)
Kammersänger Ludwig Weber (Baß)
Der Singverein der Gesellschaft der Musikfreunde

---

7. Abonnement-Konzert

Sonntag, den 4. April 1948, 11 Uhr, im Großen Musikvereins-Saal
Öffentliche Generalprobe: Samstag, den 3. April 1948, 15 Uhr

Dirigent: Dr. Volkmar Andreae

PROGRAMM:

Carl Maria von Weber . . . . Freischütz-Ouverture
Igor Strawinsky . . . . Feuervogel-Suite
Hector Berlioz . . . . Phantastische Symphonie

Das 6. Abonnement-Konzert unter Herbert von Karajan ist auf
den 8. und 9. Mai 1948 verschoben!

vienna
20 and 21
march 1948
vienna philharmonic
wiener singverein

wagner parsifal, act three
taubmann/schöffler/weber; concert performance

vienna
25 and 26
march 1948
vienna symphony
wiener singverein
seefried
höngen
dermota
patzak
frantz
schöffler

bach matthäus-passion

london
11 april 1948
philharmonia
lipatti

strauss don juan/schumann piano concerto/
beethoven symphony 5
first appearance in london

vienna
17 and 18
april 1948
vienna philharmonic
neveu

beethoven violin concerto/schumann symphony 4

rome
25 april 1948
santa cecilia
orchestra

haydn symphony 104/strauss metamorphosen/
beethoven symphony 5

rome
28 april 1948
santa cecilia
orchestra
uninsky

cherubini anacréon overture/beethoven
piano concerto 5/tchaikovsky symphony 5

rome
2 may 1948
santa cecilia
orchestra

mozart symphony 35/vaughan williams tallis fantasia/brahms symphony 1

vienna
8 and 9
may 1948
vienna philharmonic

bartok music for strings, percussion and celesta/schubert symphony 9

turin
14 may 1948
rai torino orchestra

mozart symphony 41/ravel rapsodie espagnole/ beethoven symphony 5

vienna
12 and 13
june 1948
vienna symphony
vienna opera chorus
schöffler

berger homerische sinfonie/walton belshazzar's feast

salzburg
28 july and
2, 7, 10, 13 and
16 august 1948
vienna philharmonic
vienna opera chorus

gluck orfeo ed euridice
höngen/cebotari/jurinac/schwarzkopf

salzburg
11, 14, 17, 21 and
27 august 1948
vienna philharmonic
vienna opera chorus

mozart le nozze di figaro
schwarzkopf/seefried/jurinac/taddei/
höfermayer

salzburg
18 august 1948
vienna philharmonic

haydn symphony 103/strauss metamorphosen/ beethoven symphony 5

salzburg
22 august 1948
vienna philharmonic
wiener singverein
schwarzkopf
schöffler

brahms ein deutsches requiem

STAGIONE SINFONICA
1947-1948
(LI - 3047 dalla fondazione dei Concerti)

TEATRO ARGENTINA

Domenica 2 maggio 1948 - Ore 17,30

HERBERT von KARAJAN

PROGRAMMA

1. **MOZART** — Sinfonia in *re maggiore* detta
   Salisburgo 1756 - Vienna 1791   "di Haffner" K 385
   Allegro con spirito
   Andante
   Minuetto
   Presto

2. **VAUGHAN WILLIAMS** — Fantasia sopra un tema di Thomas Tallis (prima esecuzione nei concerti dell'Istituzione)
   Down Ampney 1872

---

3. **JOHANNES BRAHMS** — Sinfonia n. 1 in *do minore*
   Amburgo 1833 - Vienna 1897
   Un poco sostenuto, Allegro
   Andante sostenuto
   Un poco allegretto e grazioso
   Adagio. Più andante. Allegro non troppo ma con brio

COMUNE DI ROMA - ACCADEMIA DI SANTA CECILIA
ISTITUZIONE DEI CONCERTI

ORCHESTRA STABILE
DELL'ACCADEMIA DI SANTA CECILIA

PHILHARMONISCHE KONZERTE
106. BESTANDSJAHR 1947/48

Sonntag, den 9. Mai 1948, 11 Uhr vormittags
im Großen Musikvereins-Saal

6. Abonnement-Konzert

verschoben vom 6. und 7. März 1948
Öffentliche Generalprobe: Samstag, den 8. Mai 1948, 15 Uhr

Dirigent:

HERBERT von KARAJAN

PROGRAMM:

Béla Bartók	Musik für Saiteninstrumente, Schlagwerk und Celesta
	1. Andante tranquillo
	2. Allegro
	3. Adagio
	4. Allegro molto
Franz Schubert	Symphonie Nr. 7, C-Dur
	1. Andante — Allegro ma non troppo
	2. Andante con moto
	3. Scherzo: Allegro vivace
	4. Allegro vivace

SALZBURGER FESTSPIELE 1948

FÜNFTES ORCHESTERKONZERT

DIE WIENER PHILHARMONIKER

DER SINGVEREIN DER GESELLSCHAFT DER MUSIKFREUNDE IN WIEN

UNTER DER LEITUNG VON

HERBERT KARAJAN

MITWIRKEND:
ELISABETH SCHWARZKOPF (SOPRAN)
PAUL SCHÖFFLER (BASS)
ALOIS FORER (ORGEL)

lucerne
25 august 1948
lucerne festival orchestra
backhaus

mozart symphony 33/brahms piano concerto 2/
beethoven symphony 5
first appearance at lucerne festival

vienna
2 and 3
october 1948
vienna symphony
wiener singverein
seefried
schöffler

brahms ein deutsches requiem

milan
21 october 1948
la scala orchestra
de vito

brahms programme
violin concerto/symphony 1

milan
23 october 1948
la scala orchestra

mozart symphony 33/strauss don juan/
schumann symphony 4

vienna
27 and 28
november 1948
vienna symphony

cherubini anacréon overture/debussy la mer/
tchaikovsky symphony 6

vienna
11 and 12
december 1948
vienna symphony
wiener singverein

bruckner programme
symphony 9/te deum

milan
28 and 31
december 1948
and 2 and 4
january 1949
vienna philharmonic
vienna opera chorus

mozart le nozze di figaro
schwarzkopf/cebotari (2 and 4 january 1949)/
seefried/jurinac/taddei/höfermayer; guest
performances by vienna staatsoper

vienna
8 and 9
january 1949
vienna symphony
seefried

dvorak symphony 9/prokofiev peter and the wolf/
ravel boléro

vienna
15 and 16
january 1949
vienna symphony
wiener singverein
seefried
höngen
patzak
schöffler

beethoven missa solemnis

havana
20 and 21
march 1949
havana philharmonic

weber der freischütz overture/strauss don juan/
brahms symphony 4

havana
3 and 4
april 1949
havana philharmonic
and chorus
menzel
peres
dillon
schon

beethoven symphony 9

buenos aires
20 april 1949
teatro colon
orchestra

mozart symphony 35/strauss don juan/brahms
symphony 1

buenos aires
4 may 1949
teatro colon
orchestra

haydn symphony 104/suffern la noche/beethoven
symphony 5

concerts on this central and southern american tour also given with local orchestras in brazil
and chile

lucerne
10 august 1949
lucerne festival orchestra
fischer

martinu concerto grosso/beethoven piano concerto 3/brahms symphony 1

salzburg
14 august 1949
vienna philharmonic
wiener singverein
zadek
klose
rosvaenge
christoff

messa da requiem

salzburg
17 august 1949
vienna philharmonic
wiener singverein
seefried
höngen
w.ludwig
christoff

beethoven symphony 9

stockholm
5, 6 and 7
october 1949
stockholm philharmonic

weber der freischütz overture/sibelius symphony 5/beethoven symphony 7

vienna
15 and 16
october 1949
vienna symphony

hindemith mathis der maler/beethoven symphony 3

vienna
29 and 30
october 1949
vienna symphony
wiener singverein
güden
jurinac
w.ludwig
braun
hotter

haydn die schöpfung

vienna
12 and 13
november 1949
vienna symphony
badura-skoda

martinu concerto grosso/brahms symphony 3/ franck variations symphoniques pour piano et orchestre/strauss till eulenspiegel

london
25 november 1949
philharmonia
bbc chorus
schwarzkopf
watson
w.ludwig
christoff

beethoven symphony 9

london
2 december 1949
philharmonia

tchaikovsky symphony 6/strauss till eulenspiegel/ravel boléro
this was a revised programme: lipatti was originally scheduled to play bartok piano concerto 3

vienna
10 and 11
december 1949
vienna symphony
schneiderhan

brahms violin concerto/tchaikovsky symphony 4

vienna
17 and 18
december 1949
vienna philharmonic

mozart symphony 39/ravel daphnis et chloé second suite/brahms symphony 2

rome
21 december 1949
santa cecilia
orchestra

locatelli concerto grosso op 4 no 10/strauss don juan/brahms symphony 2

vienna
7 and 8
january 1950
vienna symphony
gulda

weber der freischütz overture/schumann piano concerto/brahms symphony 1

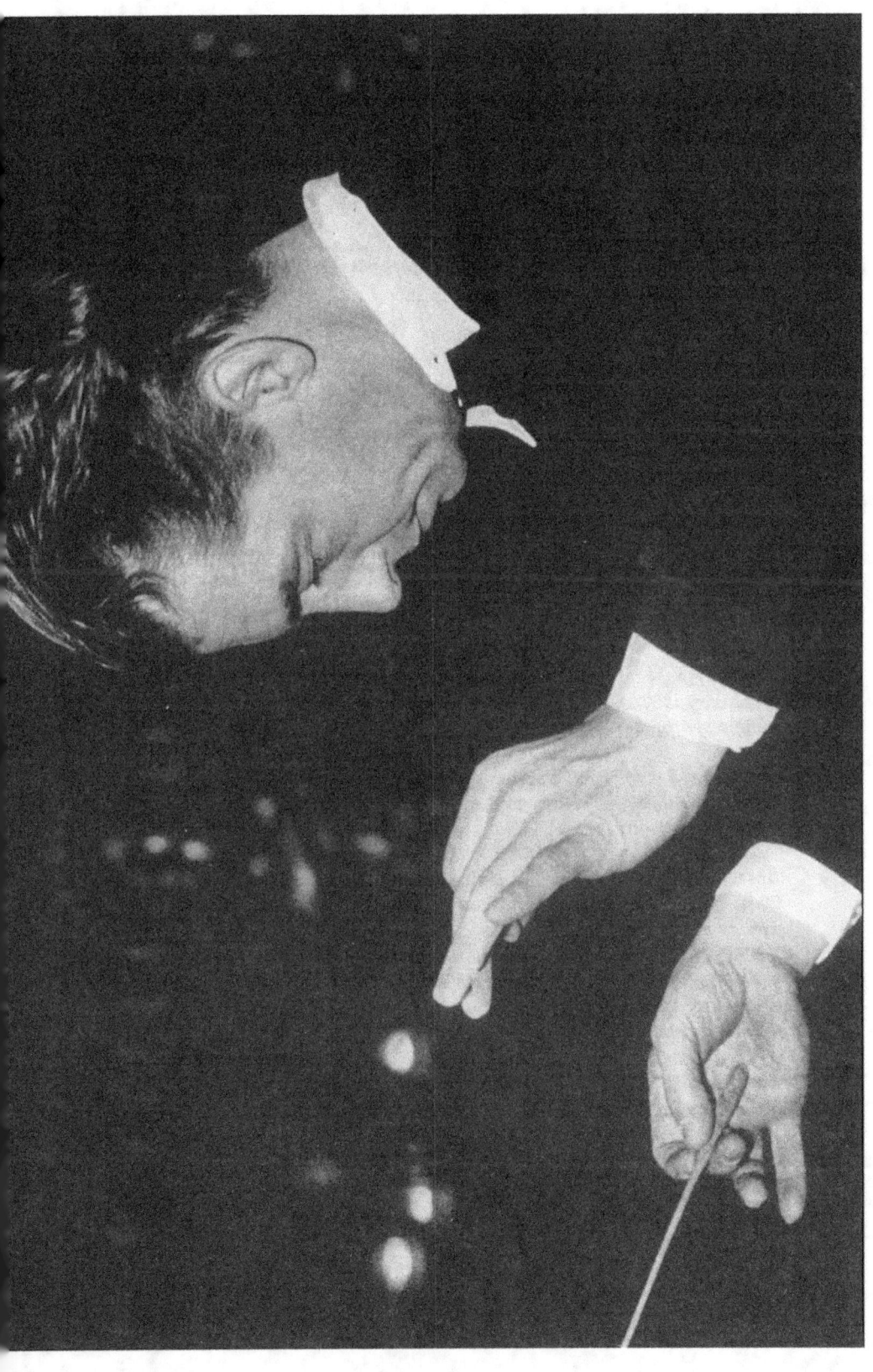

tour of west germany by vienna symphony orchestra

ulm
13 january 1950
vienna symphony

haydn symphony 104/strauss till eulenspiegel/
brahms symphony 1

munich
14 january 1950
vienna symphony

haydn symphony 104/strauss till eulenspiegel/
brahms symphony 1

frankfurt
15 january 1950
vienna symphony

hannover
16 january 1950
vienna symphony

hamburg
17 january 1950
vienna symphony

mozart symphony 35/hindemith mathis der
maler/beethoven symphony 5

berlin
18 january 1950
vienna symphony

haydn symphony 104/strauss till eulenspiegel/
brahms symphony 1

essen
19 january 1950
vienna symphony

weber der freischütz overture/schumann
symphony 4/tchaikovsky symphony 5

düsseldorf
20 january 1950
vienna symphony

weber der freischütz overture/schumann
symphony 4/tchaikovsky symphony 5

duisburg
21 january 1950
vienna symphony

haydn symphony 104/strauss till eulenspiegel/
brahms symphony 1

dortmund
22 january 1950
vienna symphony

mozart symphony 35/hindemith mathis der
maler/beethoven symphony 5

solingen haydn symphony 104/strauss till eulenspiegel/
23 january 1950 brahms symphony 1
vienna symphony

aachen haydn symphony 104/strauss till eulenspiegel/
25 january 1950 brahms symphony 1
vienna symphony

stuttgart
27 january 1950
vienna symphony

augsburg haydn symphony 104/strauss till eulenspiegel/
28 january 1950 beethoven symphony 5
vienna symphony

munich
29 january 1950
vienna symphony
encore pieces on this tour included j.strauss kaiserwalzer and wagner meistersinger overture

vienna bruckner symphony 5
4 and 5
february 1950
vienna symphony

bayreuth wagner lohengrin prelude and gralserzählung/
28 may 1950 bruckner symphony 8
vienna symphony *concert in festspielhaus to raise funds for*
hopf *re-opening of bayreuth festival*

vienna *bach bi-centenary programme*
1 june 1950 brandenburg concerto 2/double violin concerto/
vienna philharmonic cantata 50
wiener singverein
menuhin
schneiderhan

vienna
4 june 1950
vienna philharmonic
wiener singverein
seefried
höngen
w.ludwig
braun

mozart coronation mass
performed as part of service for holy mass in karlskirche to mark the bach bi-centenary celebrations

vienna
9 june 1950
vienna symphony
wiener singverein
seefried
ferrier
w.ludwig
edelmann
schöffler

bach bi-centenary programme
matthäus-passion

vienna
15 june 1950
vienna symphony
wiener singverein
schwarzkopf
ferrier
w.ludwig
schöffler
poell

bach bi-centenary programme
mass in b minor

milan
29 and 30
june 1950
vienna symphony
wiener singverein
schwarzkopf
höngen
w.ludwig
christoff

beethoven missa solemnis

milan bach mass in b minor
2, 3 and 7
july 1950
vienna symphony
wiener singverein
schwarzkopf
ferrier
w.ludwig
christoff

lucerne roussel symphony 4/mozart piano concerto 21/
23 august 1950 tchaikovsky symphony 5
lucerne festival
orchestra
lipatti

graz bruckner symphony 8
14 september 1950
vienna symphony

venice beethoven missa solemnis
16 september 1950
vienna symphony
wiener singverein
seefried
höngen
w.ludwig
schöffler

venice bach mass in b minor
17 september 1950
vienna symphony
wiener singverein
schwarzkopf
höngen
patzak
schöffler
poell

l'aquila
20 september 1950
*vienna symphony
wiener singverein
seefried
höngen
w.ludwig
schöffler*

beethoven programme
symphony 1/symphony 9

l'aquila
22 september 1950
*vienna symphony
wiener singverein
seefried
höngen
w.ludwig
schöffler*

beethoven missa solemnis

perugia
24 september 1950
*vienna symphony
wiener singverein
schwarzkopf
höngen
patzak
schöffler
poell*

bach mass in b minor

milan
12 and 14
october 1950
la scala orchestra

strauss metamorphosen/strauss till eulenspiegel/beethoven symphony 3

milan
16 and 17
october 1950
la scala orchestra

berlioz symphonie fantastique/vaughan williams tallis fantasia/mussorgsky pictures at an exhibition

vienna
21 and 22
october 1950
vienna symphony

bruckner symphony 8

vienna
4 and 5
november 1950
vienna symphony

berlioz symphonie fantastique/mussorgsky pictures at an exhibition

vienna
11 and 12
november 1950
vienna symphony

beethoven symphony 2/mozart piano concerto 21/sibelius symphony 5

vienna
18 and 19
november 1950
vienna symphony
wiener singverein
ilitsch
höngen
dermota
london

verdi messa da requiem

rome
3 december 1950
santa cecilia orchestra

beethoven egmont overture/beethoven symphony 2/mussorgsky pictures at an exhibition

milan
27 and 30
december 1950
and 6, 9 and 14
january 1951
la scala orchestra and chorus

wagner tannhäuser
schwarzkopf/cavelti/dow (14 january)/ beirer/braun/frick

milan
15, 18, 21, 23 and
28 january 1951
la scala orchestra and chorus

mozart don giovanni
schwarzkopf/de los angeles/noni/duval (28 january)/prandelli/petri/taddei/bruscantini

vienna
3 and 4
february 1951
vienna symphony
wiener singverein

verdi aida
martinis/rankin/fehenberger/savarese/ petri/pernerstorfer; these were concert performances of the opera

85

linz
5 february 1951
vienna symphony

bruckner symphony 8

vienna
21 and 22
march 1951
vienna symphony
wiener singverein
schwarzkopf
höngen
dermota
petri

bach mass in b minor

tour of west germany, paris and switzerland by vienna symphony orchestra
munich
25 may 1951
vienna symphony

mozart symphony 39/ravel daphnis et chloé
second suite/beethoven symphony 7

stuttgart
26 may 1951
vienna symphony

mozart symphony 39/ravel daphnis et chloé
second suite/beethoven symphony 7

frankfurt
27 may 1951
vienna symphony

mozart symphony 39/ravel daphnis et chloé
second suite/brahms symphony 2

heidelberg
28 may 1951
vienna symphony

mozart symphony 39/ravel daphnis et chloé
second suite/beethoven symphony 7

paris
30 may 1951
vienna symphony
fischer

haydn symphony 104/mozart piano
concerto 22/brahms symphony 1

paris
31 may 1951
vienna symphony

beethoven programme
symphony 2/leonore 3 overture/symphony 7

bern
1 june 1951
vienna symphony

beethoven programme
symphony 2/leonore 3 overture/symphony 7

geneva
2 june 1951
vienna symphony

mozart symphony 39/ravel daphnis et chloé
second suite/beethoven symphony 7

lausanne
3 june 1951
vienna symphony

mozart symphony 39/beethoven leonore 3
overture/brahms symphony 2

basel
4 june 1951
vienna symphony

mozart symphony 39/beethoven leonore 3
overture/brahms symphony 2

zürich
5 june 1951
vienna symphony

beethoven symphony 2/beethoven leonore 3
overture/mussorgsky pictures at an
exhibition

milan
18 and 19
june 1951
*la scala orchestra
fournier*

cherubini anacréon overture/beethoven
symphony 5/strauss don quixote

bayreuth
5, 8, 16, 19 and
21 august 1951
*bayreuth festival
orchestra and chorus*

wagner die meistersinger von nürnberg
*schwarzkopf/malaniuk/hopf/unger/
edelmann/dalberg/kunz; further
performances on 24 and 26 august were
conducted by hans knappertsbusch*

bayreuth
11 august 1951
*bayreuth festival
orchestra*

wagner das rheingold
*malaniuk/siewert/schwarzkopf/kuen/
fritz/s.bjoerling/pflanzl*

bayreuth
12 august 1951
*bayreuth festival
orchestra*

wagner die walküre
*rysanek/varnay/h.ludwig/treptow/
s.bjoerling/van mill*

bayreuth
13 august 1951
bayreuth festival orchestra

wagner siegfried
varnay/lipp/siewert/aldenhoff/kuen/
s.bjoerling/dalberg/pflanzl

bayreuth
15 august 1951
bayreuth festival orchestra and chorus

wagner götterdämmerung
varnay/mödl/töpper/schwarzkopf/uhde/
aldenhoff/weber/pflanzl

lucerne
1 and 2
september 1951
*vienna symphony
wiener singverein
schwarzkopf
simionato (1)
cavelti (2)
haefliger
braun*

bach mass in b minor

trieste
21 september 1951
*vienna symphony
wiener singverein
mack
braun*

brahms ein deutsches requiem

perugia
23 september 1951
*vienna symphony
wiener singverein
mack
l.fischer
haefliger
braun
rehfuss*

bach matthäus-passion

rome   beethoven missa solemnis
24 september 1951
vienna symphony
wiener singverein
trötschel
wagner
haefliger
rehfuss

rome   brahms ein deutsches requiem
25 september 1951
vienna symphony
wiener singverein
mack
braun

genua   beethoven missa solemnis
26 september 1951
vienna symphony
wiener singverein
trötschel
wagner
haefliger
rehfuss

bologna   mozart symphony 39/ravel daphnis et chloé
27 september 1951   second suite/beethoven symphony 7
vienna symphony

milan   haydn symphony 104/martinu concerto grosso/
12 and 13   sibelius symphony 5/sibelius finlandia
october 1951
la scala orchestra

vienna   bruckner symphony 9/verdi te deum
20, 21 and 22
october 1951
vienna symphony
wiener singverein

vienna   smetana vysherad/bartok piano concerto 3/
27 and 28   brahms symphony 2
october 1951
vienna symphony
baumgartner

vienna
17, 18 and 19
november 1951
vienna symphony
wiener singverein
schwarzkopf
s.bjoerling

brahms ein deutsches requiem

vienna
23, 24 and 25
november 1951
vienna symphony
tortelier

berger concerto manuale/mozart symphony 41/
strauss don quixote

vienna
8, 9 and 10
december 1951
vienna symphony
wiener singverein

handel concerto grosso op 6 no 12/stravinsky
symphony of psalms/tchaikovsky symphony 5

vienna
14, 15 and 16
december 1951
vienna symphony
rysanek
goltz
treptow
l.hofmann

wagner programme
die walküre act one/götterdämmerung
funeral march and immolation scene

milan
9, 12, 15, 20 and
22 january 1952
la scala orchestra
and chorus

beethoven fidelio
mödl/della casa/windgassen/majkut/
edelmann/uhde/london

milan
26 and 31
january and
3, 6, 13 and 17
february 1952
la scala orchestra
and chorus

strauss der rosenkavalier
schwarzkopf/della casa/jurinac/edelmann/
kunz; these were schwarzkopf's debut
performances in the role of marschallin

rome 10 february 1952 *santa cecilia* *orchestra*	mozart symphony 39/ravel rapsodie espagnole/ beethoven symphony 7
rome 12 february 1952 *santa cecilia* *orchestra* *zuccarini*	mozart symphony 39/schumann piano concerto/tchaikovsky symphony 5
london 6 may 1952 *philharmonia*	mozart divertimento 15/strauss don juan/ beethoven symphony 7
london 9 may 1952 *philharmonia*	handel water music suite/stravinsky jeu de cartes/brahms symphony 1

first european tour by philharmonia orchestra

paris 12 may 1952 *philharmonia*	handel water music suite/stravinsky jeu de cartes/tchaikovsky symphony 5
paris 13 may 1952 *philharmonia*	mozart divertimento 17/strauss don juan/ beethoven symphony 5
bern 14 may 1952 *philharmonia*	mozart divertimento 17/strauss don juan/ beethoven symphony 5
geneva 15 may 1952 *philharmonia*	mozart divertimento 17/stravinsky jeu de cartes/beethoven symphony 5
zürich 16 may 1952 *philharmonia*	handel water music suite/stravinsky jeu de cartes/beethoven symphony 7
basel 17 may 1952 *philharmonia*	handel water music suite/mozart divertimento 17/tchaikovsky symphony 5

turin
18 may 1952
philharmonia

handel water music suite/stravinsky jeu de cartes/brahms symphony 1

milan
19 and 20
may 1952
philharmonia

vivaldi concerto in d minor (madrigalesco)/handel water music suite/strauss don juan/beethoven symphony 7

vienna
22 may 1952
philharmonia
schneiderhan

handel water music suite/mozart violin concerto 5/beethoven symphony 7

vienna
23 may 1952
philharmonia

mozart divertimento 15/strauss don juan/brahms symphony 1

linz
24 may 1952
philharmonia

handel water music suite/stravinsky jeu de cartes/beethoven symphony 5

munich
26 may 1952
philharmonia

stravinsky jeu de cartes/strauss don juan/beethoven symphony 5

hamburg
27 may 1952
philharmonia

mozart divertimento 17/stravinsky jeu de cartes/brahms symphony 1

berlin
29 may 1952
philharmonia

handel water music suite/strauss don juan/brahms symphony 1
karajan's first post-war appearance in berlin

berlin
30 may 1952
philharmonia

mozart divertimento 17/stravinsky jeu de cartes/tchaikovsky symphony 5

bayreuth
23 july and
2, 7, 20 and 25
august 1952
*bayreuth festival
orchestra and chorus*

wagner tristan und isolde
mödl/malaniuk/vinay/weber/hotter/uhde

lucerne   beethoven symphony 8/mozart piano concerto
16 august 1952   24/sibelius symphony 5
lucerne festival
orchestra
casadesus

perugia   brahms ein deutsches requiem
28 september 1952
vienna symphony
wiener singverein
streich
braun

perugia   *bruckner programme*
29 september 1952   symphony 9/te deum
vienna symphony
wiener singverein
streich
d.hermann
haefliger
braun

tour of west germany and antwerp by vienna symphony orchestra
munich   mozart symphony 29/blacher paganini
3 october 1952   variations/beethoven symphony 3
vienna symphony

baden-baden   beethoven symphony 1/blacher paganini
4 october 1952   variations/tchaikovsky symphony 5
vienna symphony

mannheim   debussy la mer/mozart symphony 29/
5 october 1952   brahms symphony 2
vienna symphony

aachen   debussy la mer/beethoven symphony 1/
6 october 1952   tchaikovsky symphony 5
vienna symphony

wuppertal   beethoven symphony 1/blacher paganini
7 october 1952   variations/tchaikovsky symphony 5
vienna symphony

dortmund
8 october 1952
vienna symphony

tchaikovsky symphony 5/blacher paganini
variations/mozart symphony 29

bielefeld
9 october 1952
vienna symphony

beethoven symphony 1/debussy la mer/
brahms symphony 2

krefeld
10 october 1952
vienna symphony

beethoven symphony 1/debussy la mer/
tchaikovsky symphony 5

hamburg
11 october 1952
vienna symphony

debussy la mer/mozart symphony 29/
beethoven symphony 3

lübeck
13 october 1952
vienna symphony

beethoven symphony 1/blacher paganini
variations/brahms symphony 2

antwerp
14 october 1952
vienna symphony

mozart symphony 29/beethoven symphony 3
j.strauss kaiserwalzer played as an encore

cologne
15 october 1952
vienna symphony

beethoven symphony 1/debussy la mer/
brahms symphony 2

vienna
18, 19 and 20
october 1952
vienna symphony
schneiderhan

beethoven cycle
symphony 1/symphony 3/violin concerto

vienna
22 october 1952
vienna symphony

twentieth-century cycle
blacher paganini variations/martinu concerto
grosso/roussel symphony 3

vienna
25, 26 and 27
october 1952
vienna symphony
haskil

beethoven cycle
symphony 8/symphony 2/piano concerto 4

vienna
8, 9 and 10
november 1952
vienna symphony

beethoven cycle
egmont overture/symphony 4/symphony 7

vienna
12 november 1952
vienna symphony
kann

twentieth-century cycle
britten frank bridge variations/francaix concertino for piano/bartok concerto for orchestra

vienna
14, 15 and 16
november 1952
vienna symphony

beethoven cycle
coriolan overture/symphony 6/symphony 5

rome
6 december 1952
rai roma orchestra
meyer

pizzetti preludio a un altro giorno/mozart piano concerto 23/brahms symphony 2

rome
20 december 1952
rai roma orchestra
and chorus
laszlo
gedda
catalani
petri
bertocci
foa

stravinsky oedipus rex

rome
24 december 1952
rai roma orchestra

beethoven programme
symphony 4/symphony 7

milan
10, 13, 17, 20 and
25 january and
1 february 1953
la scala orchestra
and chorus

wagner lohengrin
schwarzkopf/mödl/windgassen/neidlinger/
edelmann/metternich/campi (20 and 25)

milan
28 and 31
january and
5, 8 and 11
february 1953
*la scala orchestra
and chorus*

mozart don giovanni
*schwarzkopf/martinis/noni/simoneau
(january)/gedda (february)/petri/panerai/
bruscantini*

milan
14, 16, 18 and 24
february 1953
*la scala orchestra
and chorus*

orff carmina burana/catulli carmina/
trionfo di afrodite
*schwarzkopf/amaro/bertasi/gedda/
zampieri/pirino/panerai/campi/ego;
these were staged versions of the works*

turin
20 february 1953
*rai torino orchestra
and chorus
schwarzkopf
cavelti
gedda
petri*

tippett a child of our time
*rehearsals and performance attended by
the composer*

turin
27 february 1953
rai torino orchestra

honegger symphony 2/strauss tod und
verklärung/tchaikovsky symphony 5
*recording for later radio transmission
on 1 march 1953*

vienna
13, 14 and 15
march 1953
*vienna symphony
wiener singverein
della casa
rössl-majdan
kmennt
edelmann*

beethoven cycle
symphony 9

vienna
18 march 1953
*vienna symphony
wiener singverein
stich-randall
leimer*

twentieth-century cycle
honegger symphony 2/leimer piano
concerto for left hand/schmitt psalm 47

rome 26 march 1953 *rai roma orchestra*	brahms symphony 2 *recording for later radio transmission*
turin 10 april 1953 *rai torino orchestra*	beethoven symphony 2/bartok concerto for orchestra
turin 11 april 1953 *rai torino orchestra*	beethoven symphony 2/sibelius finlandia *recording for later radio transmission*
turin 24 april 1953 *rai torino orchestra* *leimer*	britten frank bridge variations/leimer piano concerto for the left hand/mozart symphony 41
vienna 1, 2, 3 and 4 june 1953 *vienna symphony* *führer*	mozart symphony 29/bartok concerto for orchestra/rachmaninov piano concerto 2
vienna 5, 6 and 7 june 1953 *vienna symphony* *wiener singverein*	*beethoven cycle* fidelio *mödl/schwarzkopf/windgassen/schock/* *edelmann/braun/metternich;* *these were concert performances of the opera*
london 22 june 1953 *philharmonia*	mozart symphony 35/bartok concerto for orchestra/beethoven symphony 3
ostend 23 july 1953 *philharmonia*	mozart symphony 35/strauss don juan/beethoven symphony 3
ostend 24 july 1953 *philharmonia*	handel water music suite/britten frank bridge variations/tchaikovsky symphony 5

lucerne 15 august 1953 *lucerne festival orchestra* *laszlo* *gedda* *petri* *huggler* *woester*	mozart symphony 41/stravinsky oedipus rex
munich 19 and 21 august 1953 *bavarian state orchestra and chorus*	mozart don giovanni *schwarzkopf/martinis/noni/simoneau/* *petri/bruscantini/panerai; these were* *guest performances by the company of la* *scala milan*
edinburgh 1 september 1953 *philharmonia*	britten frank bridge variations/debussy la mer/ beethoven symphony 7 *first appearance at the edinburgh festival*
edinburgh 2 september 1953 *philharmonia* *menuhin*	handel water music suite/beethoven violin concerto/bartok concerto for orchestra
edinburgh 4 september 1953 *philharmonia*	mozart divertimento 15/ravel rapsodie espagnole/tchaikovsky symphony 5
berlin 8 september 1953 *berlin philharmonic*	bartok concerto for orchestra/beethoven symphony 3 *first post-war appearance with the berlin* *philharmonic*
venice 16 september 1953 *rai torino orchestra* *michelangeli*	debussy nuages et fetes/ravel piano concerto in g/debussy la mer/ravel daphnis et chloé second suite
venice 17 september 1953 *rai torino orchestra*	mozart symphony 40/pizzetti preludio ad un altro giorno/brahms symphony 1
tunis september 1953	lieder recital by elisabeth schwarzkopf *karajan acted as piano accompanist*

vienna
2, 3 and 4
october 1953
vienna symphony

mozart symphony 40/debussy nuages et fetes/
brahms symphony 1

vienna
9, 10 and 11
october 1953
vienna symphony

dvorak symphony 9/barber adagio for strings/
respighi pini di roma

tour of west germany, belgium, paris and switzerland by vienna symphony orchestra
munich
12 october 1953
vienna symphony

düsseldorf
13 october 1953
vienna symphony

mozart symphony 41/respighi pini di roma/
tchaikovsky symphony 6

essen
14 october 1953
vienna symphony

mozart symphony 41/strauss tod und
verklärung/brahms symphony 2

viersen
15 october 1953
vienna symphony

mozart symphony 41/strauss tod und
verklärung/brahms symphony 2

wuppertal
16 october 1953
vienna symphony

mozart symphony 40/ravel daphnis et chloé
second suite/tchaikovsky symphony 6

liege
17 october 1953
vienna symphony

mozart symphony 41/strauss tod und
verklärung/beethoven symphony 7

bruges
18 october 1953
vienna symphony

brussels
19 october 1953
vienna symphony

strauss tod und verklärung/mozart symphony 40/
beethoven symphony 7

antwerp
21 october 1953
vienna symphony

beethoven coriolan overture/beethoven symphony 2/tchaikovsky symphony 6

paris
22 october 1953
vienna symphony

beethoven programme
coriolan overture/symphony 2/symphony 3

paris
23 october 1953
vienna symphony

mozart symphony 41/strauss tod und verklärung/brahms symphony 2

baden-baden
25 october 1953
vienna symphony

mozart symphony 40/ravel daphnis et chloé second suite/brahms symphony 2

fribourg
26 october 1953
vienna symphony

beethoven programme
symphony 2/symphony 3

basel
28 october 1953
vienna symphony
wiener singverein

beethoven fidelio
schwarzkopf/felbermayer/fehenberger/majkut/schlott/metternich/uhde; this was a concert performance of the opera

geneva
29 october 1953
vienna symphony
wiener singverein

beethoven fidelio
details as above

zürich
30 october 1953
vienna symphony
wiener singverein

beethoven fidelio
details as above

vienna
31 october and
1 and 3
november 1953
vienna symphony

bruckner symphony 8

vienna
6, 7 and 8
november 1953
vienna symphony
wiener singverein
schwarzkopf
höffgen
haefliger
edelmann
rehfuss

bach matthäus-passion

london
20 november 1953
philharmonia

britten frank bridge variations/beethoven symphony 6/sibelius symphony 5

vienna
27, 28 and 29
november 1953
vienna symphony
wiener singverein
laszlo
haefliger
rehfuss

stravinsky oedipus rex

rome
5 december 1953
rai roma orchestra
giuranna

weber euryanthe overture/ghedini viola concerto/walton symphony 1

rome
11 december 1953
rai roma orchestra

beethoven programme
symphony 4/symphony 5

rome
12, 15, 20 and
22 december 1953
rome opera
orchestra and chorus

mozart don giovanni
schwarzkopf/martinis/noni/gedda/petri/
bruscantini

rome
19 december 1953
rai roma
orchestra and chorus

mozart die zauberflöte
schwarzkopf/streich/noni/gedda/taddei/
petri; concert performance sung in italian
and recorded for later radio transmission on
20 december 1953

rome
21 december 1953
rai roma
orchestra and chorus
schwarzkopf
orell
dominguez
gedda
petri
tadeo

bach magnificat/sutermeister messa da requiem

milan
18, 21, 24, 27
and 31 january
and 5 and 7
february 1954
la scala orchestra
and chorus

lucia di lammermoor
callas/villa/di stefano/poggi (7 february)/
zampieri/panerai/modesti

milan
4, 6, 9, 14 and 20
february 1954
la scala orchestra
and chorus

mozart le nozze di figaro
schwarzkopf/seefried (4 and 6 february)/
gatta/jurinac/falcon (20 february)/petri/
panerai

milan
6 february 1954
rai milano
orchestra and chorus

humperdinck hänsel und gretel
schwarzkopf/jurinac/streich/palombini/
panerai; concert performance sung in
italian and recorded for later radio
transmission on 25 december 1954

turin
12 february 1954
rai torino orchestra
anda

rosenberg concerto for strings/bartok piano concerto 3/beethoven symphony 6

turin
15 february 1954
rai torino orchestra

beethoven egmont overture/beethoven symphony 1/tchaikovsky symphony 6

turin
19 february 1954
rai torino
orchestra and chorus
micheau

mozart symphony 41/handel concerto grosso op 6 no 12/schmitt psalm 47

karajan's first appearances in japan

tokyo
7 april 1954
nhk symphony
sonoda

brahms symphony 1/beethoven piano concerto 4/strauss till eulenspiegel

tokyo
8 april 1954
nhk symphony
naito

brahms symphony 1/beethoven piano concerto 4/strauss till eulenspiegel

tokyo
14, 15 and 16
february 1954
nhk symphony
kling

beethoven egmont overture/beethoven symphony 5/mozart violin concerto 5/ mussorgsky pictures at an exhibition

tokyo
21 april 1954
nhk symphony

cherubini anacréon overture/handel water music suite/prokofiev symphony 1/ tchaikovsky symphony 6

kyoto
26 april 1954
nhk symphony
kling

beethoven egmont overture/beethoven symphony 5/mozart violin concerto 5/ mussorgsky pictures at an exhibition

takarazuka
27 and 28
april 1954
nhk symphony
and chorus
miyake
kawasaki
shibata
ito

beethoven programme
leonore 3 overture/symphony 9

nagoya 30 april and 1 may 1954 *nhk symphony and chorus miyake kawasaki shibata ito*	*beethoven programmr* leonore 3 overture/symphony 9
tokyo 7, 8 and 9 may 1954 *nhk symphony and chorus miyake kawasaki shibata ito*	matsudaira theme and variations/ beethoven symphony 9
london 24 june 1954 *philharmonia sutcliffe walton james brain*	mozart sinfonia concertante for winds/ ravel rapsodie espagnole/beethoven symphony 5
london 29 june 1954 *philharmonia*	vaughan williams tallis fantasia/debussy la mer/brahms symphony 1
aix-en-provence 28 july 1954 *philharmonia*	beethoven leonore 3 overture/debussy la mer/ berlioz symphonie fantastique
aix-en-provence 30 july 1954 *philharmonia*	britten frank bridge variations/strauss don juan/beethoven symphony 5
lucerne 8 august 1954 *philharmonia*	divertimento 15/ravel rapsodie espagnole/ brahms symphony 1

lucerne
12 august 1954
philharmonia
gieseking

strauss don juan/mozart piano concerto 23/
berlioz symphonie fantastique

ottobeuren
15 august 1954
vienna symphony

bruckner symphony 8

edinburgh
6 september 1954
philharmonia
arrau

berlioz symphonie fantastique/schumann
piano concerto/wagner tristan prelude and
liebestod

edinburgh
7 september 1954
philharmonia

beethoven programme
egmont overture/symphony 4/symphony 3

edinburgh
8 september 1954
philharmonia

mozart symphony 35/strauss till eulenspiegel/
brahms symphony 1

berlin
23 september 1954
berlin philharmonic

mozart symphony 39/bartok piano concerto 3/
brahms symphony 1

vienna
1, 2 and 3
october 1954
vienna symphony

mozart symphony 39/bruckner symphony 5

vienna
8 and 10
october 1954
vienna symphony
wiener singverein

bizet carmen
simionato/güden/gedda/roux; these were
concert performances of the opera

london
15 october 1954
philharmonia
fischer

berlioz symphonie fantastique/mozart piano
concerto 22/mussorgsky pictures at an
exhibition

tour of belgium, bern, italy and paris by philharmonia orchestra
antwerp
17 october 1954
philharmonia

brussels
18 and 19
october 1954
philharmonia

bern
20, 21 and 22
october 1954
philharmonia

milan   cherubini anacréon overture/britten frank
23 and 24   bridge variations/strauss till eulenspiegel/
october 1954   beethoven symphony 5
philharmonia

perugia   mozart symphony 35/vaughan williams
25 october 1954   tallis fantasia/beethoven symphony 3
philharmonia

rome   cherubini anacréon overture/strauss till
26 october 1954   eulenspiegel/beethoven symphony 3
philharmonia

naples   beethoven symphony 5/vaughan williams
27 october 1954   tallis fantasia/wagner meistersinger overture
philharmonia

palermo   vaughan williams tallis fantasia/strauss
28 october 1954   till eulenspiegel/tchaikovsky symphony 5
philharmonia

turin   vaughan williams tallis fantasia/strauss
31 october 1954   don juan/tchaikovsky symphony 4
philharmonia

paris
2 november 1954
philharmonia
encore pieces on this tour included wagner meistersinger and verdi forza del destino overtures

vienna
16, 17 and 18
november 1954
vienna symphony

handel concerto grosso op 6 no 12/honegger symphony 3/tchaikovsky symphony 4

berlin
21 and 22
november 1954
berlin philharmonic

vaughan williams tallis fantasia/bruckner symphony 9

vienna
26, 27 and 28
november 1954
vienna symphony
wiener singverein
stella
dominguez
gedda
modesti

verdi messa da requiem

rome
4 december 1954
rai roma orchestra
and chorus
stich-randall
rössl-majdan
kmennt
frick

beethoven symphony 9

rome
11 december 1954
rai roma orchestra
and chorus
pirino
boriello
anda

bartok cantata profana/brahms piano concerto 2

rome
15 december 1954
rai roma orchestra

mozart symphony 39/honegger symphony 3
recording for later radio transmission

rome
19 december 1954
rai roma orchestra
and chorus

debussy pelléas et mélisande
*schwarzkopf/haefliger/roux/petri; this was
a concert performance of the opera*

turin
15 january 1955
rai torino orchestra
and chorus
haefliger

handel concerto grosso op 6 no 12/kodaly
psalmus hungaricus/prokofiev symphony 5
*recording for later radio transmission on
21 december 1955*

turin
16 january 1955
rai torino orchestra
yanagawa

stravinsky symphony in three movements/
strauss tod und verklärung/rachmaninov
piano concerto 2
*recording for later radio transmission on
16 december 1955*

milan
18, 20, 22, 25 and
30 january and
1 february 1955
*la scala orchestra
and chorus*

bizet carmen
*simionato/carteri/angelici (25 january)/
di stefano/roux*

wolfsburg
13 february 1955
berlin philharmonic

strauss don juan/beethoven leonore 3
overture/tchaikovsky symphony 5

hannover
14 february 1955
berlin philharmonic

haydn symphony 104/wagner tristan
prelude and liebestod/beethoven symphony 7

hamburg
15 february 1955
berlin philharmonic

mozart symphony 35/strauss till eulenspiegel/
brahms symphony 1

berlin
21 and 22
february 1955
berlin philharmonic

haydn symphony 104/wagner tristan
prelude and liebestod/beethoven symphony 5

first tour of usa and canada by berlin philharmonic orchestra

washington 27 february 1955 *berlin philharmonic*	mozart symphony 35/wagner tristan prelude and liebestod/brahms symphony 1 *karajan's north american début*
philadelphia 28 february 1955 *berlin philharmonic*	haydn symphony 104/wagner tristan prelude and liebestod/beethoven symphony 5
new york 1 march 1955 *berlin philharmonic*	haydn symphony 104/wagner tristan prelude and liebestod/beethoven symphony 5
harrisburg 2 march 1955 *berlin philharmonic*	haydn symphony 104/wagner tristan prelude and liebestod/beethoven symphony 5
pittsburgh 3 march 1955 *berlin philharmonic*	handel concerto grosso op 6 no 12/strauss don juan/brahms symphony 2
cleveland 4 march 1955 *berlin philharmonic*	mozart symphony 35/wagner tristan prelude and liebestod/brahms symphony 1
cincinnatti 5 march 1955 *berlin philharmonic*	handel concerto grosso op 6 no 12/blacher concertante musik/strauss don juan/ beethoven symphony 5
lexington 7 march 1955 *berlin philharmonic*	beethoven egmont overture/barber adagio for strings/strauss till eulenspiegel/beethoven symphony 7
bloomington 8 march 1955 *berlin philharmonic*	mozart symphony 35/strauss don juan/ beethoven symphony 5
milwaukee 10 march 1955 *berlin philharmonic*	handel concerto grosso op 6 no 12/beethoven symphony 7/strauss till eulenspiegel/wagner tannhäuser overture
chicago 11 march 1955 *berlin philharmonic*	haydn symphony 104/wagner tristan prelude and liebestod/beethoven symphony 5

chicago
12 march 1955
berlin philharmonic
brice

beethoven leonore 3 overture/barber adagio for strings/mahler lieder eines fahrenden gesellen/tchaikovsky symphony 5

chicago
13 march 1955
berlin philharmonic

mozart symphony 35/strauss till eulenspiegel/brahms symphony 1

ann arbor
15 march 1955
berlin philharmonic

mozart symphony 35/wagner tristan prelude and liebestod/brahms symphony 1

columbus
16 march 1955
berlin philharmonic

beethoven egmont overture/beethoven symphony 7/blacher concertante musik/wagner tannhäuser overture

detroit
17 march 1955
berlin philharmonic

handel concerto grosso op 6 no 12/blacher concertante musik/strauss don juan/beethoven symphony 5

toronto
18 march 1955
berlin philharmonic

handel concerto grosso op 6 no 12/brahms symphony 2/strauss till eulenspiegel/wagner tannhäuser overture

rochester
20 march 1955
berlin philharmonic

mozart symphony 35/strauss till eulenspiegel/brahms symphony 2

montreal
21 march 1955
berlin philharmonic

beethoven egmont overture/strauss don juan/berlioz marche hongroise/tchaikovsky symphony 5

syracuse
22 march 1955
berlin philharmonic
brice

strauss don juan/mahler lieder eines fahrenden gesellen/brahms symphony 2

boston
24 march 1955
berlin philharmonic

haydn symphony 104/wagner tristan prelude and liebestod/beethoven symphony 5

hartford
25 march 1955
berlin philharmonic

beethoven egmont overture/barber adagio for strings/blacher concertante musik/tchaikovsky symphony 5

baltimore
26 march 1955
berlin philharmonic

haydn symphony 104/strauss till eulenspiegel/ beethoven symphony 7

washington
27 march 1955
berlin philharmonic

beethoven leonore 3 overture/barber adagio for strings/blacher concertante musik/ tchaikovsky symphony 5

newark
29 march 1955
berlin philharmonic

new york
30 march 1955
berlin philharmonic

beethoven leonore 3 overture/barber adagio for strings/blacher concertante musik/ tchaikovsky symphony 5

new york
1 april 1955
berlin philharmonic

mozart symphony 35/strauss till eulenspiegel/ brahms symphony 1

berlin
4 and 5
april 1955
berlin philharmonic

mozart symphony 35/strauss till eulenspiegel/ brahms symphony 1

london
1 may 1955
philharmonia

mozart symphony 35/sibelius symphony 4/ tchaikovsky symphony 4

vienna
31 may and
1 and 2
june 1955
vienna symphony
schneiderhan

beethoven coriolan overture/beethoven violin concerto/brahms symphony 4

ROYAL FESTIVAL HALL
General Manager: T. E. Bean

PHILHARMONIA CONCERT SOCIETY
Artistic Director:
WALTER LEGGE

PHILHARMONIA
ORCHESTRA
(Leader: MANOUG PARIKIAN)

HERBERT von KARAJAN

PROGRAMME

MOZART: Symphony No. 35, "Haffner"
SIBELIUS: Symphony No. 4

INTERVAL

TCHAIKOVSKY: Symphony No. 4

Sunday, May 1, 1955
at 7.30 p.m.

Management: IBBS & TILLETT LTD., 124 WIGMORE STREET, W.1

vienna
25 and 26
june 1955
vienna symphony
wiener singverein
della casa
rössl-majdan
kmennt
edelmann

beethoven symphony 9

lucerne
10 august 1955
lucerne festival
orchestra
haskil
anda

bach concerto for two pianos/honegger symphony 3/brahms symphony 2

lucerne
27 august 1955
lucerne festival
orchestra
schneiderhan

beethoven programme
coriolan overture/violin concerto/symphony 7

berlin
29 september and
2 october 1955
rias orchestra
la scala chorus

lucia di lammermoor
callas/villa/di stefano/zampieri/panerai/
zaccaria; these were guest performances by
company of la scala

berlin
30 september and
1 october 1955
berlin philharmonic
gieseking

beethoven programme
coriolan overture/piano concerto 5/
symphony 7

vienna
7, 8 and 9
october 1955
vienna symphony
wiener singverein
haefliger
badura-skoda
demus
karajan

mozart concerto for three pianos/beethoven symphony 2/kodaly psalmus hungaricus

london vaughan williams tallis fantasia/bartok concerto
14 october 1955 for orchestra/sibelius symphony 5
philharmonia

london britten frank bridge variations/ravel rapsodie
18 october 1955 espagnole/berlioz symphonie fantastique
philharmonia

first tour of north america by philharmonia orchestra
washington mozart divertimento 15/debussy la mer/berlioz
23 october 1955 symphonie fantastique
philharmonia

new york mozart divertimento 15/debussy la mer/berlioz
25 october 1955 symphonie fantastique
philharmonia

new york mozart symphony 39/brahms haydn variations/
26 october 1955 sibelius symphony 5
philharmonia

new haven handel water music suite/beethoven symphony 6/
27 october 1955 debussy la mer
philharmonia

new york handel water music suite/beethoven symphony 6/
28 october 1955 bartok concerto for orchestra
philharmonia

washington handel water music suite/beethoven symphony 6/
29 october 1955 bartok concerto for orchestra
philharmonia

huntington mozart symphony 39/brahms haydn variations/
31 october 1955 sibelius symphony 5
philharmonia

charleston vaughan williams tallis fantasia/debussy la mer/
1 november 1955 tchaikovsky symphony 4
philharmonia

columbus mozart divertimento 15/ravel rapsodie espagnole/
2 november 1955 berlioz symphonie fantastique
philharmonia

toledo
3 november 1955
philharmonia

mozart symphony 39/brahms haydn variations/
sibelius symphony 5

chicago
5 november 1955
philharmonia

mozart divertimento 15/ravel rapsodie
espagnole/berlioz symphonie fantastique

chicago
6 november 1955
philharmonia

handel water music suite/beethoven symphony 6/
bartok concerto for orchestra

grand rapids
7 november 1955
philharmonia

handel water music suite/beethoven symphony 6/
debussy la mer

kalamazoo
8 november 1955
philharmonia

mozart symphony 39/ravel rapsodie espagnole/
beethoven symphony 6

ann arbor
9 november 1955
philharmonia

mozart symphony 39/brahms haydn vatiations/
sibelius symphony 5

detroit
10 november 1955
philharmonia

handel water music suite/brahms haydn
variations/tchaikovsky symphony 4

toronto
11 november 1955
philharmonia

britten frank bridge variations/beethoven
symphony 6/debussy la mer

new york
13 november 1955
philharmonia

vaughan williams tallis fantasia/ravel rapsodie
espagnole/tchaikovsky symphony 4

baltimore
14 november 1955
philharmonia

vaughan williams tallis fantasia/brahms
haydn variations/tchaikovsky symphony 4

philadelphia
15 november 1955
philharmonia

mozart divertimento 15/beethoven symphony 6/
bartok concerto for orchestra

amherst
16 november 1955
philharmonia

handel water music suite/brahms haydn variations/tchaikovsky symphony 4

burlington
17 november 1955
philharmonia

vaughan williams tallis fantasia/ravel rapsodie espagnole/berlioz symphonie fantastique

portland
18 november 1955
philharmonia

mozart divertimento 15/brahms haydn variations/beethoven symphony 6/ verdi forza del destino overture

boston
19 november 1955
philharmonia

mozart divertimento 15/sibelius symphony 5/ bartok concerto for orchestra

many concerts on this american tour were prefaced with british national anthem in a new arrangement by william walton; encore pieces included sibelius finlandia, verdi forza del destino overture and the sousa marches stars and stripes forever and el capitan

milan
10, 13, 18, 20 and
22 december 1955
*la scala orchestra
and chorus*

mozart die zauberflöte
schwarzkopf/sciutti/köth/gedda/taddei/ zaccaria

berlin
4, 5 and 6
january 1956
*berlin philharmonic
fournier*

beethoven symphony 4/saint cello concerto in a minor/strauss don quixote

vienna
9 and 10
january 1956
*vienna symphony
mainardi*

mozart symphony 38/haydn cello concerto in d/strauss don quixote

berlin
21, 22 and 23
january 1956
*berlin philharmonic
kempff*

mozart bi-centenary concert
divertimento 17/piano concerto 20/ symphony 41

vienna   *mozart bi-centenary concert*
26 and 27   symphony 40/piano concerto 20/symphony 41
january 1956
vienna symphony
haskil

mozart bi-centenary european tour by philharmonia orchestra
salzburg   divertimento 15/piano concerto 20/
28 january 1956   symphony 39
philharmonia
haskil

munich   divertimento 15/piano concerto 20/
29 january 1956   symphony 40
philharmonia
haskil

freiburg   divertimento 15/piano concerto 20/
30 january 1956   symphony 39
philharmonia
haskil

bern   divertimento 15/piano concerto 20/
31 january 1956   symphony 40
philharmonia
haskil

zürich   divertimento 15/piano concerto 20/
1 february 1956   symphony 40
philharmonia
haskil

strassburg   divertimento 15/violin concerto 5/symphony 35
2 february 1956
philharmonia
parikian

paris   divertimento 15/piano concerto 20/
3 february 1956   symphony 41
philharmonia
haskil

paris
4 february 1956
philharmonia
haskil

symphony 39/piano concerto 20/symphony 35

london
6 february 1956
philharmonia
haskil

symphony 35/piano concerto 20/symphony 41

berlin
19 and 20
february 1956
berlin philharmonic
saint hedwig's choir
mödl
haefliger
dickie
zaccaria
neidlinger

stravinsky oedipus rex

vienna
24, 25 and 26
february 1956
vienna symphony
ferras

mozart mauerische trauermusik/brahms
violin concerto/prokofiev symphony 5

milan
14, 17, 20, 22 and
25 march 1956
la scala orchestra

strauss salome
goltz/kenney/lorenz/hotter

berlin
27, 28 and 29
april 1956
berlin philharmonic

handel concerto grosso op 6 no 12/honegger
symphony 3/tchaikovsky symphony 6

tour of west germany, belgium and paris by berlin philharmonic orchestra

kiel 30 april 1956 *berlin philharmonic* *menuhin*	*beethoven programme* coriolan overture/violin concerto/symphony 7
hamburg 1 may 1956 *berlin philharmonic*	handel concerto grosso op 6 no 12/honegger symphony 3/tchaikovsky symphony 6
bremen 2 may 1956 *berlin philharmonic*	haydn symphony 104/wagner tristan prelude and liebestod/brahms symphony 2
oldenburg 3 may 1956 *berlin philharmonic*	schubert symphony 8/strauss till eulenspiegel/ beethoven symphony 7
hannover 4 may 1956 *berlin philharmonic* *menuhin*	beethoven coriolan overture/beethoven violin concerto/brahms symphony 2
bielefeld 5 may 1956 *berlin philharmonic*	handel concerto grosso op 6 no 12/wagner tristan prelude and liebestod/beethoven symphony 3
bochum 6 may 1956 *berlin philharmonic*	haydn symphony 104/wagner tristan prelude and liebestod/beethoven symphony 7
dortmund 7 may 1956 *berlin philharmonic*	schubert symphony 8/strauss till eulenspiegel/ beethoven symphony 5
essen 8 may 1956 *berlin philharmonic*	handel concerto grosso op 6 no 12/wagner tristan prelude and liebestod/tchaikovsky symphony 6
düsseldorf 9 may 1956 *berlin philharmonic*	haydn symphony 104/strauss till eulenspiegel/ beethoven symphony 5

viersen
10 may 1956
berlin philharmonic

handel concerto grosso op 6 no 12/honegger
symphony 3/tchaikovsky symphony 6

antwerp
11 may 1956
berlin philharmonic

haydn symphony 104/wagner tristan prelude
and liebestod/brahms symphony 2

ostend
12 may 1956
berlin philharmonic

handel concerto grosso op 6 no 12/strauss
till eulenspiegel/beethoven symphony 7

paris
14 may 1956
berlin philharmonic

haydn symphony 104/strauss till eulenspiegel/
beethoven symphony 3

paris
15 may 1956
berlin philharmonic

handel concerto grosso op 6 no 12/honegger
symphony 3/brahms symphony 2

cologne
18 may 1956
berlin philharmonic

haydn symphony 104/strauss till eulenspiegel/
tchaikovsky symphony 6

wolfsburg
19 may 1956
berlin philharmonic

schubert symphony 8/strauss till eulenspiegel/
beethoven symphony 7

berlin
21 may 1956
berlin philharmonic

beethoven symphony 7/wagner tannhäuser
overture/strauss till eulenspiegel/j.strauss
kaiserwalzer/berlioz marche hongroise

munich
4 june 1956
berlin philharmonic

strauss don juan/honegger symphony 3/
brahms symphony 2

vienna
5 and 6
june 1956
berlin philharmonic

mozart symphony 35/wagner tristan prelude
and liebestod/beethoven symphony 3
*first post-war appearances of berlin
philharmonic orchestra in vienna*

vienna
7 june 1956
berlin philharmonic

mozart divertimento 17/strauss till eulenspiegel/
brahms symphony 2

graz
8 june 1956
berlin philharmonic

vienna
12, 14 and 16
june 1956
*la scala orchestra
orchestra and chorus*

donizetti lucia di lammermoor
*callas/villa/di stefano/zampieri/panerai/
zaccaria; guest performances by company of
la scala milan*

london
20 june 1956
*philharmonia
schwarzkopf*

beethoven symphony 2/strauss vier letzte lieder/
brahms symphony 4

lucerne
15 august 1956
*lucerne festival
orchestra
schneiderhan
seefried*

mozart bi-centenary programme
symphony 38/violin concerto 5/ch'io mi scordi
di te/symphony 39

lucerne
6 september 1956
philharmonia

beethoven symphony 6/brahms symphony 4

berlin
23, 24 and 25
september 1956
*berlin philharmonic
anda*

brahms programme
piano concerto 2/symphony 4

second tour of north america by berlin philharmonic orchestra

washington
7 october 1956
berlin philharmonic
schneiderhan

strauss don juan/mozart violin concerto 5/ beethoven symphony 3

princeton
8 october 1956
berlin philharmonic

cherubini anacréon overture/honegger symphony 3/berger rondo giocoso/beethoven symphony 7

new haven
9 october 1956
berlin philharmonic

weber oberon overture/schumann symphony 4/ strauss till eulenspiegel/wagner tannhäuser overture

new york
10 october 1956
berlin philharmonic
schneiderhan

strauss don juan/mozart violin concerto 5/ beethoven symphony 3

washington
11 october 1956
berlin philharmonic

new york
12 october 1956
berlin philharmonic

cherubini anacréon overture/honegger symphony 3/brahms symphony 2

new brunswick
13 october 1956
berlin philharmonic

boston
14 october 1956
berlin philharmonic

montreal
15 october 1956
berlin philharmonic

cherubini anacréon overture/beethoven symphony 7/smetana moldau/tchaikovsky romeo and juliet

ottawa
16 october 1956
berlin philharmonic

beethoven symphony 7/strauss don juan/ wagner meistersinger overture

ALLIED ARTS CORPORATION

HARRY ZELZER, *Managing Director*

Presents

Berlin Philharmonic Orchestra

conductor

HERBERT VON KARAJAN

SATURDAY EVENING, OCTOBER 27th, 1956
at 8:30 P.M.
ORCHESTRA HALL   CHICAGO

OPENING EVENT ON THE 1956-57
ZELZER CONCERT SERIES

hamilton
17 october 1956
berlin philharmonic

mozart symphony 35/strauss till eulenspiegel/
brahms symphony 1

toronto
18 october 1956
berlin philharmonic

mozart symphony 35/strauss don juan/
beethoven symphony 3

ann arbor
21 october 1956
berlin philharmonic

cherubini anacréon overture/honegger
symphony 3/beethoven symphony 7

saginaw
22 october 1956
berlin philharmonic

weber der freischütz overture/schumann
symphony 4/smetana moldau/wagner
meistersinger overture

east lansing
23 october 1956
berlin philharmonic

beethoven symphony 7/tchaikovsky
romeo and juliet/wagner tannhäuser overture

kalamazoo
24 october 1956
berlin philharmonic

chicago
26 october 1956
berlin philharmonic
schneiderhan

strauss don juan/mozart violin concerto 5/
beethoven symphony 3

chicago
27 october 1956
berlin philharmonic

weber oberon overture/schubert symphony 8/
schumann symphony 4

chicago
28 october 1956
berlin philharmonic

cherubini anacréon overture/honegger
symphony 3/brahms symphony 2

milwaukee
29 october 1956
berlin philharmonic

weber der freischütz overture/beethoven
symphony 5/wagner tristan prelude and
liebestod/wagner meistersinger overture

urbana
30 october 1956
berlin philharmonic

cherubini anacréon overture/strauss don juan/
berger rondo giocoso/beethoven symphony 3

saint louis
1 november 1956
berlin philharmonic

haydn symphony 104/wagner tristan prelude
and liebestod/brahms symphony 2

tobeka
2 november 1956
berlin philharmonic

cherubini anacréon overture/schumann
symphony 4/smetana moldau/wagner
meistersinger overture

denver
4 november 1956
berlin philharmonic

haydn symphony 104/wagner tristan prelude
and liebestod/brahms symphony 2

salt lake city
7 november 1956
berlin philharmonic

mozart symphony 35/strauss till eulenspiegel/
schumann symphony 4

provo
8 november 1956
berlin philharmonic

beethoven egmont overture/beethoven
symphony 7/smetana moldau/wagner
meistersinger overture

san francisco
10 november 1956
berlin philharmonic

haydn symphony 104/wagner tristan prelude
and liebestod/beethoven symphony 5

berkeley
12 and 13
november 1956
berlin philharmonic

weber oberon overture/schumann symphony 4/
tchaikovsky romeo and juliet/wagner
tannhäuser overture

sacramento
14 november 1956
berlin philharmonic

fresno
15 november 1956
berlin philharmonic

beethoven egmont overture/schumann
symphony 4/smetana moldau/wagner
meistersinger overture

UNIVERSITY OF KANSAS
CONCERT COURSE
presents the

Berlin Philharmonic Orchestra

Herbert von Karajan, *Conductor*

Under the Patronage of
His Excellency, HEINZ L. KREKELER
German Ambassador to the United States

PROGRAM

SYMPHONY IN D MAJOR, OPUS 104 (LONDON
    SYMPHONY) .... *Haydn*
    Adagio—Allegro
    Andante
    Menuetto
    Allegro spiritoso

PRELUDE AND LOVE-DEATH FROM "TRISTAN
    UND ISOLDE" .... *Wagner*

INTERMISSION

SYMPHONY No. 2 IN D MAJOR, OPUS 73 .... *Brahms*
    Allegro non troppo
    Adagio non troppo
    Allegretto grazioso (quasi andantino)
    Allegro con spirito

This concert is part of the second American tour of
the Berlin Philharmonic Orchestra presented by:
    Columbia Artists Management Inc.
    Personal Direction: Andre Mertens
    BERLIN PHILHARMONIC RECORDINGS:
    DECCA GOLD LABEL, RCA VICTOR RED SEAL
        AND HIS MASTER'S VOICE
    HERBERT VON KARAJAN'S RECORDINGS: ANGEL

HOCH AUDITORIUM – THURSDAY, NOVEMBER 1, 1956 – 8:20 P.M.

san diego
17 november 1956
berlin philharmonic

los angeles
18 november 1956
berlin philharmonic

santa barbara   haydn symphony 104/wagner tristan prelude
19 november 1956   and liebestod/schumann symphony 4
berlin philharmonic

berlin   haydn symphony 104/strauss don juan/
22, 23 and 24   schumann symphony 4
november 1956
berlin philharmonic

vienna   brahms ein deutsches requiem
1 and 2
december 1956
vienna symphony
wiener singverein
grümmer
hotter

berlin   blacher orchesterfantasie/strauss ariadne
8, 9 and 10   es gibt ein reich/tchaikovsky symphony 5
december 1956
berlin philharmonic
schwarzkopf

berlin   bruckner symphony 8
6, 7 and 8
january 1957
berlin philharmonic

vienna   mozart maurerische trauermusik
17 january 1957   *played in memory of arturo toscanini before*
vienna philharmonic   *a staatsoper performance which was not*
                            otherwise conducted by karajan

vienna
19 and 20
january 1957
vienna symphony

bruckner symphony 5

vienna
13 and 14
february 1957
vienna symphony

cherubini anacréon overture/hindemith
mathis der maler/beethoven symphony 7

berlin
17, 18 and 19
february 1957
berlin philharmonic

cherubini anacréon overture/schubert
symphony 8/prokofiev symphony 5

milan
11, 14, 16, 19 and
23 march 1957
*la scala orchestra
and chorus*

verdi falstaff
*schwarzkopf/moffo/barbieri/palombini/
alva/gobbi/panerai*

vienna
2 and 5
april 1957
vienna philharmonic

wagner die walküre
*nilsson/rysanek/madeira/suthaus/hotter/
frick; karajan's first appearances as
director of vienna staatsoper*

vienna
15, 18, 21, 27 and
30 april 1957
*vienna philharmonic
vienna opera chorus*

verdi otello
rysanek/canali/del monaco/colzani

vienna
17 april 1957
vienna philharmonic

bruckner symphony 8

vienna
20 april 1957
vienna philharmonic

wagner die walküre
*mödl/nordmo-lövberg/malaniuk/suthaus/
hotter/frick*

berlin beethoven symphony 9
25 and 26 *concert to mark the orchestra's seventy-fifth*
april 1957 *anniversary*
berlin philharmonic
saint hedwig's choir
grümmer
höffgen
haefliger
frick

vienna wagner die walküre
1 may 1957 *nilsson/nordmo-lövberg/malaniuk/suthaus/*
vienna philharmonic *hotter/frick*

vienna verdi otello
3 and 6 *rysanek/canali/del monaco/colzani*
may 1957
vienna philharmonic
vienna opera chorus

vienna martin études for orchestra/mozart piano
4 and 5 concerto 23/brahms symphony 4
may 1957
vienna symphony
klien

berlin hindemith mathis der maler/beethoven piano
24, 25 and 26 concerto 3/sibelius symphony 5
may 1957
berlin philharmonic
gould

vienna wagner die walküre
2 june 1957 *nilsson/rysanek/höngen/suthaus/edelmann/*
vienna philharmonic *frick*

vienna verdi otello
5 and 9 *jurinac/canali/guichandut/schöffler*
june 1957
vienna philharmonic
vienna opera chorus

vienna
7, 10, 13 and
15 june 1957
vienna philharmonic
vienna opera chorus

verdi la traviata
zeani/raimondi/panerai; performances originally planned for maria callas

vienna
12 june 1957
vienna philharmonic

wagner die walküre
mödl/cunitz/malaniuk/suthaus/edelmann/ frick

vienna
15 and 16
june 1957
vienna philharmonic
wiener singverein
stich-randall
höffgen
haefliger
zaccaria

beethoven missa solemnis

vienna
17 and 20
june 1957
vienna philharmonic
vienna opera chorus

verdi la traviata
gencer/raimondi/panerai

vienna
19 june 1957
vienna philharmonic
vienna opera chorus

bizet carmen
madeira/güden/di stefano/london

salzburg
27 july and
6, 12, 20 and 26
august 1957
vienna philharmonic
vienna opera chorus

beethoven fidelio
goltz/jurinac/zampieri/kmentt/edelmann/ schöffler/zaccaria; karajan's first appearances as artistic director of salzburg festival

salzburg
28 july 1957
vienna philharmonic

bruckner symphony 8

salzburg mozart programme
29 july 1957 symphony 35/piano concerto 21/symphony 41
berlin philharmonic first appearance of berlin philharmonic
anda orchestra at salzburg festival

salzburg verdi falstaff
10, 14, 21 and *schwarzkopf/moffo/simionato/alva/gobbi/*
27 august 1957 *panerai*
vienna philharmonc
vienna opera chorus

salzburg *twentieth century programme*
13 august 1957 berger sinfonia parabolica/einem piano
berlin philharmonic concerto/honegger symphony 3
herzog

lucerne brahms violin concerto/tchaikovsky
17 august 1957 symphony 6
lucerne festival
orchestra
milstein

salzburg brahms ein deutsches requiem
22 august 1957
vienna philharmonic
wiener singverein
della casa
fischer-dieskau

vienna verdi falstaff
15, 17, 20 and *schwarzkopf/moffo/simionato/alva/*
23 september 1957 *zampieri (23)/gobbi/panerai*
vienna philharmonic
vienna opera chorus

vienna bizet carmen
21 september and *madeira/güden/micheau (10 october)/*
8 and 10 *filacuridi/london/panerai (8 and 10 october)*
october 1957
vienna philharmonic
vienna opera chorus

STAATSOPER

Freitag, den 20. September 1957
Im Abonnement V. Gruppe. Beschränkter Kartenverkauf
Besondere Preise

FALSTAFF

Komische Oper in drei Akten (sechs Bildern)
von Arrigo Boito

Musik von Giuseppe Verdi

Musikalische Leitung u. Inszenierung: Herbert v. Karajan
Bühnenbilder und Kostüme: G. Bartolini-Salimbeni
Choreographie: Willy Fränzl
Einstudierung der Chöre: Roberto Benaglio
von der Radiotelevisione Italiana

Sir John Falstaff	Tito Gobbi
Ford, Alicens Mann	Rolando Panerai
Fenton	Giuseppe Zampieri
Dr. Cajus	Tomaso Spataro
Bardolph } in Falstaffs Diensten	Renato Ercolani
Pistol	Mario Petri
Mrs. Alice Ford	Elisabeth Schwarzkopf
Aennchen, deren Tochter	Anna Moffo
Mrs. Quickly	Giulietta Simionato
Mrs. Meg Page	Annemarie Canali
Der Wirt vom Gasthause „zum Hosenbande"	Josef Hauer
Rubin, Falstaffs Page	Günther Falusy
Ein Page Fords	Christian Hudec

Schauplatz: Windsor
Zeit: Während der Regierungszeit Heinrich IV.

Technische Einrichtung: Hans Felkel — Beleuchtung: Albin Rotter

Nach dem zweiten Bild eine kleinere, nach dem vierten
Bild eine größere Pause

Anfang 19½ Uhr   Ende nach 22 Uhr

berlin   martin études for orchestra/bruckner symphony 5
28, 29 and 30
september 1957
berlin philharmonic

vienna   verdi otello
3 and 6   *jurinac/rössl-majdan/guichandut/schöffler*
october 1957
vienna philharmonic
vienna opera chorus

vienna   handel concerto grosso op 6 no 5/einem piano
5 and 6   piano concerto/dvorak symphony 9
october 1957
vienna symphony
herzog

berlin   mozart symphony 38/martinu cello concerto/
26, 27 and 28   dvorak symphony 9
october 1957
berlin philharmonic
finke

first tour of japan by berlin philharmonic orchestra
tokyo   wagner meistersinger overture/strauss don
3 november 1957   juan/beethoven symphony 5
berlin philharmonic

tokyo   mozart symphony 35/wagner tristan prelude
4 november 1957   and liebestod/brahms symphony 2
berlin philharmonic

tokyo   wagner meistersinger overture/mozart
5 november 1957   symphony 38/brahms symphony 1
berlin philharmonic

tokyo   schubert symphony 8/beethoven symphony 3
6 november 1957
berlin philharmonic

nagoya   beethoven symphony 7/smetana moldau/
7 november 1957   wagner tannhäuser overture
berlin philharmonic

nagoya
8 november 1957
berlin philharmonic

weber oberon overture/strauss till eulenspiegel/
brahms symphony 2

fukuoka
10 november 1957
berlin philharmonic

weber oberon overture/hindemith mathis der
maler/beethoven symphony 5

yahata
11 november 1957
berlin philharmonic

wagner meistersinger overture/mozart
symphony 38/brahms symphony 1

hiroshima
13 november 1957
berlin philharmonic

mozart symphony 35/strauss don juan/
brahms symphony 2

osaka
15 november 1957
berlin philharmonic

schubert symphony 8/beethoven symphony 3

osaka
16 november 1957
berlin philharmonic

dvorak symphony 9/smetana moldau/
stravinsky firebird suite

kobe
17 november 1957
berlin philharmonic

stravinsky firebird suite/mozart symphony 38/
beethoven symphony 7

tokyo
19 november 1957
berlin philharmonic

beethoven symphony 7/smetana moldau/
stravinsky firebird suite

tokyo
20 november 1957
berlin philharmonic

wagner meistersinger overture/hindemith
mathis der maler/beethoven symphony 5

tokyo
22 november 1957
berlin philharmonic

weber oberon overture/mozart symphony 35/
beethoven symphony 5

*encore pieces on this tour included wagner meistersinger overture and bach air (suite 3);
an additional concert in sendai on 21 november was conducted by wilhelm schüchter*

berlin
27, 28 and 29
november 1957
berlin philharmonic

mozart symphony 38/stravinsky firebird suite/
brahms symphony 1

vienna
8 december 1957
vienna philharmonic

wagner die walküre
*mödl/rysanek/malaniuk/windgassen/hotter/
frick*

vienna
11 december 1957
*vienna philharmonic
vienna opera chorus*

verdi otello
rysanek/rössl-majdan/guichandut/neralic

vienna
15 december 1957
vienna opera chorus

palestrina missa papae marcelli
*thirty-year jubilee concert of vienna opera
chorus*

vienna
23 and 27
december 1957
vienna philharmonic

wagner siegfried
*nilsson/lipp/rössl-majdan/windgassen/klein/
hotter/neidlinger/frick*

berlin
5, 6 and 7
january 1958
*berlin philharmonic
ferras*

beethoven symphony 6/mendelssohn violin
concerto/ravel daphnis et chloé second suite

london
12 january 1958
philharmonia

bach brandenburg concerto 2/brahms haydn
variations/prokofiev symphony 5

vienna
22 january 1958
*vienna philharmonic
vienna opera chorus*

verdi otello
rysanek/rössl-majdan/guichandut/schöffler

vienna
23 january 1958
vienna philharmonic

strauss festfanfare für die wiener philharmoniker/
j.strauss kaiserwalzer
performed at wiener-philharmoniker-ball

vienna
25 and 26
january 1958
vienna symphony

bruckner symphony 9

vienna
25 and 27
january 1958
*vienna philharmonic
vienna opera chorus*

mozart le nozze di figaro
schwarzkopf/seefried/ludwig/wächter/kunz

vienna
31 january 1958
*vienna philharmonic
vienna opera chorus*

beethoven fidelio
*nilsson/lipp/zampieri/kmennt/frick/uhde/
metternich*

vienna
1 february 1958
*vienna philharmonic
vienna opera chorus*

puccini madama butterfly
scheyrer/rössl-majdan/zampieri/sordello

vienna
5 february 1958
vienna philharmonic

wagner die walküre
*nilsson/nordmo-lövberg/malaniuk/
windgassen/hotter/frick*

vienna
7 february 1958
vienna philharmonic

wagner siegfried
*nilsson/lipp/rössl-majdan/windgassen/
klein/hotter/neidlinger/frick*

vienna
8 and 9
february 1958
*vienna symphony
richter-haaser*

webern passacaglia/schumann piano
concerto/tchaikovsky symphony 4

berlin
21, 22 and 23
february 1958
*berlin philharmonic
saint hedwig's choir
grümmer
fischer-dieskau*

brahms ein deutsches requiem

tour of west germany and paris by berlin philharmonic orchestra

kiel 24 february 1958 *berlin philharmonic*	mozart symphony 35/strauss till eulenspiegel/ tchaikovsky symphony 5
hamburg 25 february 1958 *berlin philharmonic*	beethoven symphony 6/stravinsky firebird suite/ravel daphnis et chloé second suite
hannover 26 february 1958 *berlin philharmonic* *cherkassky*	strauss don juan/schumann symphony 4/ tchaikovsky piano concerto 1
bielefeld 27 february 1958 *berlin philharmonic*	beethoven symphony 6/stravinsky firebird suite/ravel daphnis et chloé second suite
wuppertal 28 february 1958 *berlin philharmonic*	mozart symphony 35/strauss till eulenspiegel/ schumann symphony 4
düsseldorf 1 march 1958 *berlin philharmonic*	beethoven symphony 6/hindemith mathis der maler/ravel daphnis et chloé second suite
viersen 2 march 1958 *berlin philharmonic*	mozart symphony 35/wagner tristan prelude and liebestod/schumann symphony 4
paris 4 march 1958 *berlin philharmonic*	*beethoven programme* coriolan overture/symphony 6/symphony 3
dortmund 6 march 1958 *berlin philharmonic*	weber oberon overture/beethoven symphony 7/ wagner tristan prelude and liebestod/wagner tannhäuser overture
essen 7 march 1958 *berlin philharmonic*	mozart symphony 35/strauss till eulenspiegel/ beethoven symphony 5
cologne 8 march 1958 *berlin philharmonic*	mozart symphony 35/wagner tristan prelude and liebestod/brahms symphony 2

vienna
23 march 1958
vienna philharmonic
vienna opera chorus

puccini madama butterfly
jurinac/rössl-majdan/zampieri/sordello

vienna
26 march 1958
vienna philharmonic
vienna opera chorus

verdi otello
jurinac/rössl-majdan/guichandut/schöffler

vienna
29 and 30
march 1958
vienna philharmonic
wiener singverein
güden
ludwig
kmennt
hotter

beethoven symphony 9

vienna
3 and 6
april 1958
vienna philharmonic
vienna opera chorus

puccini tosca
tebaldi/zampieri/gobbi

vienna
9 april 1958
vienna philharmonic
vienna opera chorus

verdi otello
tebaldi/rössl-majdan/guichandut/gobbi

milan
21, 24, 26 and
29 april 1958
la scala orchestra

wagner die walküre
nilsson/rysanek/madeira/suthaus/hotter/
frick

bari
1 may 1958
vienna philharmonic

mozart symphony 40/strauss till eulenspiegel/
beethoven symphony 5/wagner tannhäuser
overture

bari
2 may 1958
vienna philharmonic

strauss till eulenspiegel/wagner tristan prelude
and liebestod/tchaikovsky symphony 5/wagner
j.strauss kaiserwalzer

two concerts for brussels world fair

brussels	beethoven symphony 9
6 may 1958	
vienna philharmonic	
vienna opera chorus	
della casa	
rössl-majdan	
dermota	
hotter	

brussels	*j.strauss programme*
7 may 1958	fledermaus overture/kaiserwalzer/annen polka/
vienna philharmonic	unter donner und blitz/frühlingsstimmen/
männergesangverein	pizzicato polka/auf der jagd/an der schönen
güden	blauen donau/radetzky march

berlin	bartok music for strings percussion and celesta/
18, 19 and 20	beethoven symphony 3
may 1958	
berlin philharmonic	

vienna	wagner siegfried
22 may 1958	*mödl/lipp/madeira/windgassen/klein/*
vienna philharmonic	*hotter/neidlinger/weber*

vienna	verdi aida
24 and 28	*price/simionato/guichandut/protti/weber*
may 1958	
vienna philharmonic	
vienna opera chorus	

vienna	wagner die walküre
27 may 1958	*mödl/rysanek/madeira/windgassen/hotter/*
vienna philharmonic	*frick*

vienna	bizet carmen
2 and 4	*madeira/güden/di stefano/london*
june 1958	
vienna philharmonic	
vienna opera chorus	

vienna verdi falstaff
8 and 10 *schwarzkopf/moffo/simionato/zampieri/*
june 1958 *gobbi/panerai*
vienna philharmonic
vienna opera chorus

vienna stravinsky oedipus rex
11 june 1958 *mödl/kmennt/böhme/frick*
vienna philharmonic
vienna opera chorus

vienna puccini tosca
14 june 1958 *brouwenstijn/di stefano/gobbi*
vienna philharmonic
vienna opera chorus

two further concerts for brussels world fair
brussels **beethoven programme**
16 june 1958 **symphony 6/symphony 5**
berlin philharmonic

brussels **schubert symphony 8/blacher konzertante musik/**
17 june 1958 **brahms symphony 2**
berlin philharmonic

vienna puccini madama butterfly
18 june 1958 *jurinac/rössl-majdan/filacuridi/panerai*
vienna philharmonic
vienna opera chorus

vienna puccini tosca
21 june 1958 *rysanek/fernandi/london*
vienna philharmonic
vienna opera chorus

vienna bach mass in b minor
22 and 23
june 1958
vienna symphony
wiener singverein
grümmer
höffgen, gedda,
wächter, berry

salzburg
26 july and
2, 13, 20 and
27 august 1958
vienna philharmonic
vienna opera chorus

verdi don carlo
jurinac/simionato/fernandi/bastianini/siepi

salzburg
5, 9, 15 and
25 august 1958
vienna philharmonic
vienna opera chorus

beethoven fidelio
*goltz/jurinac/zampieri/christ/edelmann/
schöffler/zaccaria*

salzburg
21 august 1958
vienna philharmonic
wiener singverein
rysanek
ludwig
zampieri
siepi

verdi messa da requiem

munich
28 august 1958
berlin philharmonic
munich philharmonic
chorus
güden
höffgen
haefliger
frick

beethoven symphony 9

lucerne
30 and 31
august 1958
berlin philharmonic
lucerne festival
chorus
della casa
höffgen
haefliger
frick

beethoven symphony 9

vienna
9 september 1958
vienna philharmonic
vienna opera chorus

verdi aida
nilsson/simionato/di stefano/london/zaccaria

vienna
11 september 1958
vienna philharmonic
vienna opera chorus

bizet carmen
madeira/güden/di stefano/london

vienna
14 and 17
september 1958
vienna philharmonic
vienna opera chorus

verdi falstaff
schwarzkopf/beltrami/simionato/alva/gobbi/
wächter

berlin
21 and 22
september 1958
berlin philharmonic
gould

fortner impromptus for orchestra/bach piano concerto in d minor/beethoven symphony 5

vienna
11 and 12
october 1958
vienna philharmonic

beethoven programme
coriolan overture/symphony 1/symphony 3

vienna
11 october 1958
vienna philharmonic
vienna opera chorus

beethoven fidelio
mödl/lipp/zampieri/kmennt/edelmann/
uhde/böhme

vienna
13 october 1958
vienna philharmonic
vienna opera chorus

puccini tosca
borkh/zampieri/hotter

vienna
15 october 1958
vienna philharmonic

wagner siegfried
schech/lipp/madeira/windgassen/klein/
hotter/neidlinger/frick

berlin
18, 19 and 20
october 1958
berlin philharmonic
fournier

bach brandenburg concerto 2/schumann cello concerto/strauss ein heldenleben

tour of europe by berlin philharmonic orchestra

wolfsburg
21 october 1958
berlin philharmonic

mozart symphony 35/wagner tristan prelude and liebestod/dvorak symphony 9

stuttgart
22 october 1958
berlin philharmonic

mozart symphony 35/wagner tristan prelude and liebestod/brahms symphony 2

mannheim
23 october 1958
berlin philharmonic

weber oberon overture/hindemith mathis der maler/brahms symphony 1

freiburg
24 october 1958
berlin philharmonic

blacher konzertante musik/schumann symphony 4/beethoven symphony 7

zürich
26 october 1958
berlin philharmonic

schubert symphony 8/beethoven symphony 3

basel
27 october 1958
berlin philharmonic

blacher konzertante musik/schumann symphony 4/beethoven symphony 7

milan
28 and 29
october 1958
berlin philharmonic

beethoven programme
coriolan overture/symphony 6/symphony 5

rome
30 october 1958
berlin philharmonic

cherubini anacréon overture/hindemith mathis der maler/brahms symphony 2/ wagner tannhäuser overture

rome
31 october 1958
berlin philharmonic

beethoven programme
coriolan overture/symphony 6/symphony 5

paris
3 november 1958
berlin philharmonic

blacher konzertante musik/schumann symphony 4/strauss ein heldenleben

paris
4 november 1958
berlin philharmonic

bach brandenburg concerto 3/webern five pieces/schubert symphony 8/brahms symphony 1

london
5 november 1958
berlin philharmonic

beethoven programme
coriolan overture/symphony 6/symphony 3
wagner meistersinger overture played as an encore; karajan's first london appearance with the berlin philharmonic

london
6 november 1958
berlin philharmonic

mozart symphony 35/wagner tristan prelude and liebestod/brahms symphony 1
wagner tannhäuser overture played as an encore

new york
13, 14, 15 and
16 november 1958
new york philharmonic

webern five pieces/mozart symphony 41/strauss ein heldenleben
karajan's first appearance with an american orchestra

new york
20, 21, 22 and
23 november 1958
new york philharmonic
nypo chorus
price
forrester
simoneau
scott

beethoven programme
symphony 1/symphony 9

vienna
2 and 5
december 1958
vienna philharmonic
vienna opera chorus

verdi otello
jurinac/rössl-majdan/guichandut/schöffler/protti (5)

vienna
6 and 7
december 1958
vienna philharmonic

beethoven programme
egmont overture/symphony 6/symphony 5

vienna
14 december 1958
vienna philharmonic

wagner die walküre
*mödl/brouwenstijn/malaniuk/windgassen/
hotter/frick*

vienna
21 december 1958
vienna philharmonic

wagner siegfried
*mödl/lipp/höffgen/windgassen/klein/
neidlinger/pernerstorfer/frick*

vienna
23 december 1958
and 25 january 1959
vienna philharmonic

wagner das rheingold
*malaniuk/höffgen/windgassen/klein/
hotter/wächter/pernerstorfer/frick/czerwenka*

berlin
29, 30 and 31
december 1958
*berlin philharmonic
saint hedwig's choir
dickie
prey*

stravinsky canticum sacrum/bruckner
symphony 7

berlin
21, 22 and 23
january 1959
berlin philharmonic

strauss don juan/beethoven symphony 1/
respighi pini di roma

vienna
27 and 31
january 1959
*vienna philharmonic
vienna opera chorus*

mozart le nozze di figaro
*jurinac/seefried/berganza/sjöstedt (31)/
kunz/wächter*

vienna
31 january and
1 february 1959
vienna philharmonic

webern five pieces/strauss don juan/brahms
symphony 2

vienna
2 february 1959
*vienna philharmonic
vienna opera chorus*

puccini madama butterfly
jurinac/rössl-majdan/zampieri/wächter

tour of west germany by berlin philharmonic orchestra

hannover 18 february 1959 *berlin philharmonic* *i.oistrakh*	weber der freischütz overture/tchaikovsky violin concerto/beethoven symphony 5
bremen 19 february 1959 *berlin philharmonic*	bach brandenburg concerto 3/strauss till eulenspiegel/beethoven symphony 7
hamburg 20 february 1959 *berlin philharmonic*	bach brandenburg concerto 3/schubert symphony 8/strauss ein heldenleben
lübeck 21 february 1959 *berlin philharmonic*	bach brandenburg concerto 3/strauss don juan/beethoven symphony 7
kiel 22 february 1959 *berlin philharmonic* *i.oistrakh*	weber der freischütz overture/tchaikovsky violin concerto/beethoven symphony 5
essen 23 february 1959 *berlin philharmonic*	bach brandenburg concerto 3/beethoven symphony 1/brahms symphony 2
dortmund 24 february 1959 *berlin philharmonic*	weber der freischütz overture/strauss don juan/dvorak symphony 9
düsseldorf 25 february 1959 *berlin philharmonic*	bach brandenburg concerto 3/schubert symphony 8/strauss ein heldenleben
frankfurt 26 february 1959 *berlin philharmonic*	mozart symphony 35/wagner tristan prelude and liebestod/brahms symphony 2

KONZERTDIREKTION FÜR NIEDERSACHSEN
HEINRICH SCHUMACHER - HANNOVER

NIEDERSACHSENHALLE

MITTWOCH, 18. FEBRUAR 1959, 20 UHR

*

PROGRAMMFOLGE

CARL MARIA VON WEBER
    Ouvertüre zu der Oper „Der Freischütz"

PETER ILJITSCH TSCHAIKOWSKY
    Konzert für Violine und Orchester
    D-dur, op. 35
        Allegro moderato
        Canzonetta - Andante
        Finale - Allegro vivacissimo
    Solist: Igor Oistrach

PAUSE

LUDWIG VAN BEETHOVEN
    Sinfonie Nr. 5, c-moll, op. 67
        Allegro con brio
        Andante con moto
        Allegro
        Allegro

Tourneeleitung: Konzertbüro E. Berry, Dortmund

berlin
1, 2 and 3
march 1959
berlin philharmonic
schwalbé

webern five pieces/mendelssohn violin concerto/shostakovich symphony 10

london
7 march 1959
philharmonia

dvorak symphony 9/strauss don juan/ravel daphnis et chloé second suite

vienna
10 march 1959
vienna philharmonic
vienna opera chorus

verdi otello
jurinac/rössl-majdan/guichandut/protti

vienna
25 and 26
march 1959
vienna symphony
wiener singverein
stader
rössl-majdan
kmennt
dickie
wächter
berry

bach matthäus-passion

vienna
29 march 1959
vienna philharmonic

wagner das rheingold
malaniuk/höffgen/stolze/klein/hotter/
wächter/pernerstorfer/frick/czerwenka

vienna
30 march 1959
vienna philharmonic

wagner die walküre
nilsson/konetzni/malaniuk/vickers/
hotter/frick

vienna
5 april 1959
vienna philharmonic

wagner das rheingold
malaniuk/höffgen/charlebois/klein/hotter/
wächter/o.kraus/frick/czerwenka

vienna
8 april 1959
vienna philharmonic

wagner siegfried
nilsson/rothenberger/rössl-majdan/
windgassen/klein/edelmann/frick/
neidlinger

STAATSOPER

Mittwoch, den 27. Mai 1959
Bei aufgehobenem Abonnement

XV. Kongreß der Internationalen Verleger-Union
FESTVORSTELLUNG

In italienischer Sprache

Die Hochzeit des Figaro

Komische Oper in vier Akten
von Wolfgang Amadeus Mozart
Text nach Beaumarchais von Lorenzo da Ponte
Musikalische Leitung: Herbert v. Karajan
Inszenierung: Günther Rennert
Bühnenbild und Kostüme: Ita Maximowna

Graf Almaviva	Eberhard Wächter
Gräfin Almaviva	Elisabeth Schwarzkopf
Susanne, deren Kammermädchen	Irmgard Seefried
Figaro, Kammerdiener des Grafen	Erich Kunz
Cherubino, Page des Grafen	Christa Ludwig
Marcelline, Haushälterin im Schlosse des Grafen	Hilde Rössel-Majdan
Basilio, Musikmeister im Dienste des Grafen	Peter Klein
Don Curzio, Richter	Erich Majkut
Bartolo, Arzt aus Sevilla	Alois Pernerstorfer
Antonio, Gärtner des Grafen und Onkel der Susanne	Ljubo Pantscheff
Barbarina, seine Tochter	Anny Felbermayer
Erstes Bauernmädchen	Alberta Kolm
Zweites Bauernmädchen	Else Haller

Ort der Handlung ist das Schloß des Grafen Almaviva

Choreographie: Erika Hanka
Ausführende: Die Damen Greger, Philipp, Wittek;
die Herren Fränzl Wilfr., Mikura, Zajetz

Technische Einrichtung: Hans Felkel
Beleuchtung: Albin Rotter

Nach dem zweiten Akt eine größere Pause

Anfang 20 Uhr   Ende nach 23¼ Uhr

milan
28 and 30
april and
4 and 6
may 1959
*la scala orchestra
and chorus*

wagner tristan und isolde
*nilsson/rössl-majdan/windgassen/hotter/
neidlinger*

vienna
16 and 17
may 1959
vienna philharmonic

mozart symphony 40/brahms symphony 1

berlin
20 may 1959
berlin philharmonic

strauss don juan/beethoven symphony 1/
respighi pini di roma

berlin
21, 23 and 24
may 1959
*berlin philharmonic
kallir*

henze sonata per archi/mozart piano
concerto 21/brahms symphony 2

vienna
26 may 1959
vienna philharmonic

wagner das rheingold
*rössl-majdan/madeira/klein/windgassen/
hotter/wächter/greindl/pernerstorfer/frick*

vienna
27 may 1959
vienna philharmonic

mozart le nozze di figaro
schwarzkopf/seefried/ludwig/wächter/kunz

vienna
28 may 1959
vienna philharmonic

wagner die walküre
*nilsson/brouwenstijn/madeira/windgassen/
hotter/greindl*

vienna
30 may 1959
*vienna philharmonic
vienna opera chorus
lipp
rössl-majdan
dermota
berry*

150 th anniversary of haydn's death
nelson mass

vienna
31 may 1959
vienna philharmonic

wagner siegfried
*nilsson/rothenberger/madeira/windgassen/
klein/hotter/neidlinger/frick*

vienna
7 june 1959
*vienna philharmonic
vienna opera chorus*

mozart le nozze di figaro
schwarzkopf/güden/ludwig/london/kunz

vienna
8 june 1959
*vienna philharmonic
vienna opera chorus*

bizet carmen
madeira/güden/di stefano/uhde

vienna
12 june 1959
*vienna philharmonic
vienna opera chorus*

puccini tosca
tebaldi/fernandi/london

vienna
14 and 18
june 1959
*vienna philharmonic
vienna opera chorus*

wagner tristan und isolde
*nilsson/rössl-majdan/windgassen/frick/
wiener*

vienna
15 june 1959
*vienna philharmonic
vienna opera chorus*

verdi otello
tebaldi/rössl-majdan/guichandut/gobbi

vienna
20 and 21
june 1959
*vienna symphony
wiener singverein
price
dominguez
zampieri
zaccaria*

verdi messa da requiem

vienna
22 june 1959
*vienna philharmonic
vienna opera chorus*

verdi aida
tebaldi/simionato/fernandi/gobbi/frick

los angeles
2 july 1959
los angeles
philharmonic

wagner meistersinger overture/ives the unanswered question/mozart symphony 35/ strauss ein heldenleben

salzburg
5, 10, 15, 22 and
27 august 1959
vienna philharmonic
vienna opera chorus

gluck orfeo ed euridice
simionato/jurinac/sciutti

salzburg
19 august 1959
vienna philharmonic
wiener singverein
price
ludwig
gedda
zaccaria

beethoven missa solemnis

munich
21 august 1959
vienna philharmonic

bruckner symphony 8

lucerne
31 august 1959
philharmonia
gould
fournier

handel water music suite/bach piano concerto in d minor/strauss don quixote

vienna
1 september 1959
vienna philharmonic
vienna opera chorus

wagner die meistersinger von nürnberg
jurinac/rössl-majdan/windgassen/dickie/
wiener/van mill/dönch

vienna
3 september 1959
vienna philharmonic
vienna opera chorus

mozart le nozze di figaro
jurinac/güden/ludwig/wächter/kunz

BAYERISCHE STAATSOPER · MÜNCHNER OPERNFESTSPIELE
KONGRESS-SAAL DES DEUTSCHEN MUSEUMS

München, Freitag, den 21. August 1959

Orchesterkonzert

WIENER PHILHARMONIKER

Dirigent

HERBERT VON KARAJAN

ANTON BRUCKNER VIII. SYMPHONIE c-moll

Allegro moderato
Scherzo: Allegro moderato
Adagio: Feierlich, langsam, doch nicht schleppend
Finale: Feierlich, nicht schnell

Anfang 20 Uhr   *Ende nach 21.30 Uhr*

vienna puccini tosca
9 september 1959 *tebaldi/fernandi/gobbi*
vienna philharmonic
vienna opera chorus

vienna wagner tristan und isolde
12 september 1959 *mödl/rössl-majdan/windgassen/wiener/frick*
vienna philharmonic
vienna opera chorus

vienna verdi aida
13 september 1959 *davy/simionato/bergonzi/gobbi/kreppel*
vienna philharmonic
vienna opera chorus

berlin handel concerto grosso op 6 no 5/liebermann
20 and 21 capriccio/schumann symphony 4
september 1959
berlin philharmonic
seefried
schneiderhan

berlin mozart symphony 29/messiaen reveil des
23, 24 and 25 oiseaux/beethoven symphony 7
september 1959
berlin philharmonic
loriod

vienna mozart eine kleine nachtmusik/berger
14 and 15 legende vom prinzen eugen/brahms
october 1959 symphony 4
vienna philharmonic

world tour by vienna philharmonic orchestra
new delhi weber euryanthe overture/strauss till
19 october 1959 eulenspiegel/beethoven symphony 5
vienna philharmonic

bombay beethoven symphony 6/strauss till
20 october 1959 eulenspiegel/j.strauss fledermaus overture
vienna philharmonic

manila beethoven symphony 7/strauss don juan/
22 october 1959 j.strauss blue danube waltz
vienna philharmonic

manila brahms symphony 1/works by j.strauss
23 october 1959
vienna philharmonic

hong kong beethoven symphony 7/strauss till eulenspiegel/
25 october 1959 works by j.strauss
vienna philharmonic

tokyo mozart symphony 40/brahms symphony 1
27 october 1959
vienna philharmonic

tokyo mozart eine kleine nachtmusik/bruckner
28 october 1959 symphony 8
vienna philharmonic

tokyo *beethoven programme*
29 october 1959 coriolan overture/symphony 6/symphony 5
vienna philharmonic

osaka haydn symphony 103/beethoven leonore 3
31 october 1959 overture/brahms symphony 2
vienna philharmonic

osaka beethoven symphony 7/strauss don juan/
1 november 1959 wagner tannhäuser overture
vienna philharmonic

osaka mozart symphony 40/schubert symphony 8/
2 november 1959 works by j.strauss
vienna philharmonic

nakaya mozart symphony 40/schubert symphony 8/
3 november 1959 works by j.strauss
vienna philharmonic

j.strauss programme in tokyo on 5 november was conducted by willy boskovsky

tokyo berger legende vom prinzen eugen/schubert
6 november 1959 symphony 8/brahms symphony 4
vienna philharmonic

tokyo haydn symphony 103/beethoven leonore 3
7 november 1959 overture/brahms symphony 2
vienna philharmonic

honolulu beethoven symphony 7/strauss don juan/
8 november 1959 wagner meistersinger overture
vienna philharmonic

concert scheduled for 10 november in san francisco was cancelled due to airline delays

los angeles weber euryanthe overture/schubert symphony 8/
11 november 1959 beethoven symphony 5
vienna philharmonic

provo handel water music suite/beethoven symphony 1/
12 november 1959 strauss don juan/wagner tannhäuser overture
vienna philharmonic

chicago beethoven symphony 7/strauss don juan/
14 november 1959 wagner meistersinger overture
vienna philharmonic

cleveland handel water music suite/strauss till
15 november 1959 eulenspiegel/beethoven symphony 5
vienna philharmonic

new york bruckner symphony 8
17 november 1959
vienna philharmonic

boston mozart eine kleine nachtmusik/bruckner
18 november 1959 symphony 8
vienna philharmonic

new york schubert symphony 8/mozart symphony 40/
19 november 1959 works by j.strauss
vienna philharmonic

atlanta
21 november 1959
vienna philharmonic

beethoven symphony 7/strauss don juan/
wagner meistersinger overture

washington
22 november 1959
vienna philharmonic

beethoven symphony 1/brahms symphony 2

montreal
23 november 1959
vienna philharmonic

handel water music suite/strauss till
eulenspiegel/beethoven symphony 5

encore pieces on this tour included j.strauss radetzky march, blue danube waltz and delirien waltz

vienna
5 and 6
december 1959
*vienna symphony
a.fischer*

beethoven piano concerto 4/shostakovich
symphony 10

vienna
8 december 1959
*vienna philharmonic
vienna opera chorus*

beethoven fidelio
*brouwenstijn/lipp/windgassen/kmennt/
frick/hotter/berry*

vienna
11 december 1959
*vienna philharmonic
vienna opera chorus*

mozart le nozze di figaro
*stich-randall/güden/simionato/wächter/
berry*

vienna
12 and 13
december 1959
*vienna philharmonic
curzon*

bach suite 2/mozart piano concerto 23/
beethoven symphony 7
*concert marking fifth anniversary of the
death of wilhelm furtwängler*

vienna
15 and 20
december 1959 and
2 january 1960
*vienna philharmonic
vienna opera chorus*

gluck orfeo ed euridice
simionato/lipp/rothenberger

vienna 18 december 1959 *vienna philharmonic*	wagner das rheingold *malaniuk/rössl-majdan/stolze/klein/hotter/* *wächter/pernerstorfer/frick/van mill*
berlin 29, 30 and 31 december 1959 *berlin philharmonic* *richter-haaser*	blacher musica giocosa/brahms symphony 3/ schumann piano concerto/beethoven leonore 3 overture
vienna 6 january 1960 *vienna philharmonic* *vienna opera chorus*	mozart le nozze di figaro *schwarzkopf/seefried/jurinac/wächter/kunz*
vienna 9 and 10 january 1960 *vienna symphony* *wiener singverein* *dermota* *wiener*	stravinsky canticum sacrum/bruckner symphony 7
berlin 30 and 31 january and 1 february 1960 *berlin philharmonic* *rias choir* *stader* *von stein* *wunderlich* *kreppel*	mozart requiem
vienna 3 february 1960 *vienna philharmonic* *vienna opera chorus*	wagner tristan und isolde *mödl/rössl-majdan/beirer/wiener/hotter*
vienna 7 february 1960 *vienna philharmonic*	wagner das rheingold *malaniuk/rössl-majdan/holm/klein/hotter/* *wächter/pernerstorfer/frick/kreppel*

vienna
12 february 1960
vienna philharmonic
vienna opera chorus

beethoven fidelio
*brouwenstijn/seefried/zampieri/dickie/wiener/
frick/hotter*

berlin
28 and 29
february and
1 march 1960
berlin philharmonic
rössl-majdan
konya

mozart symphony 29/mahler das lied von
der erde

vienna
9 and 11
march and
10 april 1960
vienna philharmonic
vienna opera chorus

pizzetti assassino nella cattedrale
zadek/ludwig/dermota/hotter

vienna
12 march 1960
vienna philharmonic
vienna opera chorus

mozart le nozze di figaro
della casa/sciutti/ludwig/wächter/kunz

london
1 april 1960
philharmonia

bach suite 2/strauss tod und verklärung/
schumann symphony 4
*final public appearance with philharmonia
orchestra*

vienna
13 and 14
april 1960
vienna symphony
wiener singverein
lipp
rössl-majdan
dermota
edelmann
wächter

mozart requiem

berlin   mozart eine kleine nachtmusik/stravinsky
18, 19 and 20   symphony in c/tchaikovsky piano concerto 1
april 1960
berlin philharmonic
cherkassky

tour of paris and west germany by berlin philharmonic orchestra
paris   *beethoven cycle*
21 april 1960   egmont overture/symphony 4/symphony 7
berlin philharmonic

paris   *beethoven cycle*
22 april 1960   symphony 1/symphony 3
berlin philharmonic

paris   *beethoven cycle*
23 april 1960   coriolan overture/symphony 6/symphony 5
berlin philharmonic

paris   *beethoven cycle*
25 april 1960   symphony 2/leonore 3 overture/piano
berlin philharmonic   concerto 5
richter-haaser

paris   *beethoven cycle*
26 april 1960   symphony 8/symphony 9
berlin philharmonic
brasseur choir
lipp
ludwig
kmennt
frick

cologne   bach brandenburg concerto 3/beethoven
27 april 1960   symphony 1/strauss ein heldenleben
berlin philharmonic

bonn   bach brandenburg concerto 3/schumann
28 april 1960   symphony 4/beethoven symphony 5
berlin philharmonic

bielefeld   bach brandenburg concerto 3/beethoven
29 april 1960   symphony 1/strauss ein heldenleben
berlin philharmonic

wiesbaden
1 and 2
may 1960
vienna philharmonic
vienna opera chorus

mozart le nozze di figaro
schwarzkopf/stich-randall (2)/seefried/ludwig/wächter/kunz; guest performances by vienna staatsoper

milan
6, 10, 12 and 14
may 1960
la scala orchestra and chorus

mozart le nozze di figaro
jurinac/sciutti/belini/fusco/wächter/evans

vienna
21 and 22
may 1960
vienna philharmonic
wiener singverein
güden
ludwig
dermota
wiener

beethoven symphony 9

vienna
26 may 1960
vienna philharmonic
vienna opera chorus

wagner tristan und isolde
nilsson/gorr/windgassen/wiener/frick

vienna
29 may 1960
vienna philharmonic
vienna opera chorus

pizzetti assassino nella cattedrale
scheyrer/ludwig/dermota/hotter

vienna
31 may 1960
vienna philharmonic

karajan's first complete ring cycle in vienna
wagner das rheingold
malaniuk/rössl-majdan/windgassen/stolze/hotter/wächter/pernerstorfer/frick/böhme

vienna
1 june 1960
vienna philharmonic

wagner die walküre
nilsson/brouwenstijn/gorr/windgassen/hotter/frick

vienna
5 june 1960
vienna philharmonic

wagner siegfried
nilsson/lipp/madeira/windgassen/stolze/edelmann/pernerstorfer/frick

vienna
10 june 1960
vienna philharmonic
vienna opera chorus

verdi aida
rysanek/simionato/ottolini/bastianini/frick

vienna
12 and 14
june 1960
vienna philharmonic
vienna opera chorus

wagner götterdämmerung
*nilsson/brouwenstijn/gorr/windgassen/
uhde/pernerstorfer/frick*

vienna
18 and 19
june 1960
vienna philharmonic
rössl-majdan
wunderlich

mahler das lied von der erde

vienna
20 june 1960
vienna philharmonic
vienna opera chorus

puccini tosca
tebaldi/bastianini/zampieri

vienna
26 june 1960
vienna philharmonic
rössl-majdan
dermota
wellesz, speaker

mahler das lied von der erde
*matinee performance in the staatsoper to
mark centenary of mahler's birth*

salzburg
26 july 1960
vienna philharmonic
vienna opera chorus
price
ludwig
kmennt

mozart gloria from mass in c minor
*performed during opening ceremony of
grosses festspielhaus*

salzburg
26 july 1960
vienna philharmonic
vienna opera chorus

strauss der rosenkavalier
*della casa/güden/jurinac/edelmann/kunz;
first opera performance in grosses festspielhaus*

SALZBURGER FESTSPIELE 1960

40 JAHRE SALZBURGER FESTSPIELE

DER ROSENKAVALIER

KOMÖDIE FÜR MUSIK IN DREI AUFZÜGEN
VON HUGO VON HOFMANNSTHAL

MUSIK VON
RICHARD STRAUSS

DIRIGENT
HERBERT VON KARAJAN

INSZENIERUNG
RUDOLF HARTMANN

BÜHNENBILD
TEO OTTO

KOSTÜME
ERNI KNIEPERT

ORCHESTER
DIE WIENER PHILHARMONIKER
CHOR DER WIENER STAATSOPER

salzburg
3, 10, 17, 25 and
29 august 1960
vienna philharmonic
vienna opera chorus

mozart don giovanni
schwarzkopf/price/sciutti/valletti/wächter/
berry/zaccaria

salzburg
4 august 1960
vienna philharmonic
vienna opera chorus

strauss der rosenkavalier
della casa/rothenberger/jurinac/edelmann/
kunz

salzburg
6 august 1960
vienna philharmonic
vienna opera chorus

strauss der rosenkavalier
schwarzkopf/rothenberger/jurinac/edelmann/
poell

salzburg
7 august 1960
berlin philharmonic

bach suite 2/stravinsky symphony in c/
strauss ein heldenleben

salzburg
13, 18 and 28
august 1960
vienna philharmonic
vienna opera chorus

strauss der rosenkavalier
della casa/rothenberger/jurinac/edelmann/
kunz

salzburg
24 august 1960
vienna philharmonic
wiener singverein
price
rössl-majdan
wunderlich
berry
wächter

mozart requiem/bruckner te deum

vienna
1 september 1960
vienna philharmonic

wagner das rheingold
gorr/rössl-majdan/stolze/klein/hotter/
wächter/pernerstorfer/frick/böhme

vienna
3 september 1960
vienna philharmonic

wagner die walküre
nilsson/crespin/gorr/windgassen/hotter/
frick

STAATSOPER

Samstag, den 3. September 1960
Beschränkter Kartenverkauf — Erhöhte Preise

DER RING DES NIBELUNGEN

Erster Tag

Die Walküre

In drei Aufzügen von Richard Wagner

Musikalische Leitung: Herbert v. Karajan
Inszenierung: Herbert v. Karajan
Bühnenbilder und Kostüme: Emil Preetorius

Siegmund	Wolfgang Windgassen
Hunding	Gottlob Frick
Wotan	Hans Hotter
Sieglinde	Regine Crespin
Brünnhilde	Birgit Nilsson
Fricka	Rita Gorr
Helmwige	Lotte Rysanek
Gerhilde	Gerda Scheyrer
Ortlinde	Judith Hellwig
Waltraute ⎫	Traute Richter
Siegrune ⎬ Walküren	Margareta Sjöstedt
Roßweiße	Rosette Anday
Grimgerde	Dagmar Hermann
Schwertleite ⎭	Hilde Rössel-Majdan

Walkürenrufe: Berta Seidl, Dorothea Frass

Schauplatz der Handlung:
Erster Aufzug: Das Innere der Wohnung Hundings
Zweiter Aufzug: Wildes Felsengebirge
Dritter Aufzug: Auf dem Gipfel eines Felsenberges
(des „Brünnhildensteines")

Technische Einrichtung: Hans Felkel — Beleuchtung: Albin Rotter

Nach dem ersten u. zweiten Aufzug eine größere Pause

Anfang 18 Uhr   Ende etwa 22½ Uhr

Preis des Programms S 4,—

STAATSOPER

Montag, den 5. September 1960
Im Abonnement XVI. Gruppe. Beschränkter Kartenverkauf
Erhöhte Preise

DER RING DES NIBELUNGEN

Zweiter Tag

Siegfried

In drei Aufzügen von Richard Wagner

Musikalische Leitung: Herbert v. Karajan
Inszenierung: Herbert v. Karajan
Bühnenbilder und Kostüme: Emil Preetorius

Siegfried	Wolfgang Windgassen
Brünnhilde	Birgit Nilsson
Der Wanderer	Hans Hotter
Alberich	Alois Pernerstorfer
Erda	Hilde Rössel-Majdan
Mime	Peter Klein
Fafner	Gottlob Frick
Stimme des Waldvogels	Wilma Lipp

Schauplatz der Handlung:
Erster Aufzug: Eine Felsenhöhle im Walde — Zweiter Aufzug: Tiefer Wald — Dritter Aufzug: Wilde Gegend am Fuße eines Felsenberges, dann: Auf dem Gipfel des „Brünnhildensteines"

Technische Einrichtung: Hans Felkel
Beleuchtung: Albin Rotter

Nach jedem Aufzug eine größere Pause

Anfang 17 Uhr   Ende etwa 21¾ Uhr

Preis des Programms S 4,—

vienna
5 september 1960
vienna philharmonic

wagner siegfried
nilsson/lipp/madeira/windgassen/klein/
hotter/pernerstorfer/frick

vienna
8 september 1960
vienna philharmonic
vienna opera chorus

wagner götterdämmerung
nilsson/brivkalne/gorr/windgassen/frick/
alexander/pernerstorfer

vienna
11 september 1960
vienna philharmonic
vienna opera chorus

wagner tristan und isolde
nilsson/rössl-majdan/windgassen/frick/
neidlinger

vienna
13 september 1960
vienna philharmonic
vienna opera chorus

verdi aida
price/simionato/bergonzi/bastianini/
zaccaria

berlin
18 and 19
september 1960
berlin philharmonic
price

webern six pieces/handel v'adoro pupille
from giulio cesare/verdi o patria mia from
aida/brahms symphony 1

berlin
22, 23 and 24
october 1960
berlin philharmonic
francescatti

bach brandenburg concerto 4/mozart
symphony 39/brahms violin concerto

tour of west germany, switzerland and milan by berlin philharmonic orchestra
hannover
25 october 1960
berlin philharmonic

bach brandenburg concerto 4/beethoven
symphony 6/tchaikovsky symphony 4

frankfurt
26 october 1960
berlin philharmonic

stravinsky symphony in c/beethoven
symphony 3

munich
27 october 1960
berlin philharmonic

bach suite 2/beethoven symphony 4/
strauss ein heldenleben

40 JAHRE
FÜHRER DURCH DIE Konzertsäle Berlins
1920-1960

Konzert-Übersicht vom 16. September
bis 30. September 1960 u. Voranzeigen

Berliner Philharmonisches Orchester

KONZERTSAAL DER HOCHSCHULE FÜR MUSIK

Mittwoch, 21. Sept., Donnerstag, 22. Sept., jeweils 20 Uhr — Freitag, 23. Sept., 19.30 Uhr

I. Philharmonisches Konzert

Dirigent: **KARL BÖHM** — Solist: **WOLFGANG SCHNEIDERHAN**

Hindemith: Symphonische Metamorphosen Carl Maria von Weber'scher Themen · Mozart: Violinkonzert D-Dur KV. 218 · Schubert: Symphonie Nr. VII C-Dur

Donnerstag, 6. Okt., 20 Uhr
Freitag, 7. Okt., 20 Uhr
2. Konzert der Reihe „B"
Dirigent: **PIERRE MONTEUX**
Solist: **MICHEL SCHWALBÉ**

Sonnabend, 8. Okt., 20 Uhr: Geschl. Veranstaltung für das „Theater der Schulen" u. „Die Freie Volksbühne"

Beethoven: Ouvertüre „Leonore" Nr. III — Saint-Saëns: Violinkonzert h-Moll
Strauss: Till Eulenspiegels lustige Streiche — Strawinsky: „Petruschka", Ballett-Suite

Kartenverkauf ab Sonntag, 25. September

FESTWOCHEN-KONZERTE
Eröffnung der Berliner Festwochen

Sonntag, 18. Sept., 11.30 Uhr — Wiederholung: Montag, 19. Sept., 20 Uhr

Dirigent: **HERBERT VON KARAJAN**

Solistin: **LEONTYNE PRICE**

Webern: Sechs Stücke für großes Orchester op. 6 — Händel: Arie „Es blaut die Nacht" aus „Julius Cäsar" — Verdi: „Nilarie" aus „Aida" — Brahms: Symphonie Nr. I

Montag, 26. Sept., 20 Uhr   Dirigent: **KARL FORSTER**

CHOR DER ST. HEDWIGS-KATHEDRALE

Brahms: Schicksalslied · Nänie — Blacher: Requiem (Erstaufführung)

Mittwoch, 28. Sept., 20 Uhr   Dirigent: **HANS ERISMANN**

Solisten: MARIA STADER, MARGRIT CONRAD-AMBERG, VERENA GOHL
JOSEF GREINDL — SÄNGERVEREINIGUNG HARMONIE ZÜRICH

Huber: „Cuius legibus rotandur poli" (Augustinus) — Martin: Monologe aus „Jedermann" (Hofmannsthal) — Sutermeister: Missa da Requiem

stuttgart28 october 1960*berlin philharmonic*

bach brandenburg concerto 3/mozart symphony 39/tchaikovsky symphony 4

basel
30 october 1960
berlin philharmonic

bach brandenburg concerto 3/beethoven symphony 4/brahms symphony 2

bern
31 october 1960
berlin philharmonic

handel concerto grosso op 5 no 6/mozart symphony 39/beethoven symphony 7

geneva
1 november 1960
berlin philharmonic

beethoven programme
coriolan overture/symphony 6/symphony 5

zürich
2 november 1960
berlin philharmonic

bach brandenburg concerto 4/mozart symphony 39/tchaikovsky symphony 5

milan
3 and 4
november 1960
berlin philharmonic

puccini manon lescaut intermezzo/bach suite 2/beethoven symphony 4/strauss ein heldenleben
puccini item played in memory of dimitri mitropoulos

freiburg
5 november 1960
berlin philharmonic

bach brandenburg concerto 4/stravinsky symphony in c/brahms symphony 2

kassel
6 november 1960
berlin philharmonic

beethoven coriolan overture/beethoven symphony 6/tchaikovsky symphony 4

berlin
9, 10 and 11
november 1960
berlin philharmonic

voss variations for brass and percussion/bartok music for strings percussion and celesta/tchaikovsky symphony 4

vienna
27 november 1960
vienna philharmonic
vienna opera chorus

beethoven fidelio
*nordmo-lövberg/lipp/windgassen/dickie/
kreppel/hotter/wiener*

vienna
30 november 1960
vienna philharmonic

wagner das rheingold
*malaniuk/rössl-majdan/windgassen/klein/
hotter/wächter/roth-ehrang/pernerstorfer/
kreppel*

vienna
3 and 4
december 1960
vienna philharmonic

brahms symphony 3/bartok concerto for orchestra

vienna
5 december 1960
vienna philharmonic

wagner die walküre
*mödl/nordmo-lövberg/malaniuk/
windgassen/hotter/böhme*

berlin
11, 12 and 13
december 1960
*berlin philharmonic
rias choir
lipp
dermota
crass*

haydn die schöpfung

milan
17, 20 and 22
december 1960
and 3 and 5
january 1961
*la scala orchestra
and chorus*

beethoven fidelio
*nilsson/lipp/vickers/unger/frick/crass/
hotter*

vienna
31 december 1960
and 1 and 7
january 1961
*vienna philharmonic
vienna opera chorus*

j.strauss die fledermaus
*güden/streich/zampieri/stolze/wächter/
kunz*

vienna
8 january 1961
vienna philharmonic

wagner die walküre
nilsson/zadek/malaniuk/vickers/hotter/
kreppel

vienna
10 january 1961
vienna philharmonic
vienna opera chorus

wagner götterdämmerung
nilsson/scheyrer/ludwig/windgassen/hotter/
pernerstorfer/roth-ehrang

vienna
28 and 29
january 1961
vienna symphony

webern six pieces/mozart symphony 39/
prokofiev symphony 7

vienna
3 february 1961
vienna philharmonic
vienna opera chorus

verdi aida
davy/cvejic/vickers/protti/kreppel

vienna
5 february 1961
vienna philharmonic
vienna opera chorus

j.strauss die fledermaus
rethy/streich/zampieri/dickie/rootering/
kunz

vienna
11 and 12
february 1961
vienna philharmonic
wiener singverein
lipp
rössl-majdan
dermota
zaccaria

beethoven missa solemnis

berlin
15, 16 and 17
february 1961
berlin philharmonic
koch

strauss programme
oboe concerto/also sprach zarathustra/
metamorphosen

paris
20 february 1961
vienna philharmonic
backhaus

mozart eine kleine nachtmusik/beethoven
piano concerto 4/bruckner symphony 7

paris schumann symphony 4/strauss don quixote
21 february 1961
vienna philharmonic
fournier

munich beethoven symphony 1/bruckner symphony 7
23 february 1961
vienna philharmonic

vienna j.strauss die fledermaus
4, 13 and 26 *güden/rothenberger/dickie/stolze (13)/*
march 1961 *zampieri/dermota (26)/kunz/wächter*
vienna philharmonic
vienna opera chorus

vienna bizet carmen
18 march 1961 *resnik/güden/zampieri/wiener*
vienna philharmonic
vienna opera chorus

vienna wagner das rheingold
19 march 1961 *g.hoffman/resnik/stolze/klein/hotter/*
vienna philharmonic *wächter/pernerstorfer/frick/kreppel*

vienna wagner parsifal
1 and 3 *ludwig/höngen/uhl/hotter/franc/wächter/*
april 1961 *berry*
vienna philharmonic
vienna opera chorus

tour of london and west germany by berlin philharmonic orchestra
london *beethoven cycle*
14 april 1961 symphony 1/symphony 4/symphony 7
berlin philharmonic

london *beethoven cycle*
15 april 1961 symphony 2/symphony 3
berlin philharmonic

london *beethoven cycle*
16 april 1961 symphony 6/symphony 5
berlin philharmonic

STAATSOPER

Samstag, den 1. April 1961

Beschränkter Kartenverkauf — Besondere Preise

NEUINSZENIERUNG

PARSIFAL

Ein Bühnenweihfestspiel von Richard Wagner

Musikalische Leitung: Herbert v. Karajan
Inszenierung: Herbert v. Karajan
Bühnenbilder und Kostüme: Heinrich Wendel
Choreographie: Erich Walter
Einstudierung der Chöre: Richard Rossmayer

Amfortas	Eberhard Wächter
Titurel	Tugomir Franc
Gurnemanz	Hans Hotter
Parsifal	Fritz Uhl
Klingsor	Walter Berry
Kundry	Christa Ludwig / Elisabeth Höngen
Erster Knappe	Liselotte Maikl
Zweiter Knappe	Margareta Sjöstedt
Dritter Knappe	Erich Majkut
Vierter Knappe	Kurt Equiluz
Erster Gralsritter	Ermanno Lorenzi
Zweiter Gralsritter	Kostas Paskalis
Blumenmädchen 1. Gruppe	Gundula Janowitz / Hilde Güden / Biserka Cvejic
Blumenmädchen 2. Gruppe	Anneliese Rothenberger / Gerda Scheyrer / Margareta Sjöstedt
Stimme von oben	Hilde Rössel-Majdan

Mitwirkend: Wiener Sängerknaben

Die Brüderschaft der Gralsritter, Jünglinge und Knaben

Ort der Handlung:

Auf dem Gebiete und in der Burg der Gralshüter „Monsalvat"; Gegend im Charakter der nördlichen Gebirge des gotischen Spaniens — Sodann: Klingsors Zauberschloß am Südabhange derselben Gebirge, dem arabischen Spanien zugewandt, anzunehmen

Technische Einrichtung: Hans Felkel — Beleuchtung: Albin Rotter

Nach jedem Aufzug eine größere Pause

Anfang 16½ Uhr   Ende nach 21½ Uhr

Preis des Programms S 4,—

london 17 april 1961 *berlin philharmonic* *philharmonia chorus* *lipp* *ludwig* *wunderlich* *crass*	*beethoven cycle* symphony 8/symphony 9
düsseldorf 19 april 1961 *berlin philharmonic*	bach suite 2/bartok music for strings percussion and celesta/brahms symphony 1
essen 20 april 1961 *berlin philharmonic*	brahms symphony 3/bartok music for strings percussion and celesta/beethoven leonore 3 overture
dortmund 21 april 1961 *berlin philharmonic*	beethoven coriolan overture/beethoven symphony 6/tchaikovsky symphony 4
hamburg 22 april 1961 *berlin philharmonic* *koch*	strauss oboe concerto/strauss metamorphosen/ brahms symphony 1
wolfsburg 23 april 1961 *berlin philharmonic*	beethoven coriolan overture/beethoven symphony 8/brahms symphony 2
berlin 26, 27 and 28 april 1961 *berlin philharmonic* *starker*	prokofiev sinfonia concertante/beethoven symphony 3
vienna 13 and 14 may 1961 *vienna symphony* *backhaus*	*brahms programme* piano concerto 2/symphony 4

vienna
14 may 1961
vienna philharmonic
vienna opera chorus

verdi aida
paruto/cvejic/vickers/protti/kreppel

vienna
1 june 1961
vienna philharmonic
vienna opera chorus

wagner parsifal
ludwig/höngen/uhl/hotter/franc/wächter/
berry

vienna
3, 4 and 5
june 1961
vienna philharmonic
oistrakh

webern symphony/schumann symphony 4/
brahms violin concerto

vienna
7 june 1961
vienna philharmonic

wagner das rheingold
malaniuk/madeira/windgassen/klein/hotter/
wächter/pernerstorfer/frick/kreppel

vienna
9 june 1961
vienna philharmonic

wagner die walküre
nilsson/rysanek/rössl-majdan/vickers/hotter/
frick

vienna
11 june 1961
vienna philharmonic

wagner siegfried
nilsson/lipp/madeira/windgassen/klein/
hotter/pernerstorfer/frick

vienna
13 june 1961
vienna philharmonic
vienna opera chorus

wagner götterdämmerung
nilsson/scheyrer/rössl-majdan/windgassen/
pernerstorfer/wiener/frick

vienna
14 june 1961
vienna philharmonic
vienna opera chorus

j.strauss die fledermaus
güden/rothenberger/zampieri/stolze/kunz/
wächter

vienna
17 and 18
june 1961
vienna philharmonic
wiener singverein
janowitz

handel concerto grosso op 6 no 5/verdi te
deum/strauss also sprach zarathustra

vienna verdi aida
18 june 1961 price/simionato/vickers/bastianini/zaccaria
vienna philharmonic
vienna opera chorus

turin *beethoven programme*
21 june 1961 egmont overture/symphony 6/symphony 5
berlin philharmonic

turin bach suite 2/wagner tristan prelude and
22 june 1961 liebestod/brahms symphony 2
berlin philharmonic

strassburg *beethoven programme*
24 june 1961 coriolan overture/symphony 6/symphony 5
berlin philharmonic

strassburg bach brandenburg concerto 3/stravinsky
25 june 1961 symphony in c/brahms symphony 2
berlin philharmonic

milan verdi messa da requiem
8 and 9
july 1961
la scala orchestra
and chorus
price
cossotto
bergonzi
ghiaurov

salzburg mozart don giovanni
2, 5, 11, 19 and *lipp/price/sciutti/gedda/wächter/berry/*
22 august 1961 *zaccaria*
vienna philharmonic
vienna opera chorus

salzburg bach mass in b minor
20 august 1961
vienna philharmonic
wiener singverein
price, ludwig
gedda, souzay
berry

edinburgh
25 august 1961
berlin philharmonic

webern six pieces/mozart symphony 39/
brahms symphony 1

edinburgh
26 august 1961
berlin philharmonic

bach suite 2/stravinsky symphony in c/
strauss ein heldenleben

lucerne
2 september 1961
berlin philharmonic

bach suite 2/beethoven symphony 1/
strauss ein heldenleben

lucerne
3 september 1961
berlin philharmonic
richter-haaser

mozart piano concerto 23/bruckner
symphony 8

vienna
4 september 1961
vienna philharmonic

wagner das rheingold
*malaniuk/madeira/windgassen/klein/hotter/
wächter/pernerstorfer/roth-ehrang/kreppel*

vienna
6 september 1961
vienna philharmonic

wagner die walküre
*grob-prandl/crespin/madeira/vickers/
hotter/kreppel*

vienna
13 september 1961
vienna philharmonic
vienna opera chorus

verdi aida
*arroyo/simionato/bergonzi/bastianini/
zaccaria*

milan
21 and 22
september 1961
*la scala orchestra
and chorus
price
cossotto
bergonzi
petrov*

verdi messa da requiem

vienna
26 september 1961
vienna philharmonic
vienna opera chorus

mozart le nozze di figaro
*schwarzkopf/seefried/simionato/wächter/
kunz*

vienna
29 september 1961
*vienna philharmonic
members*

**bruckner adagio from seventh symphony
arranged by löwe for brass and percussion**
*performed in burgtheater at memorial service
for the actor albin skoda*

vienna
30 september and
1 october 1961
*vienna philharmonic
wiener singverein*

**locatelli concerto grosso op 4 no 10/
stravinsky symphony of psalms/dvorak
symphony 8**

berlin
6 and 7
october 1961
*berlin philharmonic
wiener singverein
stella
dominguez
bergonzi
zaccaria*

verdi messa da requiem

berlin
10, 11 and 12
october 1961
berlin philharmonic

**brahms symphony 4/debussy prélude a
l'apres-midi/ravel daphnis et chloé second
suite**

tour of usa by berlin philharmonic orchestra
new york
27 october 1961
berlin philharmonic

**bach suite 2/stravinsky symphony in c/
beethoven symphony 3**

boston
28 october 1961
berlin philharmonic

**bach suite 2/stravinsky symphony in c/
beethoven symphony 3**

new york
29 october 1961
berlin philharmonic

washington
30 october 1961
berlin philharmonic

**bach suite 2/stravinsky symphony in c/
brahms symphony 2**

columbus
31 october 1961
berlin philharmonic

mozart symphony 29/strauss tod und verklärung/tchaikovsky symphony 4

cleveland
1 november 1961
berlin philharmonic

bach suite 2/stravinsky symphony in c/ strauss also sprach zarathustra

ann arbor
3 november 1961
berlin philharmonic

brahms symphony 4/debussy prélude a l'apres-midi/strauss tod und verklärung

lavayette
4 november 1961
berlin philharmonic

mozart symphony 29/strauss tod und verklärung/tchaikovsky symphony 4

chicago
5 november 1961
berlin philharmonic

brahms symphony 4/strauss also sprach zarathustra

bloomington
6 november 1961
berlin philharmonic

fort wayne
7 november 1961
berlin philharmonic

mozart symphony 29/strauss tod und verklärung/beethoven symphony 7

oberlin
8 november 1961
berlin philharmonic

brahms symphony 4/debussy prélude a l'apres-midi/ravel daphnis et chloé second suite

vienna
19 november 1961
vienna philharmonic
vienna opera chorus

puccini tosca
roberti/raimondi/taddei

vienna
22 and 30 november 1961
vienna philharmonic

ballet performances
holst the planets

munich 26 november 1961 *vienna philharmonic*	locatelli concerto grosso op 4 no 10/mozart symphony 41/dvorak symphony 8
vienna 29 november 1961 *vienna philharmonic* *vienna opera chorus*	verdi otello *jurinac/mccracken/protti*
vienna 1 december 1961 *vienna philharmonic*	wagner das rheingold *malaniuk/rössl-majdan/windgassen/stolze/* *hotter/imdahl/pernerstorfer/roth-ehrang/* *kreppel*
vienna 2 and 3 december 1961 *vienna philharmonic*	bach brandenburg concerto 5/bruckner symphony 4
vienna 8 december 1961 *vienna philharmonic* *vienna opera chorus*	j.strauss die fledermaus *güden/rothenberger/zampieri/dickie/* *wächter/kunz*
vienna 10 december 1961 *vienna philharmonic* *vienna opera chorus*	bizet carmen *resnik/güden/usunow/protti*
vienna 17 december 1961 *vienna philharmonic* *vienna opera chorus*	beethoven fidelio *jurinac/rothenberger/windgassen/dickie/* *kreppel/hotter/guthrie*
berlin 29, 30 and 31 december 1961 *berlin philharmonic* *brendel*	locatelli concerto grosso op 4 no 10/ thärichen piano concerto/dvorak symphony 8

vienna
6 and 8
january 1962
vienna philharmonic
vienna opera chorus

debussy pelléas et mélisande
güden/höngen/gui/wächter/zaccaria

berlin
20, 21 and 22
january 1962
berlin philharmonic

henze antigoni/beethoven symphony 2/
mussorgsky pictures at an exhibition

vienna
27 and 28
january 1962
vienna symphony

haydn symphony 103/fortner impromptus/
tchaikovsky symphony 5

vienna
28 january 1962
vienna philharmonic
vienna opera chorus

mozart le nozze di figaro
stich-randall/güden/ludwig/wächter/berry

vienna
29 january 1962
vienna philharmonic
vienna opera chorus

puccini tosca
cavalli/usunow/protti

berlin
14, 15 and 16
february 1962
berlin philharmonic

bach brandenburg concerto 5/brahms haydn
variations/bartok concerto for orchestra

berlin
11, 12 and 13
march 1962
berlin philharmonic
rias choir

mozart maurerische trauermusik/stravinsky
symphony of psalms/bruckner symphony 4
*mozart work played in memory of bruno
walter*

vienna
20 march 1962
vienna philharmonic
vienna opera chorus

verdi aida
bernard/simionato/limarilli/protti/christoff

tour of russia, scandinavia, hamburg, london and paris by vienna philharmonic orchestra

moscow 23 march 1962 *vienna philharmonic*	mozart symphony 41/bruckner symphony 7
moscow 24 march 1962 *vienna philharmonic*	mozart eine kleine nachtmusik/strauss don juan/beethoven symphony 5
leningrad 27 and 28 march 1962 *vienna philharmonic*	mozart eine kleine nachtmusik/strauss don juan/beethoven symphony 5
oslo 30 march 1962 *vienna philharmonic*	mozart eine kleine nachtmusik/strauss don juan/brahms symphony 1
stockholm 1 april 1962 *vienna philharmonic*	mozart eine kleine nachtmusik/strauss don juan/beethoven symphony 5
copenhagen 3 april 1962 *vienna philharmonic*	mozart symphony 41/strauss don juan/dvorak symphony 8
hamburg 4 april 1962 *vienna philharmonic*	mozart symphony 41/bruckner symphony 7/j.strauss an der schönen blauen donau
london 6 april 1962 *vienna philharmonic*	mozart symphony 41/bruckner symphony 7
london 7 april 1962 *vienna philharmonic*	locatelli concerto grosso op 4 no 10/mozart symphony 40/strauss also sprach zarathustra
paris 9 april 1962 *vienna philharmonic*	locatelli concerto grosso op 4 no 10/schubert symphony 8/strauss also sprach zarathustra/josef strauss delirienwalzer

paris   mozart symphony 41/strauss don juan/dvorak
11 april 1962   symphony 8
vienna philharmonic

encore pieces on this tour included wagner meistersinger overture, josef strauss delirienwalzer and j.strauss an der schönen blauen donau; j.strauss programmes on this tour were conducted by boskovsky in moscow on 25 march and in london on 8 april

four performances of debussy pelléas et mélisande scheduled by karajan at la scala milan and starting on 19 april 1962 were in fact conducted by serge baudo

vienna   puccini tosca
6 may 1962   *stella/zampieri/gobbi*
vienna philharmonic
vienna opera chorus

vienna   verdi aida
10 may 1962   *rysanek/ludwig/usunow/gobbi/kreppel*
vienna philharmonic
vienna opera chorus

vienna   mozart le nozze di figaro
19 may 1962   *della casa/güden/jurinac/wächter/evans*
vienna philharmonic
vienna opera chorus

vienna   beethoven fidelio
25 may 1962   *ludwig/janowitz/vickers/kmennt/kreppel/*
vienna philharmonic   *berry/wächter*
vienna opera chorus

vienna   *bruckner programme*
26, 27 and 28   symphony 9/te deum
may 1962
vienna philharmonic
wiener singverein
lipp
höngen
gedda
kreppel

vienna mozart die zauberflöte
30 may 1962 lipp/hallstein/sciutti/gedda/kunz/wächter/
vienna philharmonic frick; *new production in restored theater an*
vienna opera chorus *der wien*

vienna wagner das rheingold
31 may 1962 *malaniuk/rössl-majdan/windgassen/klein/*
vienna philharmonic *hotter/wächter/pernerstorfer/roth-ehrang/*
  kreppel

vienna wagner die walküre
1 june 1962 *nilsson/rysanek/rössl-majdan/windgassen/*
vienna philharmonic *hotter/kreppel*

vienna wagner siegfried
3 june 1962 *nilsson/lipp/rössl-majdan/windgassen/klein/*
vienna philharmonic *hotter/roth-ehrang/pernerstorfer*

vienna wagner götterdämmerung
6 june 1962 *nilsson/hoffman/brouwenstijn/windgassen/*
vienna philharmonic *wiener/frick/pernerstorfer*
vienna opera chorus

vienna strauss der rosenkavalier
7 june 1962 *schwarzkopf/güden/seefried/edelmann/kunz*
vienna philharmonic
vienna opera chorus

vienna wagner parsifal
9 june 1962 *ludwig/höngen/uhl/wächter/hotter/berry/*
vienna philharmonic *franc*
vienna opera chorus

vienna bruckner mass no 2
11 june 1962 *performed in vienna hofburg*
vienna philharmonic
members
vienna opera
concert chorus

vienna beethoven fidelio
12 june 1962 *ludwig/janowitz/zampieri/kmennt/berry/*
vienna philharmonic *wächter/kreppel*
vienna opera chorus

vienna
14 june 1962
vienna philharmonic
vienna opera chorus

debussy pelléas et mélisande
güden/höngen/gui/wächter/zaccaria

vienna
16 june 1962
vienna philharmonic
vienna opera chorus

wagner tristan und isolde
nilsson/rössl-majdan/windgassen/wiener/hotter

vienna
18 june 1962
berlin philharmonic

beethoven symphony 4/strauss ein heldenleben

vienna
19 june 1962
berlin philharmonic

bach suite 2/debussy prélude a l'apres-midi/stravinsky symphony in c/ravel daphnis et chloé second suite

salzburg
31 july and
4, 11, 20, 25 and
30 august 1962
vienna philharmonic
vienna opera chorus

verdi il trovatore
price/simionato/corelli/bastianini/zaccaria

salzburg
9 august 1962
berlin philharmonic
wiener singverein
price
simionato
zampieri
ghiaurov

verdi messa da requiem

lucerne
1 september 1962
vienna philharmonic

handel concerto grosso op 6 no 5/bruckner symphony 7

athens
5 september 1962
berlin philharmonic

beethoven programme
coriolan overture/symphony 6/symphony 7

athens   mozart symphony 29/strauss don juan/
6 september 1962   brahms symphony 2
berlin philharmonic

athens   brahms haydn variations/schumann symphony 4/
7 september 1962   wagner tristan prelude and liebestod/wagner
berlin philharmonic   tannhäuser overture

vienna   verdi aida
23 september 1962   *price/simionato/usunow/bastianini/frick*
vienna philharmonic
vienna opera chorus

vienna   debussy pelléas et mélisande
30 september and   *güden/höngen/gui/wächter/zaccaria*
2 october 1962
vienna philharmonic
vienna opera chorus

vienna   puccini tosca
3 october 1962   *price/di stefano/taddei/zaccaria*
vienna philharmonic
vienna opera chorus

berlin   mozart symphony 40/bruckner symphony 7
7 october 1962
vienna philharmonic

berlin   handel concerto grosso op 3 no 1/schoenberg
11, 12 and 13   orchestral variations/beethoven symphony 6
october 1962
berlin philharmonic

tour of london and west germany by berlin philharmonic orchestra
london   brahms tragic overture/brahms symphony 3/
1 november 1962   bartok concerto for orchestra
berlin philharmonic

london   bach suite 2/mozart symphony 29/strauss
2 november 1962   ein heldenleben
berlin philharmonic

düsseldorf
3 november 1962
berlin philharmonic

brahms tragic overture/brahms haydn variations/tchaikovsky symphony 4

dortmund
4 november 1962
berlin philharmonic

beethoven symphony 4/strauss ein heldenleben

münster
5 november 1962
berlin philharmonic

beethoven programme
coriolan overture/symphony 6/symphony 7

bremen
6 november 1962
berlin philharmonic

brahms symphony 3/bartok concerto for orchestra

kiel
7 november 1962
berlin philharmonic

beethoven coriolan overture/beethoven symphony 6/tchaikovsky symphony 4

hamburg
8 november 1962
berlin philharmonic

beethoven coriolan overture/beethoven symphony 4/bartok concerto for orchestra

berlin
12, 13 and 14 november 1962
berlin philharmonic
demus

brahms tragic overture/mozart piano concerto 27/tchaikovsky symphony 6

vienna
24 and 25 november 1962
vienna symphony
wiener singverein
lipp
wächter

brahms ein deutsches requiem

vienna   bach magnificat/stravinsky le sacre du printemps
8 and 9
december 1962
vienna philharmonic
wiener singverein
ludwig
kmennt
wächter

berlin   haydn symphony 103/bloch schelomo/debussy
29, 30 and 31   la mer
december 1962
berlin philharmonic
borwitzky

vienna   haydn die schöpfung
5 and 6
january 1963
vienna symphony
wiener singverein
janowitz
dermota
wächter
frick

vienna   wagner tannhäuser
8 and 11   *brouwenstijn/janowitz/ludwig/hoffman (11)/*
january 1963   *beirer/kmennt/wächter/frick*
vienna philharmonic
vienna opera chorus

milan   puccini la boheme
31 january and   *freni/ratti/raimondi/vinco/maffeo/davia/*
7, 13, 19 and 24   *panerai/sereni (24 february)*
february 1963
la scala orchestra
and chorus

vienna   wagner das rheingold
15 february 1963   *malaniuk/resnik/klein/stolze/hotter/wächter/*
vienna philharmonic   *pernerstorfer/frick/kreppel*

vienna   beethoven fidelio
17 february 1963   *ludwig/janowitz/zampieri/kmennt/wächter/*
vienna philharmonic   *berry/kreppel*
vienna opera chorus

munich
23 february 1963
vienna philharmonic

mozart symphony 29/strauss don juan/beethoven symphony 7

berlin
1, 2 and 3
march 1963
berlin philharmonic
rias choir
stader, ludwig
alva, berry

bach magnificat/stravinsky le sacre du printemps

tour of west germany by berlin philharmonic orchestra

hannover
4 march 1963
berlin philharmonic

mozart symphony 40/bruckner symphony 7

kassel
5 march 1963
berlin philharmonic

bartok concerto for orchestra/dvorak symphony 8

stuttgart
6 march 1963
berlin philharmonic

mozart symphony 40/bruckner symphony 7

freiburg
7 march 1963
berlin philharmonic

beethoven programme
coriolan overture/symphony 6/symphony 5

frankfurt
8 march 1963
berlin philharmonic

bartok concerto for orchestra/dvorak symphony 8

milan
9 and 16
march 1963
la scala orchestra
and chorus

puccini la boheme
freni/fusco/raimondi/panerai/maffeo/vinco/
davia/tadeo

vienna
24 march 1963
vienna philharmonic

wagner das rheingold
malaniuk/cervena/klein/stolze/hotter/
wächter/pernerstorfer/roth-ehrang/rohr

vienna
26 march and
4 april 1963
vienna philharmonic
vienna opera chorus

wagner tannhäuser
brouwenstijn/janowitz/hoffman/beirer/
windgassen (4)/kmennt/wächter/prey (4)/
crass/kreppel (4)

vienna monteverdi l'incoronazione di poppea
1 and 8 jurinac/janowitz/lilowa/stolze/wiener/cava
april 1963
vienna philharmonic
vienna opera chorus

vienna beethoven symphony 9
6 and 7
april 1963
vienna philharmonic
wiener singverein
janowitz, rössl-majdan
dermota, wiener

vienna wagner parsifal
14 april 1963 ludwig/höngen/uhl/wächter/berry/hotter/
vienna philharmonic franc
vienna opera chorus

milan puccini la boheme
15 and 20 freni/fusco/ratti (20)/raimondi/panerai/
april 1963 badioli/tadeo
la scala orchestra
and chorus

brussels *programme included*
22 april 1963 mozart eine kleine nachtmusik/strauss don juan
vienna philharmonic

london *beethoven programme for 150 th anniversary*
24 april 1963 *of royal philharmonic society*
vienna philharmonic symphony 1/symphony 9
philharmonia chorus
janowitz, rössl-majdan
dermota, wiener

tour of paris, switzerland and munich by berlin philharmonic orchestra
paris *brahms cycle*
26 april 1963 violin concerto/symphony 4
berlin philharmonic
gerle

paris *brahms cycle*
27 april 1963 symphony 3/symphony 2
berlin philharmonic

MUSICA VIVA

2. Sonderkonzert: Sonntag, 5. Mai 1963, 20 Uhr, im Herkules-Saal der Residenz

Gastkonzert des Berliner Philharmonischen Orchesters

Herbert von Karajan

dirigiert

das Berliner Philharmonische Orchester

den Chor des Bayerischen Rundfunks
Einstudierung des Chores: Fritz Schieri a. G.

Hans Werner Henze
Antifone per orchestra

Igor Strawinsky
Psalmensymphonie für gemischten Chor und Orchester
Viertel = 92   Achtel = 60   Viertel = 48   Text: Seite 12

Béla Bartók
Concerto für Orchester
I Introduzione   II Giuco delle Coppie   III Elegia   IV Intermezzo   V Finale

paris
28 april 1963
berlin philharmonic
backhaus

brahms cycle
piano concerto 2/symphony 1

geneva
30 april 1963
berlin philharmonic

bach suite 2/mozart symphony 29/brahms symphony 2

zürich
1 may 1963
berlin philharmonic

bartok concerto for orchestra/dvorak symphony 8

basel
3 may 1963
berlin philharmonic

beethoven symphony 2/dvorak symphony 8

munich
5 may 1963
berlin philharmonic
bavarian radio chorus

henze antifone/stravinsky symphony of psalms/
bartok concerto for orchestra
concert in the munich musica viva series

vienna
26 may 1963
vienna philharmonic
vienna opera chorus

wagner parsifal
ludwig/höngen/uhl/wächter/berry/hotter/
franc

vienna
27 may 1963
vienna philharmonic
vienna opera chorus

monteverdi l'incoronazione di poppea
jurinac/janowitz/lilowa/stolze/wiener/cava

vienna
29 may 1963
vienna philharmonic
vienna opera chorus

wagner tannhäuser
schwarzkopf/janowitz/ludwig/windgassen/
kmennt/wächter/kreppel

vienna
31 may and
13 june 1963
vienna philharmonic
vienna opera chorus

puccini tosca
price/bergonzi/raimondi (13 june)/taddei/
zaccaria

vienna
2, 3 and 4
june 1963
vienna philharmonic
francescatti
fournier

brahms programme
double concerto/symphony 1

vienna
6 june 1963
vienna philharmonic
vienna opera chorus

debussy pelléas et mélisande
güden/höngen/gui/wächter/zaccaria

vienna
8 june 1963
vienna philharmonic

wagner das rheingold
*malaniuk/rössl-majdan/windgassen/klein/
hotter/wächter/pernerstorfer/frick/kreppel*

vienna
9 june 1963
vienna philharmonic

wagner die walküre
*nilsson/rysanek/rössl-majdan/windgassen/
hotter/frick*

vienna
12 june 1963
vienna philharmonic

wagner siegfried
*nilsson/rothenberger/rössl-majdan/
windgassen/klein/hotter/frick/pernerstorfer*

vienna
15 june 1963
vienna philharmonic
vienna opera chorus

wagner götterdämmerung
*nilsson/brouwenstijn/ludwig/windgassen/
wiener/frick/pernerstorfer*

prague
18 june 1963
vienna philharmonic

mozart symphony 41/strauss don juan/
brahms symphony 1/josef strauss delirienwalzer

vienna
19 june 1963
vienna philharmonic
vienna opera chorus

beethoven fidelio
*ludwig/janowitz/usunow/kmennt/wächter/
berry/kreppel*

vienna
22 june 1963
vienna philharmonic
vienna opera chorus

mozart don giovanni
*güden/price/sciutti/wunderlich/wächter/
berry/kreppel*

vienna
24 september 1963
vienna philharmonic
vienna opera chorus

mozart don giovanni
güden/watson/sciutti/dermota/siepi/corena/ kreppel

vienna
28 and 29
september 1963
vienna philharmonic

beethoven symphony 2/leitermeyer rhapsodische skizzen/debussy la mer

vienna
3 october 1963
vienna philharmonic
vienna opera chorus

verdi otello
tucci/lilowa/guichandut/taddei

vienna
4 and 7
october 1963
vienna philharmonic
vienna opera chorus

debussy pelléas et mélisande
güden/höngen/gui/wächter/zaccaria

vienna
6 october 1963
vienna philharmonic
vienna opera chorus

verdi aida
tucci/simionato/usunow/protti/vinco

berlin
14 and 15
october 1963
berlin philharmonic
saint hedwig's
and rias choirs
janowitz
wagner
alva
wiener

beethoven symphony 9
opening concert in re-built philharmonie

berlin
15 october 1963
berlin philharmonic

beethoven leonore 3 overture
inaugural ceremony in philharmonie; other works by blacher and haydn not conducted by karajan

berlin
18 and 19
october 1963
berlin philharmonic
francescatti
fournier

brahms programme
double concerto/symphony 1

vienna
24 and 27
october 1963
vienna philharmonic
vienna opera chorus

verdi il trovatore
ligabue/cossotto/corelli/wächter/zaccaria

vienna
2 and 3
november 1963
vienna symphony
wiener singverein
lipp
rössl-majdan
wunderlich
engen

mozart requiem/bruckner te deum
final public appearances with vienna
symphony orchestra

vienna
6 and 15
november 1963
vienna philharmonic
vienna opera chorus

verdi il trovatore
ligabue/lilowa/corelli/bastianini/vinco

vienna
9, 13 and 17
november 1963
vienna philharmonic
vienna opera chorus

puccini la boheme
freni/güden/coulter (17)/raimondi/panerai/
taddei/vinco; premiere of this production
scheduled for 2 november but cancelled due
to an industrial dispute

munich
1 and 5
december 1963
bavarian state
orchestra and chorus

beethoven fidelio
ludwig/steffek/uhl/stolze/frick/berry/prey;
part of opening festival of munich national-
theater; further performance conducted by
böhm due to karajan's illness on 12 december

tour of london, brussels and paris by berlin philharmonic orchestra

london *brahms cycle*
31 january 1964 piano concerto 2/symphony 4
berlin philharmonic
anda

london *brahms cycle*
1 february 1964 symphony 3/symphony 2
berlin philharmonic

london *brahms cycle*
3 february 1964 violin concerto/symphony 1
berlin philharmonic
ferras

brussels beethoven coriolan overture/beethoven
4 february 1964 symphony 4/strauss ein heldenleben
berlin philharmonic

paris mozart symphony 41/tchaikovsky symphony 6
6 february 1964
berlin philharmonic

paris beethoven symphony 4/strauss ein heldenleben
7 february 1964
berlin philharmonic

berlin bach brandenburg concerto 6/bruckner
11 and 12 symphony 7
february 1964
berlin philharmonic

berlin britten war requiem
8 and 9
march 1964
berlin philharmonic
deutsche oper chorus
lipp
kesteren
fischer-dieskau

vienna
24 march 1964
vienna philharmonic
vienna opera chorus

beethoven fidelio
kuchta/janowitz/uhl/stolze/wächter/hotter/
kreppel

vienna
26 and 29
march 1964
vienna philharmonic
vienna opera chorus

wagner parsifal
ludwig/höngen/uhl/wächter/berry/hotter/
franc

vienna
1 april 1964
vienna philharmonic

wagner das rheingold
malaniuk/rössl-majdan/klein/stolze/
wächter/kerns/pernerstorfer/welter/
kreppel

vienna
4 and 5
april 1964
vienna philharmonic

beethoven symphony 1/tchaikovsky
symphony 6

milan
7, 9 and 18
april 1964
la scala orchestra
and chorus

puccini la boheme
freni/sciutti/raimondi/panerai/maffeo/
mercuriali/vinco/badioli/calabrese

tour of west germany by berlin philharmonic orchestra
hamburg
22 april 1964
berlin philharmonic

tchaikovsky symphony 6/debussy la mer

bremen
23 april 1964
berlin philharmonic

beethoven symphony 6/strauss ein
heldenleben

hannover
24 april 1964
berlin philharmonic

bach suite 2/strauss don juan/brahms
symphony 2

wolfsburg
25 april 1964
berlin philharmonic

mozart symphony 29/strauss don juan/
tchaikovsky symphony 6

münster
26 april 1964
berlin philharmonic

mozart symphony 29/strauss don juan/
brahms symphony 2

düsseldorf
27 april 1964
berlin philharmonic

beethoven programme
coriolan overture/symphony 6/symphony 5

kassel
28 april 1964
berlin philharmonic

beethoven symphony 4/strauss ein heldenleben

munich
30 april 1964
berlin philharmonic

tchaikovsky symphony 6/debussy la mer

stuttgart
1 may 1964
berlin philharmonic

beethoven symphony 6/strauss ein heldenleben

nürnberg
2 may 1964
berlin philharmonic

bach suite 2/strauss don juan/brahms
symphony 1

berlin
5 and 6
may 1964
berlin philharmonic
schwarzkopf
koch

strauss centenary concert
oboe concerto/4 letzte lieder/ein heldenleben

milan
9 may 1964
la scala orchestra
and chorus

puccini la boheme
cast as for 7 april 1964

vienna
17 and 18
may 1964
berlin philharmonic
backhaus

brahms programme
piano concerto 2/symphony 2

vienna
19 may 1964
berlin philharmonic

beethoven programme
coriolan overture/symphony 6/symphony 7

vienna
21 may and
3 june 1964
vienna philharmonic
vienna opera chorus

beethoven fidelio
ludwig/janowitz/mccracken/usunow (3 june)/
kmennt/berry/wächter/kreppel

vienna
24 may 1964
vienna philharmonic
vienna opera chorus

wagner parsifal
ludwig/höngen/uhl/wächter/berry/hotter/
franc

vienna
28 may 1964
vienna philharmonic
vienna opera chorus

wagner tannhäuser
brouwenstijn/janowitz/ludwig/beirer/kmennt/
imdahl/frick

vienna
31 may 1964
vienna philharmonic
vienna opera chorus

puccini la boheme
freni/sciutti/raimondi/panerai/taddei/
zaccaria

vienna
7 june 1964
vienna philharmonic
vienna opera chorus

verdi il trovatore
price/simionato/mccracken/protti/zaccaria

vienna
10 june 1964
vienna philharmonic
vienna opera chorus

puccini tosca
price/labo/taddei/zaccaria

vienna
11 june 1964
vienna philharmonic
vienna opera chorus

strauss die frau ohne schatten
rysanek/ludwig/hoffman/thomas/berry/
kreppel

vienna 14 june 1964 *vienna philharmonic* *vienna opera chorus*	verdi aida *price/simionato/labo/bastianini/zaccaria*
vienna 17 june 1964 *vienna philharmonic* *vienna opera chorus*	strauss die frau ohne schatten *janowitz/kuchts/hoffman/thomas/wiener/ kreppel; karajan's final appearance as director of vienna staatsoper*
vienna 20, 21 and 22 june 1964 *vienna philharmonic* *fournier*	*strauss centenary concert* don quixote/also sprach zarathustra
den haag 30 june 1964 *vienna philharmonic*	strauss don juan/schubert symphony 8/ beethoven symphony 7
amsterdam 1 july 1964 *vienna philharmonic*	mozart symphony 40/bruckner symphony 7
salzburg 1, 13 and 29 august 1964 *vienna philharmonic* *vienna opera chorus*	strauss der rosenkavalier *schwarzkopf/rothenberger/jurinac/ edelmann/ferenz*
salzburg 11, 17 and 27 august 1964 *vienna philharmonic* *vienna opera chorus*	strauss elektra *varnay/hillebrecht/mödl/king/wächter*
salzburg 15 august 1964 *berlin philharmonic* *schwarzkopf* *koch*	*strauss centenary concert* oboe concerto/4 letzte lieder/ein heldenleben

st moritz
20 august 1964
*berlin philharmonic
members
schneiderhan
schwalbé*

salzburg   *strauss centenary concert*
30 august 1964   *don quixote/also sprach zarathustra*
*vienna philharmonic
fournier*

lucerne   *strauss centenary concert*
1 september 1964   *don quixote/also sprach zarathustra*
*vienna philharmonic
fournier*

venice   mozart symphony 40/strauss don juan/
13 september 1964   beethoven symphony 5
vienna philharmonic

bucharest   mozart symphony 40/strauss don juan/
15 september 1964   brahms symphony 1
vienna philharmonic

bucharest   mozart eine kleine nachtmusik/schubert
16 september 1964   symphony 8/beethoven symphony 5
vienna philharmonic

moscow   puccini la boheme
20, 22, 24 and 26   *freni/vicenzi/raimondi/panerai/maffeo/*
september 1964   *mantovani (22 and 24)/vinco/calabrese*
*la scala orchestra
and chorus*

moscow   verdi messa da requiem
23 and 25
september 1964
*la scala orchestra
and chorus
price
cossotto
bergonzi
ghiaurov/zaccaria*

berlin
29 and 30
september 1964
berlin philharmonic
ferras

bach brandenburg concerto 3/bach violin concerto in e/stravinsky le sacre du printemps

berlin
16 and 17
october 1964
berlin philharmonic
price

berg three pieces/bach cantata 51/beethoven symphony 5

berlin
22, 25, 28 and 31
october 1964
deutsche oper
orchestra and chorus

verdi il trovatore
price/lazzarini/prevedi/guelfi/zaccaria

hannover
1 november 1964
berlin philharmonic

mozart divertimento 15/brahms haydn variations/tchaikovsky symphony 5

munich
6, 8, 10 and 12
november 1964
la scala orchestra
and chorus

puccini la boheme
freni/martino/raimondi/panerai/maffeo/
vinco/carbonari

berlin
24 and 25
november 1964
berlin philharmonic
deutsche oper
chorus
janowitz
wiener

brahms ein deutsches requiem

milan
17, 20 and 22
december 1964
la scala orchestra
and chorus

verdi la traviata
moffo/freni (17)/cioni/sereni/zaccaria

DEUTSCHE OPER BERLIN

DONNERSTAG, DEN 22. OKTOBER 1964

Beginn: 19.30 Uhr   Ende: 22.15 Uhr

Neuinszenierung

DER TROUBADOUR

Oper in 4 Akten (8 Bildern) von Giuseppe Verdi

(in italienischer Sprache)

Verlag: G. Ricordi & Co., Frankfurt a. M.

Musikalische Leitung und Inszenierung: Herbert von Karajan
Bühnenbild: Teo Otto · Kostüme: Georg Wakhevitch
Chöre: Walter Hagen-Groll

Graf Luna	Gian Giacomo Guelfi
Gräfin Leonore	Leontyne Price
Azucena, eine Zigeunerin	Adriana Lazzarini
Manrico	Bruno Prevedi
Ferrando, Anhänger des Luna	Nicola Zaccaria
Inez, Vertraute der Leonore	Marina Türke
Ruiz, Anhänger des Manrico	Karl Ernst Mercker
Ein Zigeuner	Walter Dicks
Ein Bote	Werner Götz

Technische Leitung: Hans Birr · Beleuchtung: Willi Rosumek

Pause nach dem 4. Bild

Einlaß für Zuspätkommende auf Klingelzeichen und nach dem 1. Bild

berlin nono incontri/haydn cello concerto in d/
29 and 30 berlioz symphonie fantastique
december 1964
berlin philharmonic
finke

tour of usa by berlin philharmonic orchestra
new york *beethoven cycle*
19 january 1965 coriolan overture/symphony 4/symphony 7
berlin philharmonic

boston
20 january 1965
berlin philharmonic

new york *beethoven cycle*
21 january 1965 symphony 2/symphony 3
berlin philharmonic

washington beethoven symphony 6/strauss ein heldenleben
23 january 1965
berlin philharmonic

washington
24 january 1965
berlin philharmonic

new york *beethoven cycle*
25 january 1965 symphony 6/symphony 5
berlin philharmonic

new york *beethoven cycle*
26 january 1965 leonore 3 overture/symphony 8/piano
berlin philharmonic concerto 3
richter-haaser

1964   Eighty-sixth Season   1965

UNIVERSITY MUSICAL SOCIETY

THE UNIVERSITY OF MICHIGAN

Charles A. Sink, President

Gail W. Rector, Executive Director   Lester McCoy, Conductor

Fourth Program   Nineteenth Annual Extra Series   Complete Series 3454

Berlin Philharmonic Orchestra

HERBERT von KARAJAN, Conductor

Under the Patronage of
The Governing Mayor of the City of Berlin
WILLY BRANDT

Under the Sponsorship of
The German Ambassador to the United States
HIS EXCELLENCY, HEINRICH KNAPPSTEIN

SATURDAY EVENING, JANUARY 30, 1965, AT 8:30
HILL AUDITORIUM, ANN ARBOR, MICHIGAN

PROGRAM

Suite No. 2 in B minor . . . . BACH
    Ouverture   Bourrée II
    Rondeau   Polonaise
    Sarabande   Menuet
    Bourrée I   Badinerie
       Soloist: KARL-HEINZ ZÖLLER, *Flutist*

Symphony No. 29 in A major, K. 201 . . . . MOZART
    Allegro moderato
     Andante
      Menuetto
       Allegro con spirito

INTERMISSION

Symphony No. 1 in C minor, Op. 68 . . . . BRAHMS
    Un poco sostenuto; allegro
    Andante sostenuto
     Un poco allegretto e grazioso
      Adagio; allegro non troppo ma con brio

Deutsche Grammophon Gesellschaft Recordings

A R S   L O N G A   V I T A   B R E V I S

new york *beethoven cycle*
28 january 1965 symphony 1/symphony 9
berlin philharmonic
westminster choir
janowitz
chookasian
konya
kwei-sze

detroit beethoven symphony 6/debussy prélude a
29 january 1965 l'apres-midi d'un faune/ravel daphnis et
berlin philharmonic chloé second suite

ann arbor bach suite 2/mozart symphony 29/brahms
30 january 1965 symphony 1
berlin philharmonic

chicago beethoven symphony 4/strauss ein heldenleben
31 january 1965
berlin philharmonic

chicago bach suite 2/mozart symphony 29/brahms
1 february 1965 symphony 2
berlin philharmonic

berlin bruckner symphony 8
25 and 26
february 1965
berlin philharmonic

tour of west germany, london, brussels and paris by vienna philharmonic orchestra
nürnberg mozart eine kleine nachtmusik/schubert
28 march 1965 symphony 8/beethoven symphony 7/josef
vienna philharmonic strauss delirienwalzer

munich mozart symphony 29/strauss don juan/
29 march 1965 beethoven symphony 7/josef strauss
vienna philharmonic delirienwalzer

stuttgart mozart symphony 29/strauss don juan/
30 march 1965 dvorak symphony 8/josef strauss delirienwalzer
vienna philharmonic

hamburg mozart eine kleine nachtmusik/schubert
31 march 1965 symphony 8/dvorak symphony 8
vienna philharmonic

hannover mozart eine kleine nachtmusik/schubert
1 april 1965 symphony 8/beethoven symphony 7/josef
vienna philharmonic strauss delirienwalzer

london mozart symphony 29/bruckner symphony 8
3 april 1965
vienna philharmonic

london haydn symphony 104/strauss don juan/
5 april 1965 dvorak symphony 8
vienna philharmonic

brussels mozart eine kleine nachtmusik/schubert
6 april 1965 symphony 8/beethoven symphony 7
vienna philharmonic

paris mozart symphony 29/bruckner symphony 8
8 april 1965
vienna philharmonic

paris mozart symphony 40/brahms haydn
9 april 1965 variations/beethoven symphony 7/josef
vienna philharmonic strauss delirienwalzer

milan puccini la boheme
22, 25 and 28 *freni/martino/raimondi/sereni/maffeo/*
april 1965 *vinco/badioli/calabrese*
*la scala orchestra
and chorus*

hamburg verdi il trovatore
9 may 1965 *ligabue/lazzarini/bergonzi/herlea; guest*
deutsche oper *performance by deutsche oper berlin*
orchestra and chorus

berlin verdi il trovatore
12 and 15 *cast as for 9 may 1965*
may 1965
*deutsche oper
orchestra and chorus*

berlin *sibelius programme*
13 and 14 symphony 4/symphony 5/finlandia
may 1965
berlin philharmonic

tour of scandinavia by berlin philharmonic orchestra

helsinki
16 may 1965
berlin philharmonic

sibelius programme
symphony 4/symphony 5/finlandia

stockholm
17 may 1965
berlin philharmonic

bach brandenburg concerto 3/schubert symphony 8/brahms symphony 1

copenhagen
18 may 1965
berlin philharmonic

sibelius symphony 5/beethoven symphony 2

bergen
19 may 1965
berlin philharmonic

schubert symphony 8/strauss don juan/beethoven symphony 5

milan
22 and 23
may 1965
berlin philharmonic

locatelli concerto grosso op 4 no 10/mozart symphony 29/brahms symphony 1

milan
24 and 25
may 1965
berlin philharmonic

tchaikovsky symphony 6/debussy prélude a l'apres-midi/ravel daphnis et chloé second suite

milan
28 and 29
may 1965
*la scala orchestra
and chorus
scotto
smith
shirley
zaccaria*

mozart requiem

salzburg
26 and 30 july
and 13, 16, 25 and
28 august 1965
*vienna philharmonic
vienna opera chorus*

mussorgsky boris godunov
jurinac/radev/usunow/stolze/ghiaurov/ghiuselev

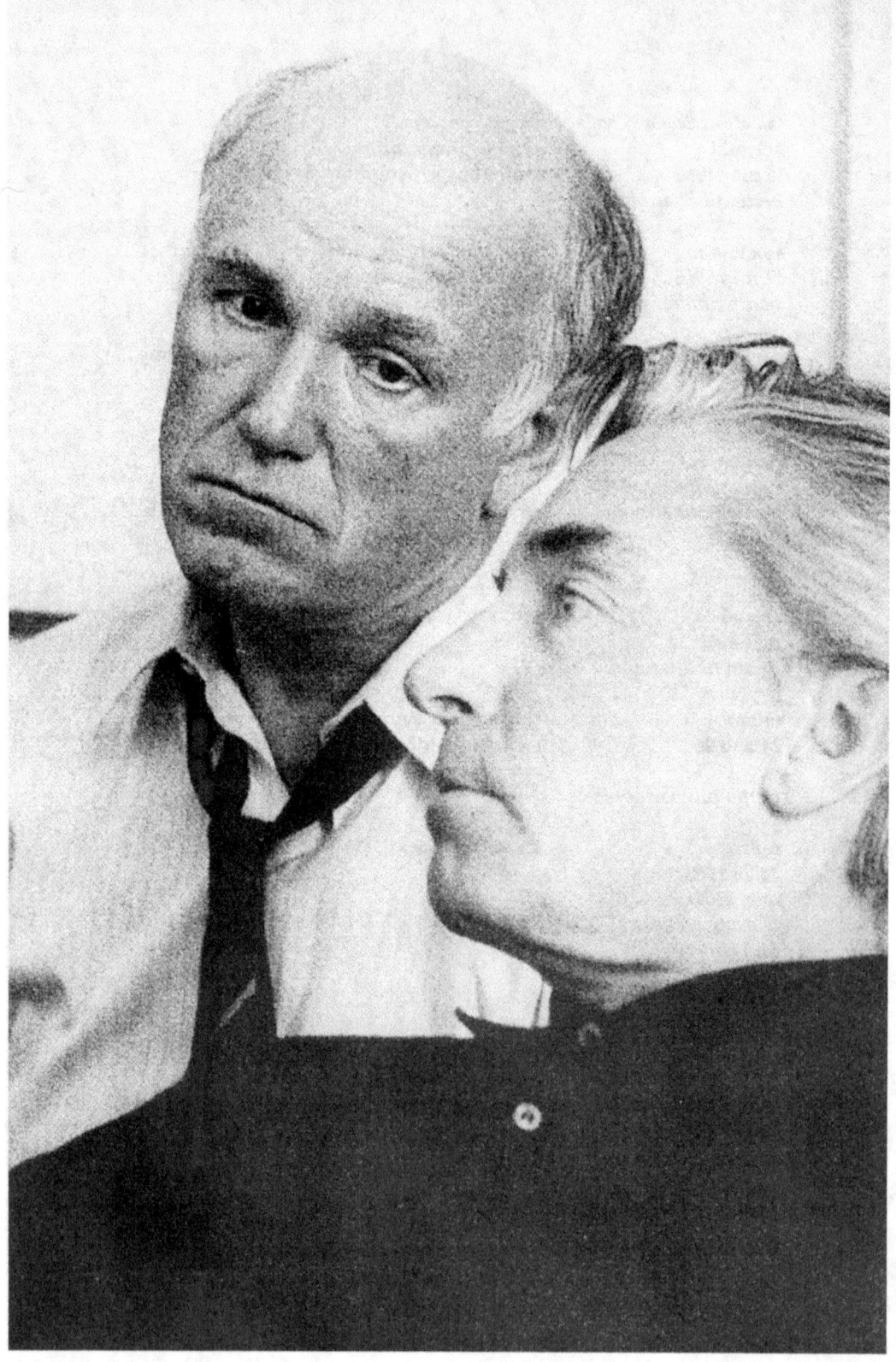

salzburg strauss elektra
29 july and *varnay/hillebrecht/mödl/stolze/wächter*
17 and 26
august 1965
vienna philharmonic
vienna opera chorus

salzburg tchaikovsky piano concerto 1/dvorak
15 august 1965 symphony 8
staatskapelle dresden
richter

salzburg haydn die schöpfung
29 august 1965
vienna philharmonic
wiener singverein
janowitz
wunderlich
prey
borg

lucerne bach brandenburg concerto 3/beethoven
4 september 1965 symphony 4/schumann symphony 4
berlin philharmonic

lucerne sibelius symphony 5/sibelius finlandia/
5 september 1965 debussy prélude a l'apres-midi/ravel
berlin philharmonic daphnis et chloé second suite

venice verdi messa da requiem
7 september 1965
berlin philharmonic
wiener singverein
scotto
simionato
bergonzi
zaccaria

athens sibelius symphony 5/debussy prélude a
9 september 1965 l'apres-midi/debussy la mer/sibelius finlandia
berlin philharmonic

athens
10 september 1965
berlin philharmonic

beethoven programme
symphony 1/leonore 3 overture/symphony 5

epidaurus
12 september 1965
berlin philharmonic
wiener singverein
scotto
ludwig
bergonzi
zaccaria

verdi messa da requiem

berlin
23 and 24
september 1965
berlin philharmonic

mozart divertimento 15/bennett aubade/
dvorak symphony 9

berlin
26 and 27
september 1965
berlin philharmonic

bartok concerto for orchestra/beethoven
symphony 4

tour of west germany by berlin philharmonic orchestra

munich
25 october 1965
berlin philharmonic

beethoven symphony 1/berlioz symphonie
fantastique

stuttgart
26 october 1965
berlin philharmonic

mozart divertimento 15/brahms haydn
variations/tchaikovsky symphony 5

nürnberg
27 october 1965
berlin philharmonic

dvorak symphony 9/debussy prélude a
l'apres-midi/ravel daphnis et chloé second
suite

frankfurt
28 october 1965
berlin philharmonic

beethoven symphony 1/berlioz symphonie
fantastique

bad godesberg
29 october 1965
berlin philharmonic

bach brandenburg concerto 3/brahms haydn
variations/dvorak symphony 9

kassel
30 october 1965
berlin philharmonic

mozart divertimento 15/brahms haydn variations/tchaikovsky symphony 5

wolfsburg
31 october 1965
berlin philharmonic

dvorak symphony 9/debussy prélude a l'apres-midi/ravel daphnis et chloé second suite

hannover
1 november 1965
berlin philharmonic

mozart divertimento 17/brahms haydn variations/tchaikovsky symphony 5

hamburg
2 november 1965
berlin philharmonic

beethoven symphony 1/berlioz symphonie fantastique

berlin
5, 6 and 7 november 1965
berlin philharmonic
michelangeli

webern five pieces/schumann piano concerto/ tchaikovsky symphony 5

berlin
29 and 30 december 1965
berlin philharmonic
fournier

strauss programme
also sprach zarathustra/don quixote

berlin
25 and 26 january 1966
berlin philharmonic

bach brandenburg concerto 3/brahms haydn variations/dvorak symphony 9

berlin
30 january 1966
berlin philharmonic

beethoven programme
symphony 2/symphony 7

berlin
25 and 26 february 1966
berlin philharmonic
wiener singverein
janowitz, ludwig,
wunderlich, berry

beethoven missa solemnis

concert in london on 13 march 1966 with the new philharmonia orchestra and chorus (verdi messa da requiem) was cancelled due to differences with the chorus-master wilhelm pitz: it was conducted by rafael frühbeck de burgos

berlin **16 and 17** **march 1966** *berlin philharmonic*	**bach brandenburg concerto 6/bruckner symphony 9**

tour of japan by berlin philharmonic orchestra

tokyo **12 april 1966** *berlin philharmonic*	*beethoven cycle* **coriolan overture/symphony 6/symphony 5**
tokyo **13 april 1966** *berlin philharmonic*	*beethoven cycle* **symphony 4/symphony 7**
tokyo **14 april 1966** *berlin philharmonic*	*beethoven cycle* **symphony 1/symphony 3**
tokyo **15 april 1966** *berlin philharmonic*	*beethoven cycle* **leonore 3 overture/symphony 2/symphony 8**
tokyo **16 april 1966** *berlin philharmonic* *nhk chorus* *janowitz* *nagano* *kesteren* *talvela*	*beethoven cycle* **symphony 9**
sendai **17 april 1966** *berlin philharmonic*	**dvorak symphony 8/debussy prélude a l'apres-midi/debussy la mer**
sapporo **19 april 1966** *berlin philharmonic*	**schubert symphony 8/brahms symphony 2**

nagoya　　　　　　　　　dvorak symphony 9/debussy prélude a l'apres-midi/
20 april 1966　　　　　　　debussy la mer
berlin philharmonic

kanazawa　　　　　　　　schubert symphony 8/beethoven symphony 3
21 april 1966
berlin philharmonic

osaka　　　　　　　　　　webern six pieces/strauss don juan/brahms
22 april 1966　　　　　　　symphony 1
berlin philharmonic

okayama　　　　　　　　　dvorak symphony 8/debussy prélude a l'apres-midi/
24 april 1966　　　　　　　debussy la mer
berlin philharmonic

takamatsu　　　　　　　　schubert symphony 8/dvorak symphony 9
25 april 1966
berlin philharmonic

matsyama　　　　　　　　bach brandenburg concerto 6/brahms haydn
26 april 1966　　　　　　　variations/beethoven symphony 7
berlin philharmonic

fukuoka　　　　　　　　　schubert symphony 8/dvorak symphony 9
28 april 1966
berlin philharmonic

hiroshima　　　　　　　　bach brandenburg concerto 6/brahms haydn
29 april 1966　　　　　　　variations/beethoven symphony 5
berlin philharmonic

osaka　　　　　　　　　　mozart divertimento 15/strauss ein heldenleben
30 april 1966
berlin philharmonic

tokyo　　　　　　　　　　bruckner symphony 8
2 may 1966
berlin philharmonic

tokyo　　　　　　　　　　mozart divertimento 15/strauss ein heldenleben
3 may 1966
berlin philharmonic

milan
12, 16, 23 and 25
may 1966
*la scala orchestra
and chorus*

mascagni cavalleria rusticana
*cossotto/bumbry (23 and 25)/martino/cecchele/
guelfi*

prague
29 may 1966
berlin philharmonic

mozart divertimento 15/beethoven symphony 3

prague
30 may 1966
berlin philharmonic

bartok concerto for orchestra/dvorak symphony 8

rotterdam
15 june 1966
berlin philharmonic

mozart divertimento 15/berlioz symphonie fantastique

amsterdam
16 june 1966
berlin philharmonic

bruckner symphony 8

scheveningen
17 june 1966
berlin philharmonic

beethoven symphony 6/debussy prélude a l'apres-midi/debussy la mer

chartres
19 june 1966
berlin philharmonic

mozart symphony 35/bruckner symphony 8

paris
20 june 1966
berlin philharmonic

mozart divertimento 15/berlioz symphonie fantastique

paris
21 june 1966
berlin philharmonic

dvorak symphony 9/debussy la mer/debussy prélude a l'apres-midi/wagner meistersinger overture

salzburg
27 and 30
july and
10, 15 and 27
august 1966
*vienna philharmonic
vienna opera chorus*

bizet carmen
bumbry/freni/vickers/vinay (27 and 30 july and 10 august)/dooley (15 august)/blanc (27 august)

salzburg mussorgsky boris godunov
13, 16, 25 and 29 *jurinac/radev/maslennikov/stolze/ghiaurov/*
august 1966 *borg*
vienna philharmonic
vienna opera chorus

salzburg mozart divertimento 15/berlioz symphonie
14 august 1966 fantastique
berlin philharmonic

st moritz
20 august 1966
*berlin philharmonic
members
ferras, schwalbé*

salzburg beethoven symphony 1/bruckner symphony 7
28 august 1966
vienna philharmonic

lucerne beethoven symphony 1/bruckner symphony 7
31 august 1966
vienna philharmonic

berlin beethoven symphony 6/schumann symphony 4
4 september 1966
berlin philharmonic

berlin handel concerto grosso op 6 no 2/berg lyric
12 and 13 suite/brahms symphony 1
september 1966
berlin philharmonic

berlin bach brandenburg concerto 3/brahms violin
10 and 11 concerto/mussorgsky pictures at an exhibition
october 1966
*berlin philharmonic
milstein*

berlin honegger symphony 3/ravel pavane pour une
14 and 15 infante défunte/ravel boléro
october 1966
berlin philharmonic

tour of west germany by berlin philharmonic orchestra

hamburg 22 november 1966 *berlin philharmonic*	bach brandenburg concerto 3/honegger symphony 3/mussorgsky pictures at an exhibition
bremen 23 november 1966 *berlin philharmonic*	honegger symphony 3/beethoven symphony 7
hannover 24 november 1966 *berlin philharmonic*	dvorak symphony 9/mussorgsky pictures at an exhibition
bielefeld 25 november 1966 *berlin philharmonic* *schwalbé*	mozart violin concerto 3/tchaikovsky symphony 4
wolfsburg 26 november 1966 *berlin philharmonic*	brahms symphony 4/schumann symphony 4
berlin 29 and 30 november 1966 *berlin philharmonic* *schwalbé*	mozart violin concerto 3/shostakovich symphony 10
berlin 16 december 1966 *berlin philharmonic*	bruckner symphony 8
berlin 31 december 1966 and 1 january 1967 *berlin philharmonic*	mozart divertimento 17/j.strauss zigeunerbaron overture/kaiserwalzer/annen polka/perpetuum mobile/fledermaus overture/josef strauss delirienwalzer

milan verdi messa da requiem
16 and 18
january 1967
*la scala orchestra
and chorus*
price
cossotto
verrett (18 january)
pavarotti
ghiaurov

berlin mozart divertimento 17/j.strauss zigeunerbaron
28 january 1967 overture/kaiserwalzer/annen polka/perpetuum
berlin philharmonic mobile/fledermaus overture/josef strauss
  delirienwalzer

berlin bruckner symphony 5
29 and 30
january 1967
berlin philharmonic

berlin schoenberg gurrelieder
24 and 25
february 1967
*berlin philharmonic
deutsche oper choir
jurinac
ludwig
kachel
stolze
talvela*

salzburg wagner die walküre
19 march 1967 *crespin/janowitz/ludwig/vickers/stewart/*
berlin philharmonic *talvela; inaugural performance of salzburg*
  osterfestspiele

salzburg *bach programme*
20 and 26 brandenburg concerto 1/violin concerto in e/
march 1967 brandenburg concerto 3/suite 2
*berlin philharmonic
ferras*

salzburg bruckner symphony 8
21 and 26
march 1967
berlin philharmonic

salzburg beethoven missa solemnis
22 and 25
march 1967
berlin philharmonic
wiener singverein
janowitz
ludwig
krenn
berry

salzburg wagner die walküre
23 march 1967 *crespin/hillebrecht/veasey/vickers/stewart/*
berlin philharmonic *talvela*

salzburg wagner die walküre
27 march 1967 *knipolva/janowitz/ludwig/parly/berry/talvela*
berlin philharmonic

berlin mozart divertimento 15/berlioz symphonie
16 april 1967 fantastique
berlin philharmonic

tour of west germany, paris, london and florence by berlin philharmonic orchestra
munich mozart divertimento 17/shostakovich
30 april 1967 symphony 10
berlin philharmonic

freiburg bach brandenburg concerto 1/honegger
1 may 1967 symphony 3/ravel pavane pour une infante
berlin philharmonic défunte/ravel boléro

stuttgart mozart divertimento 17/berlioz symphonie
2 may 1967 fantastique
berlin philharmonic

nürnberg bach brandenburg concerto 6/schumann
3 may 1967 symphony 4/ravel pavane pour une infante
berlin philharmonic défunte/ravel boléro

heidelberg
4 may 1967
berlin philharmonic

bach brandenburg concerto 1/brahms haydn variations/dvorak symphony 9

frankfurt
5 may 1967
berlin philharmonic

bach brandenburg concerto 2/brahms haydn variations/dvorak symphony 9

paris
8 may 1967
berlin philharmonic

mozart divertimento 15/shostakovich symphony 10

paris
9 may 1967
berlin philharmonic

bach brandenburg concerto 2/schumann symphony 4/ravel pavane pour une infante défunte/ravel boléro

london
11 may 1967
berlin philharmonic

mozart divertimento 15/berlioz symphonie fantastique

london
12 may 1967
berlin philharmmonic

bach brandenburg concerto 6/schumann symphony 4/ravel pavane pour une infante défunte/ravel boléro

florence
14 may 1967
berlin philharmonic

bach brandenburg concerto 3/brahms haydn variations/beethoven symphony 5

florence
15 may 1967
berlin philharmonic

beethoven symphony 4/strauss ein heldenleben

rome
20 may 1967
*rai roma orchestra
and rai choruses
donath
troyanos
krenn
crass*

concert for pope pius vi
mozart coronation mass/verdi te deum

milan
23, 26 and 30
may and
2 and 5
june 1967
*la scala orchestra
and chorus*

mascagni cavalleria rusticana
*cossotto/bumbry (30 may and 2 and 5 june)/
martino/martelli (30 may and 2 june)/cecchele/
guelfi*

salzburg
29 july and
1, 8, 14 and 28
august 1967
*vienna philharmonic
vienna opera chorus*

bizet carmen
bumbry/freni/vickers/diaz

salzburg
12, 17, 26 and 29
august 1967
*vienna philharmonic
vienna opera chorus*

mussorgsky boris godunov
*jurinac/radev/maslennikov/stolze/ghiaurov/
borg*

salzburg
16 august 1967
*cleveland orchestra
demus, eschenbach
karajan*

mozart concerto for three pianos/prokofiev symphony 5

st moritz
20 august 1967
*berlin philharmonic
members*

salzburg
27 august 1967
*vienna philharmonic
vienna opera chorus
donath*

bruckner symphony 9/verdi te deum

lucerne
31 august 1967
*cleveland orchestra
demus, eschenbach
karajan*

mozart concerto for three pianos/prokofiev symphony 5

edinburgh
3 september 1967
berlin philharmonic

mozart divertimento 15/tchaikovsky symphony 4

edinburgh
4 september 1967
berlin philharmonic

handel concerto grosso op 6 no 12/stravinsky symphony in c/beethoven symphony 5

edinburgh
5 september 1967
berlin philharmonic
edinburgh
festival chorus
donath
veasey
tear
souzay

bach magnificat/brahms symphony 1

berlin
19 and 20 september 1967
berlin philharmonic
weissenberg

bach brandenburg concerto 4/sibelius symphony 7/tchaikovsky piano concerto 1

berlin
24 and 25 september 1967
berlin philharmonic

bach brandenburg concerto 5/shostakovich symphony 10

montreal
11, 13 and 15 october 1967
la scala orchestra and chorus

puccini la boheme
sighele/collier/raimondi/panerai/maffeo/vinco/calabrese

montreal
14 october 1967
la scala orchestra and chorus
price
cossotto
bergonzi
ghiaurov

verdi messa da requiem

new york   verdi messa da requiem
18 october 1967
*la scala orchestra
and chorus*
*price
cossotto
bergonzi
ghiaurov*

berlin   mozart concerto for 3 pianos/bruckner
22 and 23   symphony 4
october 1967
*berlin philharmonic
demus
eschenbach
karajan*

berlin   bach brandenburg concerto 4/beethoven
28 october 1967   symphony 3
berlin philharmonic

new york   wagner die walküre
21, 24 and 27   *nilsson/janowitz/ludwig/vickers/stewart/*
november 1967   *berry (27)/ridderbusch; karajan's first*
metropolitan opera   *appearances at the metropolitan opera*
orchestra

new york   *bach programme*
29 november 1967   brandenburg concerto 3/brandenburg
berlin philharmonic   concerto 5/suite 2

new york   *bach programme*
30 november 1967   brandenburg concerto 6/piano concerto
berlin philharmonic   in d minor/brandenburg concerto 1
weissenberg

new york   *bach programme*
1 december 1967   brandenburg concerto 2/violin concerto
berlin philharmonic   in e/brandenburg concerto 4
ferras

new york wagner die walküre
2 and 5 *nilsson/crespin/ludwig/vickers/stewart/*
december 1967 *berry (act 2 only on 5 december)/ridderbusch*
metropolitan opera
orchestra

berlin mozart eine kleine nachtmusik/tchaikovsky
10 december 1967 symphony 4
berlin philharmonic

berlin beethoven symphony 9
31 december 1967
and 1 january 1968
berlin philharmonic
deutsche oper chorus
janowitz
ludwig
thomas
berry

berlin mozart symphony 29/wagner tristan prelude
6 january 1967 and liebestod/brahms symphony 2
berlin philharmonic

tour of west germany by berlin philharmonic orchestra
munich bach brandenburg concerto 3/bruckner
22 january 1968 symphony 4
berlin philharmonic

nürnberg mozart divertimento 15/brahms symphony 2
23 january 1968
berlin philharmonic

landau mozart symphony 29/wagner tristan prelude
24 january 1968 and liebestod/beethoven symphony 5
berlin philharmonic

stuttgart stravinsky symphony in c/beethoven symphony 3
25 january 1968
berlin philharmonic

frankfurt mozart divertimento 17/tchaikovsky symphony 4
26 january 1968
berlin philharmonic

berlin
29 and 30
january 1968
berlin philharmonic

brahms symphony 3/penderecki polymorphia/
ravel rapsodie espagnole

berlin
4 february 1968
*berlin philharmonic
deutsche oper chorus
rebmann
wagner
kesteren
ridderbusch*

beethoven symphony 9

salzburg
7, 9 and 14
april 1968
berlin philharmonic

wagner das rheingold
*veasey/dominguez/grobe/stolze/kelemen/
fischer-dieskau/talvela/ridderbusch*

salzburg
8 and 14
april 1968
berlin philharmonic

beethoven programme
coriolan overture/symphony 6/symphony 7

salzburg
10 and 15
april 1968
berlin philharmonic

wagner die walküre
*crespin/kniplova (15)/janowitz/veasey/
vickers/stewart/talvela*

salzburg
11 and 13
april 1968
*berlin philharmonic
wiener singverein
janowitz
fischer-dieskau*

brahms ein deutsches requiem

hamburg
27 april 1968
*berlin philharmonic
eschenbach
frantz
karajan*

mozart concerto for 3 pianos/prokofiev
symphony 5

hamburg bach brandenburg concerto 1/beethoven
28 april 1968 symphony 3
berlin philharmonic

bremen mozart divertimento 15/tchaikovsky symphony 4
29 april 1968
berlin philharmonic

kassel bach brandenburg concerto 2/prokofiev
30 april 1968 symphony 5
berlin philharmonic

wolfsburg mozart divertimento 17/beethoven symphony 3
1 may 1968
berlin philharmonic

berlin berg violin concerto/prokofiev symphony 5
4 and 5
may 1968
berlin philharmonic
szeryng

tour of paris, portugal and spain by berlin philharmonic orchestra
paris mozart concerto for 3 pianos/prokofiev
14 may 1968 symphony 5
berlin philharmonic
demus
eschenbach
karajan

lisbon mozart symphony 29/strauss don juan/
16 may 1968 beethoven symphony 5
berlin philharmonic

lisbon bach brandenburg concerto 3/ravel rapsodie
17 may 1968 espagnole/brahms symphony 2
berlin philharmonic

oporto mozart symphony 29/strauss till eulenspiegel/
18 may 1968 beethoven symphony 5
berlin philharmonic

madrid
20 may 1968
berlin philharmonic

mozart symphony 29/strauss till eulenspiegel/
brahms symphony 1/wagner tannhäuser overture

madrid
21 may 1968
berlin philharmonic

beethoven programme
symphony 6/symphony 7

barcelona
23 may 1968
berlin philharmonic

bach brandenburg concerto 3/ravel rapsodie
espagnole/brahms symphony 2

barcelona
24 may 1968
berlin philharmonic

beethoven symphony 6/strauss ein heldenleben

milan
6, 8 and 11
june 1968
*la scala orchestra
and chorus*

mascagni cavalleria rusticana
cossotto/martino/cecchele/guelfi

salzburg
26 and 30
july and
13 and 17
august 1968
*vienna philharmonic
vienna opera chorus*

mozart don giovanni
*zylis-gara/janowitz/freni/kraus/ghiaurov/
krause (17 august)/evans/talvela*

salzburg
14 august 1968
berlin philharmonic

bach programme
brandenburg concerti 2, 6 and 4

salzburg
15 august 1968
*berlin philharmonic
anda*

mozart piano concerto 20/bruckner symphony 4
anda replaced sviatoslav richter

salzburg
16 august 1968
berlin philharmonic

bach programme
brandenburg concerti 3, 5 and 1

st moritz
19 august 1968
*berlin philharmonic
members*

salzburg — mozart don giovanni
24 and 27 — *zylis-gara/janowitz/pilou/kraus/krause/*
august 1968 — *evans/talvela*
vienna philharmonic
vienna opera chorus

salzburg — schubert symphony 8/j.strauss zigeunerbaron
25 august 1968 — overture/kaiserwalzer/annen polka/perpetuum
vienna philharmonic — mobile/josef strauss delirienwalzer

lucerne — bach brandenburg concerto 2/shostakovich
31 august 1968 — symphony 10
berlin philharmonic

lucerne — dvorak symphony 9/ravel pavane pour une
1 september 1968 — infante défunte/ravel boléro
berlin philharmonic

baalbeck — *beethoven programme*
3 september 1968 — coriolan overture/symphony 6/symphony 5
berlin philharmonic

baalbeck — mozart symphony 29/strauss till eulenspiegel/
4 september 1968 — brahms symphony 2
berlin philharmonic

dubrovnik — *beethoven programme*
6 september 1968 — coriolan overture/symphony 6/symphony 5
berlin philharmonic

dubrovnik — mozart symphony 29/strauss till eulenspiegel/
7 september 1968 — brahms symphony 2
berlin philharmonic

berlin — bartok music for strings percussion and celesta/
20 and 21 — beethoven symphony 7
september 1968
berlin philharmonic

berlin
25 september 1968
berlin philharmonic
ferras

brahms cycle
violin concerto/symphony 1

berlin
28 september 1968
berlin philharmonic
anda

brahms cycle
piano concerto 2/symphony 4

berlin
30 september 1968
berlin philharmonic

brahms cycle
symphony 3/symphony 2

berlin
1 october 1968
berlin philharmonic
deutsche oper chorus
janowitz
fischer-dieskau

brahms cycle
ein deutsches requiem

new york
31 october and
5 and 8
november 1968
metropolitan opera
orchestra

wagner die walküre
nilsson/crespin (8 nov)/crespin/hillebrecht
(8 nov)/ludwig/vickers/king (5 nov)/
stewart/talvela

new york
22, 25 and 30
november 1968
metropolitan opera
orchestra

wagner das rheingold
veasey/chookasian/stewart/kelemen/milnes/
riddersbusch

new york
29 and 30
november 1968
berlin philharmonic
wiener singverein
price
cossotto
bergonzi
ghiaurov

messa da requiem

new york
1 december 1968
berlin philharmonic

berlin   mozart symphony 29/strauss don juan/
8 december 1968   brahms symphony 2
berlin philharmonic

berlin   beethoven symphony 1/dvorak symphony 9
13 december 1968
berlin philharmonic

berlin   mozart piano concerto 21/bruckner
31 december 1968   symphony 7
and 1 january 1969
berlin philharmonic
eschenbach

berlin   handel concerto grosso op 6 no 8/ligeti
4 and 5   atmospheres/schubert symphony 9
january 1969
berlin philharmonic

tour of west germany by berlin philharmonic orchestra
munich   bartok music for strings percussion and celesta/
25 and 26   schubert symphony 9
january 1969
berlin philharmonic

munich   mozart divertimento 15/prokofiev symphony 5
27 january 1969
berlin philharmonic

stuttgart   bartok music for strings percussion and celesta/
28 january 1969   schubert symphony 9
berlin philharmonic

nürnberg   bach brandenburg concerto 1/tchaikovsky
29 january 1969   symphony 5
berlin philharmonic

frankfurt
30 january 1969
berlin philharmonic

mozart symphony 33/strauss till eulenspiegel/
beethoven symphony 7

luxembourg
31 january 1969
berlin philharmonic

mozart divertimento 15/strauss till eulenspiegel/
beethoven symphony 5

berlin
2 and 3
february 1969
berlin philharmonic

schoenberg orchestral variations/tchaikovsky
symphony 5

new york
19 february and
1 march 1969
*metropolitan opera
orchestra*

wagner die walküre
*nilsson/crespin/veasey/vickers/adam/
ridderbusch/talvela (1 march)*

new york
22 and 26
february 1969
*metropolitan opera
orchestra*

wagner das rheingold
*reynolds/veasey (26)/chookasian/adam/
kelemen/milnes/ridderbusch*

salzburg
30 march and
2 and 7
april 1969
berlin philharmonic

wagner siegfried
*dernesch/grist/gayer (7 april)/dominguez/
thomas/stolze/stewart/ridderbusch/kelemen*

salzburg
31 march and
6 april 1969
berlin philharmonic

mozart divertimento 17/bruckner symphony 7

salzburg
1 and 6
april 1969
berlin philharmonic

wagner das rheingold
*veasey/dominguez/adam/ridderbusch/
kelemen/greindl*

salzburg   haydn die schöpfung
3 and 5
april 1969
berlin philharmonic
wiener singverein
janowitz
krenn
prey
berry

berlin   brahms double concerto/dvorak symphony 8
27 april 1969
berlin philharmonic
brandis
borwitzky

tour of west germany by berlin philharmonic orchestra
hamburg   bartok music for strings percussion and celesta/
1 may 1969   brahms symphony 2
berlin philharmonic

kiel   mozart symphony 33/strauss till eulenspiegel/
2 may 1969   beethoven symphony 7
berlin philharmonic

hamburg   mozart divertimento 17/shostakovich
3 may 1969   symphony 10
berlin philharmonic

wuppertal   mozart symphony 33/strauss till eulenspiegel/
4 may 1969   beethoven symphony 5
berlin philharmonic

düsseldorf   mozart divertimento 17/tchaikovsky symphony 5
5 may 1969
berlin philharmonic

hannover   bartok music for strings percussion and celesta/
6 may 1969   schubert symphony 9
berlin philharmonic

tour of moscow, leningrad, london and paris by berlin philharmonic orchestra
moscow   *beethoven programme*
28 may 1969   coriolan overture/symphony 6/symphony 5
berlin philharmonic

moscow   bach brandenburg concerto 1/shostakovich
29 may 1969   symphony 10
berlin philharmonic *shostakovich symphony performed in presence of the composer*

moscow   mozart divertimento 17/strauss ein heldenleben
30 may 1969
berlin philharmonic

leningrad   *beethoven programme*
1 june 1969   coriolan overture/symphony 6/symphony 5
berlin philharmonic

leningrad   mozart divertimento 17/shostakovich
2 june 1969   symphony 10
berlin philharmonic

london   mozart concerto for three pianos/prokofiev
4 june 1969   symphony 5
berlin philharmonic
eschenbach
frantz
karajan

london   bach brandenburg concerto 1/bruckner
6 june 1969   symphony 7
berlin philharmonic

paris   bartok music for strings percussion and celesta/
8 june 1969   brahms symphony 2
berlin philharmonic

amsterdam   mozart concerto for three pianos/brahms
30 june 1969   symphony 1
berlin philharmonic
eschenbach
frantz
karajan

rotterdam   bach brandenburg concerto 3/stravinsky
1 july 1969   symphony in c/dvorak symphony 8
berlin philharmonic

den haag   mozart divertimento 17/prokofiev symphony 5
2 july 1969
berlin philharmonic

aix-en-provence   mozart concerto for three pianos/berlioz
14 and 15   symphonie fantastique
july 1969
orchestre de paris
eschenbach
frantz
karajan

salzburg   mozart don giovanni
1, 4, 14, 18 and   *zylis-gara/janowitz/freni/kraus/ghiaurov/*
25 august 1969   *evans/halem*
vienna philharmonic
vienna opera chorus

salzburg   tchaikovsky rococo variations/berlioz
15 august 1969   symphonie fantastique
orchestre de paris
rostropovich

st moritz   *programme included*
22 august 1969   bach piano concerto bwv 1053
berlin philharmonic
members
richter

salzburg   bruckner symphony 5
27 august 1969
vienna philharmonic

salzburg   mozart don giovanni
29 august 1969   *zylis-gara/janowitz/miljakovic/kraus/krause/*
vienna philharmonic   *evans/halem*
vienna opera chorus

lucerne bach brandenburg concerto 1/tchaikovsky
31 august 1969 symphony 5
berlin philharmonic

lucerne bartok music for strings percussion and celesta/
1 september 1969 brahms symphony 2
berlin philharmonic

mallorca *beethoven programme for opening of new*
3 september 1969 *concert hall*
berlin philharmonic symphony 6/symphony 7

mallorca mozart symphony 29/strauss don juan/
4 september 1969 brahms symphony 2
berlin philharmonic

mallorca schubert symphony 8/tchaikovsky symphony 5
6 september 1969
berlin philharmonic

berlin beethoven symphony 8/dvorak cello concerto
18 and 19
september 1969
berlin philharmonic
rostropovich

berlin bartok music for strings percussion and celesta/
21 and 22 beethoven symphony 3
september 1969
berlin philharmonic

berlin bruckner symphony 8
25 september 1969
berlin philharmonic

paris brahms ein deutsches requiem
1, 2 and 3 *concerts in memory of charles munch*
october 1969
orchestre de paris
wiener singverein
janowitz
kerns

berlin   beethoven symphony 4/strauss ein heldenleben
12 and 21
october 1969
berlin philharmonic

berlin   schubert symphony 8/dvorak symphony 9
19 october 1969
berlin philharmonic

berlin   berg three pieces/tchaikovsky symphony 6
25 and 26
october 1969
berlin philharmonic

berlin   penderecki de natura sonoris/beethoven
31 december 1969   grosse fuge/strauss also sprach zarathustra
berlin philharmonic

berlin   mozart violin concerto 5/tchaikovsky
4 january 1970   symphony 5
berlin philharmonic
friedman

berlin   bruckner symphony 9/verdi te deum
21 and 22
january 1970
berlin philharmonic
deutsche oper chorus
gayer

tour of west germany by berlin philharmonic orchestra
hamburg   strauss metamorphosen/tchaikovsky
25 january 1970   symphony 5
berlin philharmonic

hannover   honegger symphony 3/brahms symphony 4
26 january 1970
berlin philharmonic

braunschweig   mozart divertimento 15/tchaikovsky symphony 5
27 january 1970
berlin philharmonic

kassel
28 january 1970
berlin philharmonic

strauss metamorphosen/brahms symphony 2

münster
29 january 1970
berlin philharmonic

mozart symphony 35/strauss till eulenspiegel/
beethoven symphony 5

duisburg
30 january 1970
berlin philharmonic

honegger symphony 3/beethoven symphony 7

wolfsburg
31 january 1970
berlin philharmonic

mozart symphony 35/strauss till eulenspiegel/
beethoven symphony 5

salzburg
21, 25 and 30
march 1970
berlin philharmonic
vienna opera chorus

wagner götterdämmerung
dernesch/janowitz/ludwig/brilioth/thomas
(30 march)/stewart/kelemen/ridderbusch/
greindl (25 march)

salzburg
22 and 28
march 1970
berlin philharmonic

bartok music for strings percussion and celesta/
brahms symphony 1

salzburg
23 and 29
march 1970
berlin philharmonic
eschenbach

mozart piano concerto 23/bruckner symphony 9

salzburg
24 and 27
march 1970
berlin philharmonic
wiener singverein
donath
reynolds
krenn
ridderbusch

mozart requiem/verdi te deum

berlin   honegger symphony 2/brahms symphony 4
16 and 17
april 1970
berlin philharmonic

tour of japan by berlin philharmonic orchestra
osaka   *beethoven bi-centenary cycle*
8 may 1970   coriolan overture/symphony 6/symphony 5
berlin philharmonic

osaka   *beethoven bi-centenary cycle*
9 may 1970   symphony 4/symphony 7
berlin philharmonic

osaka   *beethoven bi-centenary cycle*
10 may 1970   symphony 1/symphony 3
berlin philharmonic

osaka   *beethoven bi-centenary cycle*
11 may 1970   symphony 2/symphony 8/leonore 3 overture
berlin philharmonic

osaka   *beethoven bi-centenary cycle*
13 may 1970   symphony 9
berlin philharmonic
nhk chorus
rebmann
fassbänder
hollweg
kelemen

osaka   mozart divertimento 15/fortner marginalien/
14 may 1970   brahms symphony 2
berlin philharmonic

tokyo   *brahms programme*
16 may 1970   symphony 3/symphony 2
berlin philharmonic

tokyo   honegger symphony 3/dvorak symphony 8
17 may 1970
berlin philharmonic

tokyo
18 may 1970
berlin philharmonic

mozart divertimento 17/tchaikovsky symphony 5

tokyo
19 may 1970
berlin philharmonic

schumann symphony 4/strauss also sprach zarathustra

tokyo
21 may 1970
berlin philharmonic

berlioz symphonie fantastique/ravel pavane pour une infante défunte/ravel daphnis et chloé second suite

tokyo
22 may 1970
berlin philharmonic

beethoven programme
symphony 2/symphony 5

vienna
9 june 1970
berlin philharmonic

beethoven bi-centenary cycle
coriolan overture/symphony 6/symphony 5

vienna
10 june 1970
berlin philharmonic

beethoven bi-centenary cycle
symphony 1/symphony 3

vienna
11 june 1970
berlin philharmonic

beethoven bi-centenary cycle
symphony 4/symphony 7

vienna
12 june 1970
berlin philharmonic

beethoven bi-centenary cycle
symphony 8/symphony 2/leonore 3 overture

vienna
14 june 1970
berlin philharmonic
wiener singverein
janowitz
reynolds
hollweg
berry

beethoven bi-centenary cycle
symphony 9

paris 17, 18 and 19 june 1970 *orchestre de paris*	mozart symphony 41/franck symphony in d minor
strassburg 21 june 1970 *orchestre de paris* *andré*	handel concerto grosso op 6 no 2/haydn trumpet concerto/franck symphony in d minor
aix-en-provence 18 july 1970 *orchestre de paris* *eschenbach*	*programme included* mozart symphony 41
salzburg 27 july and 11 and 28 august 1970 *vienna philharmonic* *vienna opera chorus*	mozart don giovanni *zylis-gara/janowitz/miljakovic/burrows/* *krause/ghiaurov (27 july)/evans/halem*
salzburg 9 august 1970 *berlin philharmonic* *eschenbach*	schumann piano concerto/brahms symphony 1
salzburg 10, 13, 18, 25 and 29 august 1970 *vienna philharmonic* *vienna opera chorus*	verdi otello *freni/malagu/vickers/craig (18)/glossop*
salzburg 12 august 1970 *berlin philharmonic*	mozart sinfonia concertante for wind/ strauss also sprach zarathustra
st moritz 22 august 1970 *berlin philharmonic* *members* *kim*	

salzburg
26 august 1970
vienna philharmonic
wiener singverein
janowitz
ludwig
bergonzi
raimondi

verdi messa da requiem

lucerne
31 august 1970
berlin philharmonic

stravinsky apollon musagete/beethoven symphony 3

lucerne
1 september 1970
berlin philharmonic

honegger symphony 2/beethoven symphony 5

venice
3 september 1970
berlin philharmonic

mozart symphony 29/strauss don juan/
brahms symphony 1

venice
4 september 1970
berlin philharmonic

beethoven programme
coriolan overture/symphony 6/symphony 5

bonn
16 and 17
september 1970
berlin philharmonic
wiener singverein
donath
dominguez
hollweg
ridderbusch

beethoven bi-centenary concerts
symphony 9

berlin
20 and 21
september 1970
berlin philharmonic
vienna opera chorus

wagner götterdämmerung, act three
dernesch/hetzel/brilioth/nienstedt/ridderbusch
this was a concert performance

berlin bach brandenburg concerto 4/stravinsky
26 and 27 apollon musagete/beethoven symphony 5
september 1970
berlin philharmonic

paris honegger symphony 2/berlioz symphonie
1, 2 and 3 fantastique
october 1970
orchestre de paris

berlin mozart sinfonia concertante for winds/
11 and 12 franck symphony in d minor
october 1970
berlin philharmonic

berlin mozart violin concerto 5/franck symphony
18 october 1970 in d minor
berlin philharmonic
kim

paris mozart symphony 40/strauss don quixote
9, 10 and 11
december 1970
orchestre de paris
rostropovich

berlin mahler das lied von der erde
14 and 15
december 1970
berlin philharmonic
ludwig
spiess
laubenthal

berlin beethoven symphony 9
31 december 1970
and 1 january 1971
berlin philharmonic
deutsche oper chorus
donath
schiml
hollweg
ridderbusch

berlin
9 january 1971
berlin philharmonic

mozart sinfonia concertante for winds/
beethoven symphony 7

tour of west germany by berlin philharmonic orchestra
hannover
26 january 1971
berlin philharmonic

mozart symphony 39/franck symphony
in d minor

münster
27 january 1971
berlin philharmonic

mozart symphony 40/tchaikovsky symphony 4

bremen
28 january 1971
berlin philharmonic

mozart sinfonia concertante for winds/
brahms symphony 2

hamburg
29 january 1971
berlin philharmonic

stravinsky apollon musagete/brahms
symphony 1

wolfsburg
30 january 1971
berlin philharmonic

mozart symphony 41/tchaikovsky symphony 4

braunschweig
31 january 1971
berlin philharmonic

beethoven programme
symphony 4/symphony 7

berlin
2, 3 and 4
february 1971
berlin philharmonic

honegger symphony 2/tchaikovsky symphony 4

berlin
19 february 1971
berlin philharmonic
ferras

fortner marginalien/berg violin concerto/
stravinsky le sacre du printemps

salzburg beethoven fidelio
3, 7 and 12 *dernesch/ligendza (7)/mathis/vickers/grobe/*
april 1971 *ridderbusch/kelemen/van dam*
berlin philharmonic
vienna opera chorus

salzburg beethoven piano concerto 4/strauss ein heldenleben
4 and 10
april 1971
berlin philharmonic
weissenberg

salzburg mozart symphony 41/stravinsky le sacre du
5 and 11 printemps
april 1971
berlin philharmonic

salzburg beethoven symphony 9
6 and 9
april 1971
berlin philharmonic
wiener singverein
janowitz
reynolds
brilioth
ridderbusch

tour of west germany by berlin philharmonic orchestra
kronberg
25 april 1971
berlin philharmonic
members

munich bruckner symphony 8
26 april 1971
berlin philharmonic

stuttgart stravinsky apollon musagete/brahms symphony 1
27 april 1971
berlin philharmonic

ulm mozart divertimento 15/brahms symphony 1
28 april 1971
berlin philharmonic

nürnberg   *beethoven programme*
29 april 1971   symphony 4/symphony 7
berlin philharmonic

mainz   bach brandenburg concerto 1/brahms symphony 2
30 april 1971
berlin philharmonic

wiesbaden   stravinsky apollon musagete/beethoven
1 may 1971   symphony 5
berlin philharmonic

berlin   stravinsky apollon musagete/brahms symphony 2
5 and 6
may 1971
berlin philharmonic

tour of milan, switzerland and vienna by berlin philharmonic orchestra
milan   stravinsky apollon musagete/beethoven
23 and 24   symphony 5/wagner tannhäuser overture
may 1971   *karajan's final appearances in milan*
berlin philharmonic

geneva   bartok music for strings percussion and celesta/
25 may 1971   brahms symphony 1
berlin philharmonic

zürich   beethoven symphony 6/stravinsky le sacre
26 may 1971   du printemps
berlin philharmonic

vienna   bruckner symphony 8
27 may 1971
berlin philharmonic

vienna   *stravinsky programme*
28 may 1971   apollon musagete/le sacre du printemps
berlin philharmonic

paris   verdi messa da requiem
22, 23 and 24
june 1971
orchestre de paris
wiener singverein
freni
ludwig
cossutta
ghiaurov

rouen   verdi messa da requiem
26 june 1971
orchestra
chorus and soloists
as above

strassburg
27 june 1971
orchestre de paris

aix-en-provence
july 1971
orchestre de paris

salzburg   verdi otello
30 july and   *freni/vickers/glossop*
3, 12, 16, 27 and
30 august 1971
vienna philharmonic
vienna opera chorus

salzburg   mozart requiem
31 july 1971   *memorial performance for bernhard paumgartner*
vienna philharmonic
vienna opera
concert chorus

salzburg   bach concerto for four pianos/dvorak
15 august 1971   symphony 9
czech philharmonic
pommier
klien
frantz
karajan

st moritz
24 august 1971
berlin philharmonic
members
weissenberg

salzburg   bruckner symphony 8
29 august 1971
vienna philharmonic

lucerne   bruckner symphony 8
31 august 1971
berlin philharmonic

lucerne   honegger symphony 3/brahms symphony 1
1 september 1971
berlin philharmonic

trieste   mozart symphony 41/strauss ein heldenleben
3 september 1971
berlin philharmonic

trieste   *beethoven programme*
4 september 1971   coriolan overture/symphony 4/symphony 5
berlin philharmonic   *wagner tannhäuser overture played as encore*

venice   stravinsky apollon musagete/brahms symphony 1
5 september 1971
berlin philharmonic

venice   mozart symphony 41/strauss ein heldenleben
6 september 1971
berlin philharmonic

berlin   wagner die walküre, act one
18 and 19   *dernesch/kollo/meven; this was a concert*
september 1971   *performance*
berlin philharmonic

berlin   vivaldi concerto al santo sepolcro/sibelius
25 and 26   violin concerto/stravinsky le sacre du printemps
september 1971
berlin philharmonic
ferras

berlin honegger symphony 3/dvorak symphony 8
10 october 1971
berlin philharmonic

berlin honegger symphony 3/beethoven symphony 2
17 october 1971
berlin philharmonic

tour of west germany by berlin philharmonic orchestra
hamburg honegger symphony 3/dvorak symphony 8
2 november 1971
berlin philharmonic

hannover *beethoven programme*
3 november 1971 symphony 6/symphony 5
berlin philharmonic

braunschweig brahms symphony 4/debussy prélude a
4 november 1971 l'apres-midi/ravel daphnis et chloé second
berlin philharmonic suite

düsseldorf *beethoven programme*
5 november 1971 symphony 4/symphony 7
berlin philharmonic

wuppertal mozart symphony 38/dvorak symphony 9
6 november 1971
berlin philharmonic

berlin schoenberg orchestral variations/beethoven
13 and 14 symphony 5
november 1971
berlin philharmonic

berlin bruckner symphony 9
17 november 1971
berlin philharmonic

berlin mozart symphony 38/brahms symphony 4
5 december 1971
berlin philharmonic

PHILHARMONIE
BERLINER PHILHARMONISCHES ORCHESTER

2. ABONNEMENTSKONZERT DER SERIE C

Sonnabend, den 13. November 1971, 20.00 Uhr
Sonntag, den 14. November 1971, 11.30 Uhr

Dirigent
HERBERT VON KARAJAN

ARNOLD SCHÖNBERG
Variationen für Orchester op. 31

Introduktion und Thema
Variation I: Moderato –
II: Langsam
III: Mäßig
IV: Walzertempo
V: Bewegt
VI: Andante
VII: Langsam
VIII: Sehr rasch –
IX: L'istesso tempo; aber etwas langsamer

Finale

LUDWIG VAN BEETHOVEN
Symphonie Nr. V in c-moll op. 67

Allegro con brio · Andante con moto · Allegro – Allegro – Presto

Fotografieren, Filmen und Tonaufzeichnungen nicht gestattet

berlin
11 and 12
december 1971
berlin philharmonic

bach brandenburg concerto 6/berg lyric suite/tchaikovsky symphony 6

berlin
31 december 1971
and 1 january 1972
berlin philharmonic

rossini semiramide overture/bizet l'arlésienne suite/sibelius valse triste/puccini manon lescaut intermezzo/massenet thais méditation/mascagni amico fritz intermezzo/suppé light cavalry overture/josef strauss delirienwalzer

berlin
8, 9 and 10
january 1972
berlin philharmonic

bach brandenburg concerto 3/berg three pieces/schumann symphony 2

berlin
13 february 1972
berlin philharmonic

bach brandenburg concerto 6/berg lyric suite/tchaikovsky symphony 6

berlin
19 and 20
february 1972
berlin philharmonic

mendelssohn symphony 3/debussy prélude a l'apres-midi/ravel daphnis et chloé second suite

salzburg
25 and 29
march and
2 april 1972
berlin philharmonic
vienna opera chorus

wagner tristan und isolde
dernesch/ludwig/baldani (29 march)/vickers/berry/ridderbusch

salzburg
26 march and
1 april 1972
berlin philharmonic

stravinsky apollon musagete/brahms symphony 2

salzburg
27 march and
3 april 1972
berlin philharmonic

mozart symphony 39/debussy prélude a l'apres-midi/ravel daphnis et chloé second suite

salzburg   bach matthäus-passion
28 and 31
march 1972
berlin philharmonic
wiener singverein
janowitz
ludwig
schreier
krenn
fischer-dieskau
berry

tour of west germany by berlin philharmonic orchestra
munich   honegger symphony 3/dvorak symphony 8
18 april 1972
berlin philharmonic

stuttgart   mendelssohn symphony 3/ravel pavane pour
19 april 1972   une infante défunte/ravel boléro
berlin philharmonic

heilbronn   *beethoven programme*
20 april 1972   symphony 4/symphony 5
berlin philharmonic

karlsruhe   mozart symphony 39/brahms symphony 1
21 april 1972
berlin philharmonic

nürnberg   mozart symphony 41/dvorak symphony 8
22 april 1972
berlin philharmonic

mainz   mendelssohn symphony 3/debussy prélude
23 april 1972   a l'apres-midi/ravel daphnis et chloé second
berlin philharmonic suite

wiesbaden   honegger symphony 3/brahms symphony 2
24 april 1972
berlin philharmonic

tour of bonn, spain, london, brussels and paris by berlin philharmonic orchestra

bonn
6 may 1972
berlin philharmonic
    beethoven programme
    symphony 4/symphony 5

barcelona
9 may 1972
berlin philharmonic
    beethoven programme
    coriolan overture/symphony 4/symphony 5

barcelona
10 may 1972
berlin philharmonic
    mozart symphony 39/brahms symphony 1

madrid
11 may 1972
berlin philharmonic
    brahms symphony 4/debussy prélude a
    l'apres-midi/ravel daphnis et chloé second
    suite

madrid
12 may 1972
berlin philharmonic
    beethoven symphony 4/strauss ein heldenleben

london
15 may 1972
berlin philharmonic
    mozart divertimento 15/stravinsky le sacre
    du printemps

london
16 may 1972
berlin philharmonic
    beethoven symphony 6/strauss ein heldenleben

brussels
17 may 1972
berlin philharmonic
    mozart divertimento 15/brahms symphony 2

paris
18 may 1972
berlin philharmonic
    beethoven symphony 4/strauss ein heldenleben

paris
19 may 1972
berlin philharmonic
    mozart divertimento 15/stravinsky le sacre
    du printemps

Edinburgh International Festival 1972

Usher Hall 8 pm
Monday 4 September

Berlin Philharmonic Orchestra
leaders Michel Schwalbé, Thomas Brandis, Léon Spierer

Herbert von Karajan, conductor
Christa Ludwig mezzo soprano
Rene Kollo tenor

Mahler 1860-1911

Das Lied von der Erde (The Song of the Earth)

1 Das Trinklied vom Jammer der Erde
2 Der Einsame im Herbst
3 Von der Jugend
4 Von der Schönheit
5 Der Trunkene im Frühling
6 Der Abschied

Under the patronage of Her Majesty the Queen
and Her Majesty Queen Elizabeth the Queen Mother
In association with the Corporation of the City of Edinburgh
The Scottish Arts Council and The British Council

berlin
25 june 1972
berlin philharmonic

webern six pieces/stravinsky symphony in c/
schoenberg verklärte nacht

amsterdam
28 june 1972
berlin philharmonic

stravinsky apollon musagete/strauss ein
heldenleben

rotterdam
29 june 1972
berlin philharmonic

mendelssohn symphony 3/ravel pavane pour
une infante défunte/ravel daphnis et chloé
second suite

scheveningen
30 june 1972
berlin philharmonic

bach brandenburg concerto 6/berg three
pieces/beethoven symphony 5

salzburg
26 and 29
july and
11, 14, 26 and 29
august 1972
vienna philharmonic
vienna opera chorus

mozart le nozze di figaro
harwood/stratas/mathis (26 and 29 july)/
berganza/schiml (29 july)/krause/berry/
van dam (29 july)

salzburg
30 july 1972
vienna philharmonic
vienna opera chorus
mathis
simon
laubenthal
van dam

mozart coronation mass/bruckner te deum

salzburg
31 july and
12 and 22
august 1972
vienna philharmonic
vienna opera chorus

verdi otello
freni/vickers/glossop

salzburg bartok piano concerto 3/schumann symphony 4
13 august 1972
staatskapelle dresden
anda

st moritz
20 august 1972
berlin philhatmonic
members

salzburg schoenberg verklärte nacht/beethoven
25 august 1972 symphony 5
berlin philharmonic

salzburg mahler das lied von der erde
27 august 1972
berlin philharmonic
ludwig
kollo

munich mozart symphony 41/strauss ein heldenleben
28 august 1972
berlin philharmonic

lucerne stravinsky symphony in c/schumann symphony 4
31 august 1972
berlin philharmonic

lucerne mozart symphony 39/stravinsky le sacre du
1 september 1972 printemps
berlin philharmonic

edinburgh bach brandenburg concerto 3/berg three pieces/
3 september 1972 beethoven symphony 3
berlin philharmonic

edinburgh mahler das lied von der erde
4 september 1972
berlin philharmonic
ludwig
kollo

edinburgh stravinsky apollon musagete/brahms symphony 2
5 september 1972
berlin philharmonic

berlin stravinsky apollon musagete/strauss don juan/
11 september 1972 brahms symphony 1
berlin philharmonic

berlin brahms ein deutsches requiem
23 and 24
september 1972
berlin philharmonic
wiener singverein
janowitz
fischer-dieskau

berlin bach brandenburg concerto 1/stravinsky
26 september 1972 symphony in c/rachmaninov piano concerto 2
berlin philharmonic
weissenberg

berlin mozart violin concerto 5
september 1972
european youth
orchestra
oistrakh

tour of belgrade and west germany by berlin philharmonic orchestra
belgrade *beethoven programme*
14 october 1972 coriolan overture/symphony 4/symphony 5
berlin philharmonic

belgrade mozart symphony 29/wagner tristan prelude
15 october 1972 and liebestod/brahms symphony 1
berlin philharmonic

hamburg bach brandenburg concerto 6/berg three pieces/
17 october 1972 beethoven symphony 5
berlin philharmonic

hannover vivaldi le 4 stagioni/brahms symphony 1
18 october 1972
berlin philharmonic
schwalbé

PHILHARMONIE
BERLINER PHILHARMONISCHES ORCHESTER

ABONNEMENTSFREIES KONZERT

Sonntag, den 26. November 1972, **11.30 Uhr**

Dirigent

HERBERT VON KARAJAN

Solisten

GUNDULA JANOWITZ (Hanne)
WERNER HOLLWEG (Lukas)
WALTER BERRY (Simon)

Am Cembalo: Horst Göbel

CHOR DER DEUTSCHEN OPER BERLIN
Einstudierung: Walter Hagen-Groll

JOSEPH HAYDN
DIE JAHRESZEITEN

I. Der Frühling
II. Der Sommer
III. Der Herbst
IV. Der Winter

Fotografieren, Filmen und Tonaufzeichnungen **nicht gestattet**

braunschweig berg three pieces/beethoven symphony 3
19 october 1972
berlin philharmonic

münster mozart symphony 38/wagner tristan prelude
20 october 1972 and liebestod/beethoven symphony 7
berlin philharmonic

bonn beethoven symphony 2/tchaikovsky symphony 4
21 october 1972
berlin philharmonic

berlin *mendelssohn programme*
7 and 8 hebrides overture/violin concerto/symphony 3
november 1972
berlin philharmonic
schwalbé

berlin bruckner symphony 8
22 november 1972
berlin philharmonic

berlin haydn die jahreszeiten
25 and 26
november 1972
berlin philharmonic
deutsche oper chorus
janowitz
hollweg
berry

berlin berg three pieces/beethoven symphony 3
9, 10 and 11
december 1972
berlin philharmonic

berlin bruckner symphony 5
31 december 1972
and 1 january 1973
berlin philharmonic

london
4 january 1973
berlin philharmonic

beethoven programme
symphony 4/symphony 5
fanfare for europe concert in winter proms series

berlin
7 and 8
january 1973
berlin philharmonic
brandis

vivaldi le 4 stagioni/strauss sinfonia domestica

berlin
25 january 1973
berlin philharmonic
deutsche oper chorus

webern five pieces/schoenberg orchestral variations/stravinsky symphony of psalms

berlin
28 january 1973
berlin philharmonic
roloff

beethoven symphony 8/franck variations symphoniques/strauss till eulenspiegel

berlin
15 february 1973
berlin philharmonic

mozart symphony 41/strauss sinfonia domestica

berlin
17 and 18
february 1973
berlin philharmonic

mahler symphony 5

berlin
5 and 6
march 1973
berlin philharmonic
pommier

webern six pieces/beethoven piano concerto 3/tchaikovsky symphony 4

salzburg
15 and 21
april 1973
berlin philharmonic

wagner das rheingold
fassbänder/finnilä/schreier/stolze/stewart/kelemen/ridderbusch

salzburg
16 and 23
april 1973
berlin philharmonic

beethoven programme
symphony 4/symphony 5

salzburg wagner tristan und isolde
17 and 22 dernesch/baldani/vickers/vermeersch/
april 1973 ridderbusch
berlin philharmonic
vienna opera chorus

salzburg mozart coronation mass/verdi te deum
18 and 20
april 1973
berlin philharmonic
wiener singverein
janowitz
fassbänder
laubenthal
ridderbusch

tour of west germany by berlin philharmonic orchestra
mainz mozart symphony 39/dvorak symphony 9
13 may 1973
berlin philharmonic

karlsruhe bach brandenburg concerto 3/berg three
14 may 1973 pieces/beethoven symphony 5
berlin philharmonic

stuttgart beethoven symphony 2/strauss sinfonia
15 may 1973 domestica
berlin philharmonic

nürnberg schoenberg verklärte nacht/brahms symphony 1
16 may 1973
berlin philharmonic

augsburg mozart symphony 29/strauss don juan/
17 may 1973 brahms symphony 2
berlin philharmonic

berlin sibelius symphony 5/strauss also sprach
26 and 27 zarathustra
may 1973
berlin philharmonic

salzburg bruckner symphony 5
9 june 1973 *inaugural concert of salzburg pfingstfestspiele*
berlin philharmonic

salzburg mozart requiem/bruckner te deum
10 june 1973 *this was a matinee concert*
berlin philharmonic
wiener singverein
mathis
ludwig
laubenthal
hendriks

salzburg mozart concerto for three pianos/bruckner
10 june 1973 symphony 4
berlin philharmonic
eschenbach
frantz
karajan

salzburg bruckner symphony 8
11 june 1973
berlin philharmonic

tour of paris, zürich and granada by berlin philharmonic orchestra
paris bach brandenburg concerto 6/berg three pieces/
24 june 1973 beethoven symphony 5
berlin philharmonic

paris beethoven symphony 4/strauss sinfonia domestica
25 june 1973
berlin philharmonic

zürich bach brandenburg concerto 6/berg three pieces/
26 june 1973 beethoven symphony 5
berlin philharmonic

granada *beethoven programme*
28 june 1973 symphony 6/symphony 5
berlin philharmonic

granada 29 june 1973 *berlin philharmonic*	mozart symphony 29/strauss don juan/ brahms symphony 1
granada 1 july 1973 *berlin philharmonic*	schumann symphony 4/debussy prélude a l'apres-midi/ravel daphnis et chloé second suite
salzburg 28 july and 3, 10, 14, 18, 21 and 29 august 1973 *vienna philharmonic* *vienna opera chorus*	mozart le nozze di figaro *harwood/stratas/berganza/krause/berry*
salzburg 30 july 1973 *vienna philharmonic* *pommier*	bach piano concerto bwv 1052/bruckner symphony 7
salzburg 20, 23 and 25 august 1973 *wdr orchestra* *rias choir*	orff de temporum fine comoedia *ludwig/schreier/greindl; world premiere* *performances*
salzburg 27 august 1973 *berlin philharmonic*	bach brandenburg concerto 6/berg three pieces/brahms symphony 1
salzburg 28 august 1973 *berlin philharmonic*	mahler symphony 5
lucerne 31 august 1973 *berlin philharmonic*	honegger symphony 3/strauss sinfonia domestica
lucerne 1 september 1973 *berlin philharmonic*	honegger symphony 2/tchaikovsky symphony 6

berlin
8 september 1973
berlin philharmonic

mozart symphony 41/tchaikovsky symphony 5

berlin
26 september 1973
berlin philharmonic

beethoven symphony 7/j.strauss zigeunerbaron overture/kaiserwalzer/tritsch-tratsch polka/ fledermaus overture

berlin
29 and 30
september 1973
berlin philharmonic
wiener singverein
janowitz
finnilä
hollweg
kerns
van dam

bach mass in b minor

tour of japan by berlin philharmonic orchestra
tokyo
25 october 1973
berlin philharmonic

beethoven programme
symphony 6/symphony 5

tokyo
26 october 1973
berlin philharmonic

bach brandenburg concerto 1/bruckner symphony 7

tokyo
27 october 1973
berlin philharmonic

dvorak symphony 8/wagner tristan prelude and liebestod/wagner tannhäuser overture

tokyo
28 october 1973
berlin philharmonic

mozart symphony 41/tchaikovsky symphony 4

tokyo
29 october 1973
berlin philharmonic

brahms symphony 3/debussy la mer

tokyo
31 october 1973
berlin philharmonic

schubert symphony 8/strauss ein heldenleben

tokyo   schoenberg verklärte nacht/beethoven
1 november 1973   symphony 3
berlin philharmonic

osaka   *beethoven programme*
2 november 1973   symphony 6/symphony 5
berlin philharmonic

osaka   mozart symphony 41/tchaikovsky symphony 4
3 november 1973
berlin philharmonic

osaka   dvorak symphony 8/wagner tristan prelude
4 november 1973   and liebestod/wagner tannhäuser overture
berlin philharmonic

berlin   bruckner symphony 5
21 november 1973
berlin philharmonic

berlin   stravinsky symphony of psalms/tchaikovsky
24 and 25   symphony 6
november 1973
berlin philharmonic
deutsche oper chorus

berlin   bach magnificat/bartok concerto for orchestra
8 and 9
december 1973
berlin philharmonic
deutsche oper chorus
tomowa-sintow
angervö
kollo
van dam

berlin   *beethoven cycle*
29 december 1973   symphony 4/symphony 7
berlin philharmonic

berlin   *beethoven cycle*
30 december 1973   symphony 1/symphony 3
berlin philharmonic

berlin
31 december 1973
berlin philharmonic

beethoven cycle
symphony 2/symphony 8/leonore 3 overture

berlin
1 january 1974
berlin philharmonic
deutsche oper chorus
donath
anderson
kollo
ridderbusch

beethoven cycle
symphony 9

berlin
2 january 1974
berlin philharmonic

beethoven cycle
symphony 6/symphony 5

berlin
5 and 6
january 1974
berlin philharmonic

mozart divertimento 15/shostakovich symphony 10

berlin
21 and 22
january 1974
berlin philharmonic

brahms symphony 3/debussy la mer

berlin
27 january 1974
berlin philharmonic

bartok piano concerto 3/schoenberg pelleas und melisande

berlin
10 february 1974
berlin philharmonic

mozart divertimento 17/bartok concerto for orchestra

berlin
16, 17 and 18
february 1974
berlin philharmonic
spierer

schubert symphony 8/penderecki capriccio/
mussorgsky pictures at an exhibition

linz 23 and 24 march 1974 *vienna philharmonic*	bruckner symphony 7 *inaugural concerts in the linz brucknerhaus*
salzburg 6 and 12 april 1974 *berlin philharmonic* *wiener singverein* *harwood* *ludwig* *schreier* *kerns* *ridderbusch*	bach mass in b minor
salzburg 7, 10 and 14 april 1974 *berlin philharmonic* *vienna opera chorus* *wiener singverein*	wagner die meistersinger von nürnberg *janowitz/meyer/kollo/schreier/ridderbusch/* *leib/hendriks*
salzburg 8 and 13 april 1974 *berlin philharmonic* *pommier*	beethoven piano concerto 3/tchaikovsky symphony 5
salzburg 9 and 15 april 1974 *berlin philharmonic*	mozart divertimento 15/strauss sinfonia domestica

tour of west germany by berlin philharmonic orchestra

düsseldorf 1 may 1974 *berlin philharmonic*	brahms symphony 3/mussorgsky pictures at an exhibition
wuppertal 2 may 1974 *berlin philharmonic*	schubert symphony 8/tchaikovsky symphony 4

dortmund
3 may 1974
berlin philharmonic

beethoven symphony 2/bartok concerto for orchestra

wolfsburg
4 may 1974
berlin philharmonic

brahms symphony 4/mussorgsky pictures at an exhibition

braunschweig
5 may 1974
berlin philharmonic

mozart symphony 36/dvorak symphony 8

hamburg
6 may 1974
berlin philharmonic

brahms symphony 3/mussorgsky pictures at an exhibition

berlin
23 may 1974
berlin philharmonic

bach brandenburg concerto 6/bruckner symphony 9

berlin
25, 26 and 27 may 1974
berlin philharmonic

vaughan williams tallis fantasia/bruckner symphony 7

salzburg
1 june 1974
berlin philharmonic

vaughan williams tallis fantasia/bruckner symphony 7

salzburg
2 june 1974
berlin philharmonic
wiener singverein
janowitz
van dam

brahms ein deutsches requiem

salzburg
3 june 1974
berlin philharmonic

bach brandenburg concerto 6/bruckner symphony 9

tour of london, paris and vienna by berlin philharmonic orchestra
london   **brahms cycle**
17 june 1974   symphony 4/symphony 2
berlin philharmonic

london   **brahms cycle**
18 june 1974   symphony 3/symphony 1
berlin philharmonic

paris   schoenberg verklärte nacht/tchaikovsky
19 june 1974   symphony 5
berlin philharmonic

vienna   *bruckner programme*
21 june 1974   symphony 9/te deum
berlin philharmonic
wiener singverein
donath
reynolds
schreier
van dam

vienna   mahler symphony 5
23 june 1974
berlin philharmonic

vienna   verdi messa da requiem
24 june 1974
berlin philharmonic
wiener singverein
freni
ludwig
pavarotti
van dam

salzburg   mozart die zauberflöte
26 and 29 july   *mathis/lebrun/gruberova (26 july)/grist/kollo/*
and 12, 17, 23 and   *hollweg (29 august)/prey/meven/krause/*
29 august 1974   *van dam (26 july and 12 and 23 august)*
vienna philharmonic
vienna opera chorus

salzburg mozart le nozze di figaro
31 july and *harwood/freni/von stade/van dam/krause*
10, 13 and 24
august 1974
vienna philharmonic
vienna opera chorus

salzburg schumann piano concerto/dvorak symphony 8
15 august 1974
vienna philharmonic
pollini

salzburg mozart divertimento 17/strauss ein heldenleben
27 august 1974
berlin philharmonic

salzburg stravinsky symphony of psalms/tchaikovsky
28 august 1974 symphony 6
berlin philharmonic
vienna opera chorus

lucerne schoenberg pelleas und melisande/debussy
31 august 1974 la mer
berlin philharmonic

lucerne berg three pieces/bruckner symphony 4
1 september 1974
berlin philharmonic

berlin beethoven piano concerto 4/brahms
6 september 1974 symphony 2
berlin philharmonic
weissenberg

berlin mozart piano concerto 23/schoenberg pelleas
25 september 1974 und melisande
berlin philharmonic
pommier

berlin   beethoven missa solemnis
29 and 30
september 1974
berlin philharmonic
wiener singverein
janowitz
baltsa
hollweg/schreier
van dam

berlin   beethoven violin concerto/dvorak symphony 8
13 october 1974
berlin philhatmonic
brandis

berlin   bach brandenburg concerto 1/berlioz
19 and 20   symphonie fantastique
october 1974
berlin philharmonic

tour of usa by berlin philharmonic orchestra
washington   *beethoven programme*
2 november 1974   symphony 4/symphony 5
berlin philharmonic

washington   brahms symphony 4/wagner tristan
3 november 1974   prelude and liebestod/wagner tannhäuser
berlin philharmonic   overture

chicago   *beethoven programme*
4 november 1974   symphony 6/symphony 3
berlin philharmonic

chicago   bruckner symphony 8
5 november 1974
berlin philharmonic

boston   brahms symphony 1/wagner tristan prelude
6 november 1974   and liebestod/wagner tannhäuser overture
berlin philharmonic

boston   mozart divertimento 15/beethoven symphony 3
8 november 1974
berlin philharmonic

John F. Kennedy Center for the Performing Arts

ROGER L. STEVENS
Chairman

MARTIN FEINSTEIN
Executive Director

JULIUS RUDEL
Music Director

CONCERT HALL

Washington Performing Arts Society presents

ALDUS H. CHAPIN, *President*
PATRICK HAYES, *Managing Director*
DOUGLAS H. WHEELER, *Manager*

in association with

Columbia Artists Management, Inc.

Under the Patronage of
The Governing Mayor of the City of Berlin
The Honorable KLAUS SCHUETZ

Under the Sponsorship of
The Ambassador of the Federal Republic of Germany
His Excellency BERNDT VON STADEN

Berlin Philharmonic Orchestra
Herbert von Karajan, *Conductor and Music Director*

Sunday Afternoon, November 3, 1974 at 3:00

BRAHMS	Symphony No. 4 in E minor, Opus 98 Allegro ma non troppo Andante moderato Allegro energico e passionato (Tema con variazioni)
	Intermission
WAGNER	Prelude and Liebestod, from "Tristan and Isolde" Overture to "Tannhäuser"

COLUMBIA ARTISTS MANAGEMENT INC.
Personal Direction: RONALD A. WILFORD
165 West 57th Street, New York, N.Y. 10019

Deutsche Grammophon, Angel, London Records

new york
9 november 1974
berlin philharmonic

brahms cycle
symphony 4/symphony 2

new york
10 november 1974
berlin philharmonic

bruckner symphony 8

new york
11 november 1974
berlin philharmonic

beethoven symphony 4/strauss ein heldenleben

new york
13 november 1974
berlin philharmonic

brahms cycle
symphony 3/symphony 1

berlin
7 and 8
december 1974
berlin philharmonic

bartok music for strings percussion and celesta/dvorak symphony 9

berlin
5 and 6
january 1975
berlin philharmonic
rostropovich

haydn symphony 104/strauss don quixote

berlin
26 january 1975
berlin philharmonic

webern passacaglia/webern symphony/bartok concerto for orchestra

berlin
16, 17 and 18
february 1975
berlin philharmonic
pollini

webern five pieces/bach brandenburg concerto 2/brahms piano concerto 2

berlin
23 february 1975
berlin philharmonic

bartok music for strings percussion and celesta/beethoven symphony 7

vienna
1 and 2
march 1975
vienna philharmonic
weissenberg

beethoven piano concerto 5/bruckner symphony 7

salzburg
22, 26 and 29
march 1975
berlin philharmonic
vienna opera chorus

puccini la boheme
freni/holm/pavarotti/bonisolli (29)/panerai/
washington

salzburg
23 and 30
march 1975
berlin philharmonic
vienna opera chorus
wiener singverein

wagner die meistersinger von nürnberg
janowitz/meyer/kollo/schreier/ridderbusch/
leib/lagger

salzburg
24 and 31
march 1975
berlin philharmonic

dvorak symphony 9/ravel boléro

salzburg
25 and 28
march 1975
berlin philharmonic
wiener singverein
janowitz
ludwig/baltsa
schreier
ridderbusch

beethoven missa solemnis

berlin
17 april 1975
berlin philharmonic

schubert symphony 8/j.strauss zigeunerbaron overture/kaiserwalzer/tritsch-tratsch polka/ fledermaus overture/josef strauss delirienwalzer

berlin
19 and 20
april 1975
berlin philharmonic

berg lyric suite/bruckner symphony 4

tour of west germany by berlin philharmonic orchestra
mannheim *mozart programme*
7 may 1975 symphony 35/piano concerto 23/symphony 39
berlin philharmonic
eschenbach

karlsruhe *mozart programme*
8 may 1975 symphony 29/piano concerto 20/symphony 40
berlin philharmonic
frantz

heilbronn *mozart programme*
9 may 1975 eine kleine nachtmusik/piano concerto 23/
berlin philharmonic symphony 39
eschenbach

stuttgart *mozart programme*
10 may 1975 divertimento 15/concerto for three pianos/
berlin philharmonic symphony 35
eschenbach
frantz
karajan

nürnberg *mozart programme*
11 may 1975 divertimento 17/concerto for three pianos/
berlin philharmonic symphony 29
eschenbach
frantz
karajan

munich *mozart programme*
12 may 1975 divertimento 15/concerto for three pianos/
berlin philharmonic symphony 35
eschenbach
frantz
karajan

salzburg *brahms cycle*
17 may 1975 violin concerto/symphony 2
berlin philharmonic
shiokawa

salzburg
18 may 1975
berlin philharmonic
members
wiener singverein

bruckner mass no 2
this was a matinee concert

salzburg
18 may 1975
berlin philharmonic

brahms cycle
symphony 3/symphony 4

salzburg
19 may 1975
berlin philharmonic
pollini

brahms cycle
piano concerto 2/symphony 1

tour of paris and spain by berlin philharmonic orchestra
paris
2 june 1975
berlin philharmonic

brahms cycle
symphony 4/symphony 2

paris
3 june 1975
berlin philharmonic

brahms cycle
symphony 3/symphony 1

madrid
5 june 1975
berlin philharmonic

dvorak symphony 8/ravel pavane pour une infante défunte/ravel boléro

madrid
6 june 1975
berlin philharmonic

schoenberg verklärte nacht/beethoven symphony 3

barcelona
7 june 1975
berlin philharmonic

dvorak symphony 8/ravel pavane pour une infante défunte/ravel boléro

barcelona
8 june 1975
berlin philharmonic

schoenberg verklärte nacht/beethoven symphony 3

salzburg
30 july and
9, 14, 18 and 23
august 1975
vienna philharmonic
vienna opera chorus

mozart le nozze di figaro
harwood/mathis/von stade/krause/van dam

salzburg
11, 16, 21, 26 and
29 august 1975
vienna philharmonic
vienna opera chorus

verdi don carlo
freni/randova/ludwig (11)/domingo/ghiaurov/
cappuccilli

salzburg
24 august 1975
vienna philharmonic
wiener singverein
freni
cossotto
domingo
ghiaurov

verdi messa da requiem

salzburg
27 august 1975
berlin philharmonic
rostropovich

beethoven symphony 4/strauss don quixote

salzburg
28 august 1975
berlin philharmonic

bruckner symphony 8

lucerne
31 august 1975
berlin philharmonic

bartok concerto for orchestra/beethoven
symphony 6

lucerne
1 september 1975
berlin philharmonic

bartok music for strings percussion and celesta/
debussy prélude a l'apres-midi/ravel boléro

berlin
6 september 1975
berlin philharmonic

schoenberg verklärte nacht/beethoven
symphony 7

berlin *strauss programme*
25 september 1975 metamorphosen/also sprach zarathustra
berlin philharmonic

berlin mozart coronation mass/bruckner te deum
29 and 30
september 1975
berlin philharmonic
wiener singverein
tomowa-sintov
baltsa
krenn
van dam

berlin berg three pieces/tchaikovsky symphony 5
18 and 19
october 1975
berlin philharmonic

teheran *beethoven programme*
8 and 9 symphony 4/symphony 5
november 1975
berlin philharmonic

teheran mozart symphony 35/strauss till eulenspiegel/
11 november 1975 brahms symphony 2
berlin philharmonic

berlin bruckner symphony 9
19 november 1975
berlin philharmonic

berlin bruckner symphony 8
6 and 7
december 1975
berlin philharmonic

concert activity halted during january and february 1976 as a result of serious illness

berlin brahms violin concerto/tchaikovsky symphony 5
7 march 1976
berlin philharmonic
kremer

salzburg wagner lohengrin
10, 14 and 17 *tomowa-sintov/schröder-feinen/böhm/kollo (10)/*
april 1976 *nimsgern/ridderbusch*
berlin philharmonic
vienna opera chorus

salzburg beethoven piano concerto 5/schumann
11 and 18 symphony 4
april 1976
berlin philharmonic
weissenberg

salzburg mozart symphony 39/strauss also sprach
12 and 19 zarathustra
april 1976
berlin philharmonic

salzburg verdi messa da requiem
13 and 16
april 1976
berlin philharmonic
wiener singverein
caballé
cossotto
carreras
van dam

berlin mozart symphony 39/j.strauss zigeunerbaron
6 may 1976 overture/tritsch-tratsch polka/kaiserwalzer/
berlin philharmonic fledermaus overture/josef strauss delirienwalzer

berlin bartok piano concerto 3/beethoven symphony 3
8 and 9
may 1976
berlin philharmonic
pommier

london beethoven symphony 8/strauss ein heldenleben
12 may 1976 *concert in a series to mark the twenty-fifth*
berlin philharmonic *anniversary of royal festival hall*

tour of west germany, prague and salzburg by berlin philharmonic orchestra

hannover
27 may 1976
berlin philharmonic
eschenbach
frantz
karajan

mozart programme
divertimento 15/concerto for three pianos/symphony 35

hamburg
28 may 1976
berlin philharmonic
frantz

mozart programme
symphony 29/piano concerto 20/symphony 41

wuppertal
29 may 1976
berlin philharmonic
eschenbach
frantz
karajan

mozart programme
divertimento 15/concerto for three pianos/symphony 35

duisburg
30 may 1976
berlin philharmonic
eschenbach

mozart programme
eine kleine nachtmusik/piano concerto 23/symphony 40

mainz
31 may 1976
berlin philharmonic
eschenbach
frantz
karajan

mozart programme
symphony 29/concerto for three pianos/divertimento 17

prague
2 june 1976
berlin philharmonic

mozart programme

salzburg
5 june 1976
berlin philharmonic
weissenberg

tchaikovsky cycle
piano concerto 1/symphony 5

salzburg
6 june 1976
berlin philharmonic

tchaikovsky cycle
romeo and juliet/symphony 6

salzburg
7 june 1976
berlin philharmonic
hirschhorn

tchaikovsky cycle
violin concerto/symphony 4

salzburg
25 july 1976
vienna philharmonic
kremer

bach violin concerto 2/bruckner symphony 9

salsburg
26 and 30
july and
12, 16, 26 and
30 august 1976
vienna philharmonic
vienna opera chorus
wiener singverein

verdi don carlo
freni/cossotto/randova (30 august)/carreras/
ghiaurov/cappuccilli

salzburg
28 july and
14 and 28
august 1976
vienna philharmonic
vienna opera chorus

mozart le nozze di figaro
tomowa-sintov/harwood (28 august)/mathis/
ewing/von stade (28 august)/van dam/
berry (28 july)/krause/nicolai (28 july);
additional performances of figaro at 1976
salzburg festival conducted by bernhard klee

salzburg
15 august 1976
staatskapelle dresden
gilels

beethoven piano concerto 3/shostakovich
symphony 10

salzburg
27 august 1976
berlin philharmonic

mozart symphony 29/wimberger plays/
debussy prélude a l'apres-midi/ravel boléro

salzburg
28 august 1976
berlin philharmonic
wiener singverein
tomowa-sintov
baltsa
schreier
van dam

beethoven symphony 9

lucerne
1 september 1976
berlin philharmonic

mozart symphony 39/ravel rapsodie espagnole/
schumann symphony 4

lucerne
2 september 1976
berlin philharmonic

bruckner symphony 9

berlin
25 september 1976
berlin philharmonic
wiener singverein
cotrubas
van dam

brahms ein deutsches requiem

berlin
26 september 1976
international
youth orchestra

wagner meistersinger overture
part of a concert organised by karajan
stiftung and also featuring other youth
orchestras with other conductors

berlin
29 and 30
september 1976
berlin philharmonic
wiener singverein
zeumer
baltsa
krenn
rydl

mozart requiem/bruckner te deum

berlin
16 and 17
october 1976
berlin philharmonic

mozart sinfonia concertante for winds/
sibelius symphony 5/sibelius finlandia

berlin
24 october 1976
berlin philharmonic
hirschhorn

schoenberg verklärte nacht/tchaikovsky
violin concerto/sibelius finlandia

tour of usa by berlin philharmonic orchestra

new york schoenberg verklärte nacht/beethoven symphony 3
4 november 1976
berlin philharmonic

washington mozart symphony 39/ravel rapsodie espagnole/
6 november 1976 schumann symphony 4
berlin philharmonic

washington beethoven symphony 6/strauss ein heldenleben
7 november 1976
berlin philharmonic

chicago *brahms cycle*
9 november 1976 symphony 4/symphony 2
berlin philharmonic

chicago *brahms cycle*
10 november 1976 symphony 3/symphony 1
berlin philharmonic

new york brahms ein deutsches requiem
13 november 1976
berlin philharmonic
wiener singverein
price
van dam

new york beethoven symphony 9
14 november 1976
berlin philharmonic
wiener singverein
tomowa-sintov
baltsa
böhm
van dam

new york bruckner te deum/mozart requiem
15 november 1976
berlin philharmonic
wiener singverein
tomowa-sintov
baltsa
krenn
van dam

new york
16 november 1976
berlin philharmonic
wiener singverein
freni
cossotto
pavarotti
van dam

verdi messa da requiem

berlin
11 and 12
december 1976
berlin philharmonic

bruckner symphony 5

berlin
30 december 1976
berlin philharmonic
borwitzky

mozart/strauss cycle
symphony 39/don quixote

berlin
31 december 1976
berlin philharmonic

mozart/strauss cycle
symphony 41/ein heldenleben

berlin
1 january 1977
berlin philharmonic

mozart/strauss cycle
symphony 40/don juan/till eulenspiegel

berlin
4 and 5
january 1977
berlin philharmonic

haydn symphony 103/stravinsky le sacre du printemps

berlin
24 and 25
january 1977
berlin philharmonic

wimberger plays/berlioz symphonie fantastique

berlin
27 january 1977
berlin philharmonic

wimberger plays/webern five pieces/
honegger symphony 3

berlin
19, 20 and 21
february 1977
berlin philharmonic

mahler symphony 6

salzburg
3 and 8
april 1977
berlin philharmonic

mahler symphony 6

salzburg
4 and 11
april 1977
berlin philharmonic

bruckner symphony 5

salzburg
5 and 9
april 1977
berlin philharmonic
wiener singverein
tomowa-sintov
baldani
schreier
krenn (5 only)
kerns
nienstedt

bach matthäus-passion

salzburg
6 and 10
april 1977
berlin philharmonic
vienna opera chorus

verdi il trovatore
price/cossotto/bonisolli/capuccilli/van dam

vienna
8, 12 and 15
may 1977
vienna philharmonic
vienna opera chorus

verdi il trovatore
price/ludwig/pavarotti/capuccilli/van dam
karajan's return to vienna staatsoper

vienna
10, 14 and 18
may 1977
vienna philharmonic
vienna opera chorus

mozart le nozze di figaro
tomowa-sintov/cotrubas/von stade/van dam/
krause

ORCHESTRE PHILHARMONIQUE DE BERLIN

Direction :

Herbert von KARAJAN

JEUDI 16 JUIN 1977

BEETHOVEN

VENDREDI 17 JUIN 1977

MAHLER

THÉATRE DES CHAMPS-ÉLYSÉES
(*Directeur* : Félix VALOUSSIÈRE)

vienna
13, 16 and 20
may 1977
vienna philharmonic
vienna opera chorus

puccini la boheme
freni/holm/carreras/panerai/washington/
maffeo

salzburg
28 may 1977
berlin philharmonic

mozart/strauss cycle
symphony 39/also sprach zarathustra

salzburg
29 may 1977
berlin philharmonic
mutter

mozart/strauss cycle
violin concerto 3/don juan/till eulenspiegel

salzburg
30 may 1977
berlin philharmonic

mozart/strauss cycle
symphony 41/ein heldenleben

london
13 june 1977
berlin philharmonic

mahler symphony 6

london
15 june 1977
berlin philharmonic

beethoven programme
symphony 6/symphony 5

paris
16 june 1977
berlin philharmonic

beethoven programme
symphony 6/symphony 5

paris
17 june 1977
berlin philharmonic

mahler symphony 6

salzburg
26 and 29
july and
12 and 29
august 1977
vienna philharmonic
vienna opera chorus

strauss salome
behrens/baltsa/böhm/ochman/van dam

salzburg
30 july and
12, 16 and 26
august 1977
vienna philharmonic
vienna opera chorus

verdi don carlo
freni/cossotto/carreras/domingo (30 july)/
ghiaurov/capuccilli

salzburg
15 august 1977
vienna philharmonic
vienna opera chorus
mathis
schreier
van dam

haydn die schöpfung

salzburg
27 august 1977
berlin philharmonic

mahler symphony 6

salzburg
28 august 1977
berlin philharmonic

beethoven programme
symphony 6/symphony 3

lucerne
31 august 1977
berlin philharmonic

beethoven symphony 2/sibelius symphony 5

lucerne
1 september 1977
berlin philharmonic

mahler symphony 6

berlin
25 september 1977
berlin philharmonic
grönroos
vogler
thärichen

thärichen paukenkrieg (first performance)/
stravinsky le sacre du printemps

berlin
29 and 30
september 1977
berlin philharmonic

beethoven programme
symphony 6/symphony 5

berlin
21, 22 and 23
october 1977
berlin philharmonic
brandis
borwitzky

brahms programme
double concerto/symphony 2

salzburg
24 october 1977
berlin philharmonic

beethoven programme
symphony 6/symphony 5

brussels
25 october 1977
berlin philharmonic

beethoven programme
symphony 6/symphony 5

brussels
26 october 1977
berlin philharmonic

beethoven programme
symphony 4/symphony 7

berlin
27 october 1977
berlin philharmonic

mozart symphony 39/brahms symphony 1

tour of japan by berlin philharmonic orchestra
osaka
6 november 1977
berlin philharmonic

brahms cycle
haydn variations/symphony 4

osaka
7 november 1977
berlin philharmonic
brandis
borwitzky

brahms cycle
double concerto/symphony 2

osaka
8 november 1977
berlin philharmonic
weissenberg

brahms cycle
symphony 3/piano concerto 2

osaka
9 november 1977
berlin philharmonic
shiokawa

brahms cycle
violin concerto/symphony 1

osaka
10 november 1977
berlin philharmonic
weissenberg

beethoven piano concerto 4/strauss ein heldenleben

tokyo
13 november 1977
berlin philharmonic

beethoven cycle
symphony 1/symphony 3

tokyo
14 november 1977
berlin philharmonic
weissenberg

beethoven cycle
piano concerto 4/symphony 2

tokyo
15 november 1977
berlin philharmonic

beethoven cycle
symphony 4/symphony 7

tokyo
16 november 1977
berlin philharmonic

beethoven cycle
symphony 6/symphony 5

tokyo
17 november 1977
berlin philharmonic
weissenberg

beethoven cycle
symphony 8/piano concerto 5

tokyo
18 november 1977
berlin philharmonic
nhk choir
hendricks
angervő
winkler
sotin

beethoven cycle
symphony 9

berlin
9, 10 and 11 december 1977
berlin philharmonic

mahler symphony 5

aachen   beethoven symphony 6/brahms symphony 1
13 december 1977
berlin philharmonic

berlin   mahler symphony 6
29 december 1977
berlin philharmonic

berlin   beethoven symphony 9
31 december 1977
berlin philharmonic
deutsche oper chorus
tomowa-sintov
baltsa
kollo
van dam

berlin   mahler symphony 5
1 january 1978
berlin philharmonic

berlin   mahler das lied von der erde
4 and 5
january 1978
berlin philharmonic
baltsa
winkler

berlin   sibelius symphony 4/beethoven symphony 7
28 and 29
january 1978
berlin philharmonic

berlin   mozart violin concerto 3/bruckner
11, 12 and 18   symphony 7
february 1978
berlin philharmonic
mutter

berlin   debussy la mer/debussy prélude a l'apres-midi/
14 and 15   ravel daphnis et chloé second suite
february 1978
berlin philharmonic

salzburg
19 and 27
march 1978
berlin philharmonic
vienna opera chorus

beethoven fidelio
*behrens/mathis/winkler/zednik/plishka/
nimsgern/van dam*

salzburg
20 and 25
march 1978
berlin philharmonic
lupu

beethoven programme
piano concerto 3/symphony 3

salzburg
21 and 26
march 1978
berlin philharmonic
vienna opera chorus

verdi il trovatore
*kabaiwanska/miltschewa/bonisolli/
capuccilli/van dam*

salzburg
22 and 24
march 1978
berlin philharmonic
wiener singverein
janowitz
van dam

brahms ein deutsches requiem

vienna
24 april and
1 and 4 may 1978
vienna philharmonic
vienna opera chorus

verdi il trovatore
*kabaiwanska/cossotto/domingo/bonisolli
(24 april)/capuccilli/van dam*

vienna
28 april 1978
vienna philharmonic
vienna opera chorus

mozart le nozze di figaro
*tomowa-sintov/cotrubas/yachmi/van dam/
krause*

vienna
2 and 9
may 1978
vienna philharmonic
vienna opera chorus

puccini la boheme
*freni/holm/carreras/panerai/washington/
maffeo*

vienna   *bruckner programme*
7 and 8   symphony 9/te deum
may 1978
vienna philharmonic
wiener singverein
tomowa-sintov
baltsa
rendall
van dam

salzburg   *mahler cycle*
13 may 1978   symphony 6
berlin philharmonic

salzburg   *mahler cycle*
14 may 1978   das lied von der erde
berlin philharmonic
baltsa
winkler

salzburg   *mahler cycle*
15 may 1978   symphony 5
berlin philharmonic

berlin   bruckner symphony 7
28 may 1978
berlin philharmonic

dresden   beethoven symphony 4/strauss ein heldenleben
30 may 1978   *first public appearance of conductor and orchestra*
berlin philharmonic   *in the german democratic republic*

leipzig   mozart symphony 5/bruckner symphony 7
31 may 1978
berlin philharmonic

tour of switzerland and paris by berlin philharmonic orchestra
zürich   *beethoven programme*
18 june 1978   symphony 6/symphony 5
berlin philharmonic

zürich
19 june 1978
berlin philharmonic

dvorak symphony 9/mussorgsky pictures at an exhibition

basel
20 june 1978
berlin philharmonic

beethoven programme
symphony 4/symphony 7

paris
22 june 1978
berlin philharmonic
weissenberg

beethoven programme
piano concerto 3/symphony 3

paris
23 june 1978
berlin philharmonic

dvorak symphony 9/mussorgsky pictures at an exhibition

paris
24 june 1978
berlin philharmonic
weissenberg
mutter
rostropovich

television concert
works by massenet/mozart/mussorgsky/offenbach/sibelius/j.strauss/strauss/verdi/wagner

salzburg
29 july and
4, 14, 17 and 25 august 1978
vienna philharmonic
vienna opera chorus

verdi don carlo
freni/randova/obraztsova (29 july)/carreras/ghiaurov/raimondi (17 august)/capuccilli

salzburg
3, 12, 16 and 26 august 1976
vienna philharmonic
vienna opera chorus

strauss salome
behrens/baltsa/böhm/ochman/van dam

salzburg
15 august 1978
vienna philharmonic

bruckner symphony 8

salzburg
27 august 1978
berlin philharmonic
zeltser
mutter
ma

beethoven triple concerto/stravinsky le sacre du printemps

salzburg
28 august 1978
berlin philharmonic
wiener singverein
freni
baltsa
carreras
ghiaurov

verdi messa da requiem

lucerne
30 august 1978
berlin philharmonic
wiener singverein
freni
baltsa
carreras
ghiaurov

verdi messa da requiem

lucerne
31 august 1978
berlin philharmonic
zeltser
mutter
ma

beethoven triple concerto/stravinsky le sacre du printemps

concert activity halted in september, october and november 1978 as a result of serious illness

berlin
9 and 10
december 1978
berlin philharmonic

stravinsky apollon musagete/strauss also sprach zarathustra

berlin
30 and 31
december 1978
berlin philharmonic

verdi forza del destino overture/bizet l'arlésienne suite 2/liszt hungarian rhapsody 2/berlioz marche hongroise/mascagni l'amico fritz intermezzo/suppé light cavalry overture

berlin
1 january 1979
berlin philharmonic

rossini guillaume tell overture/bizet l'arlésienne suite 2/liszt hungarian rhapsody 2/chabrier espana/puccini manon lescaut intermezzo/mascagni l'amico fritz intermezzo/gounod faust ballet music/suppé light cavalry overture

berlin
4 and 5
january 1979
berlin philharmonic

bach brandenburg concerto 3/berg three pieces/dvorak symphony 8

berlin
27, 28 and 29
january 1979
*berlin philharmonic
zeltser*

webern five pieces/schumann symphony 4/tchaikovsky piano concerto 1

berlin
24 and 25
february 1979
*berlin philharmonic
deutsche oper chorus
mathis
wohlers
salminen*

haydn die schöpfung

berlin
12 march 1979
berlin philharmonic

webern five pieces/stravinsky apollon musagete/berg three pieces

hamburg
13 march 1979
berlin philharmonic

mozart symphony 39/brahms symphony 1

hamburg
14 march 1979
berlin philharmonic

schubert symphony 8/brahms symphony 2

berlin
2 april 1979
berlin philharmonic

strauss festliches präludium
performed at opening ceremony of icc congress centre

salzburg
7 and 13
april 1979
berlin philharmonic
wiener singverein
tomowa-sintov
baldani
tappy
salminen/van dam

beethoven missa solemnis

salzburg
8 and 15
april 1979
berlin philharmonic
vienna opera chorus

verdi don carlo
freni/baltsa/carreras/ghiaurov/cappuccilli

salzburg
9 and 14
april 1979
berlin philharmonic

bruckner symphony 7

salzburg
10 and 16
april 1979
berlin philharmonic

dvorak symphony 8/mussorgsky pictures at an exhibition

vienna
6, 11 and 20
may 1979
vienna philharmonic
vienna opera chorus

verdi don carlo
freni/baltsa/carreras/raimondi/salminen
(20)/cappuccilli

vienna
12 and 13
may 1979
vienna philharmonic

bruckner symphony 8

salzburg
1 june 1979
berlin philharmonic
zeltser
mutter
ma

beethoven programme
triple concerto/symphony 7

salzburg
2 june 1979
berlin philharmonic

bach brandenburg concerto 4/bruckner symphony 4

salzburg
3 june 1979
berlin philharmonic

debussy la mer/debussy prélude a l'apres-midi/ravel boléro

sankt florian
4 june 1979
vienna philharmonic

bruckner symphony 8

linz
5 june 1979
berlin philharmonic

bach brandenburg concerto 4/bruckner symphony 4

tour of london, paris and düsseldorf by berlin philharmonic orchestra

london
18 june 1979
berlin philharmonic
zeltser
mutter
ma

beethoven triple concerto/strauss also sprach zarathustra

london
19 june 1979
berlin philharmonic

bruckner symphony 8

paris
21 june 1979
berlin philharmonic
zeltser
mutter
ma

beethoven triple concerto/strauss also sprach zarathustra

paris
22 june 1979
berlin philharmonic

mozart symphony 41/tchaikovsky symphony 5

paris
23 june 1979
berlin philharmonic

strauss till eulenspiegel
performance for radio france

düsseldorf
24 june 1979
berlin philharmonic

schumann symphony 4/mussorgsky pictures at an exhibition

düsseldorf
25 june 1979
berlin philharmonic

mozart symphony 39/brahms symphony 2

salzburg
26 and 30
july and
10, 13, 25 and 29
august 1979
vienna philharmonic
vienna opera chorus

verdi aida
freni/horne/carreras/raimondi/ghiaurov
(26 july)/cappuccilli

salzburg
29 july 1979
vienna philharmonic

haydn symphony 104/dvorak symphony 9

salzburg
14 august 1979
vienna philharmonic
vienna opera chorus

mozart le nozze di figaro
kanawa/mathis/ewing/van dam/krause
additional performances of figaro at 1979
salzburg festival conducted by bernhard klee

salzburg
27 august 1979
berlin philharmonic

mozart divertimento 15/strauss also sprach zarathustra

salzburg
28 august 1979
berlin philharmonic

stravinsky apollon musagete/tchaikovsky symphony 6

lucerne
31 august 1979
berlin philharmonic

mozart divertimento 15/strauss also sprach zarathustra

lucerne
1 september 1979
berlin philharmonic

brahms symphony 3/respighi pini di roma

berlin
5 september 1979
berlin philharmonic

beethoven symphony 6/strauss also sprach zarathustra

berlin
28 and 29 september 1979
*berlin philharmonic
zeltser
mutter
ma*

beethoven triple concerto/tchaikovsky symphony 5

berlin
6 october 1979
*berlin philharmonic
weissenberg*

strauss till eulenspiegel/gershwin rhapsody in blue/j.strauss fledermaus overture
part of a charity evening (kanzlerfest) in which other artists also participated

tour to tokyo and peking by berlin philharmonic orchestra
tokyo
16 october 1979
berlin philharmonic

mozart symphony 39/strauss also sprach zarathustra

tokyo
17 october 1979
berlin philharmonic

mahler symphony 6

tokyo
18 october 1979
berlin philharmonic

schubert symphony 8/tchaikovsky symphony 5

tokyo
19 october 1979
berlin philharmonic

dvorak symphony 8/mussorgsky pictures at an exhibition

tokyo
21 october 1979
*berlin philharmonic
wiener singverein
tomowa-sintov
baltsa
schreier
van dam*

beethoven symphony 9

tokyo
22 october 1979
berlin philharmonic
wiener singverein
tomowa-sintov
schreier
van dam

haydn die schöpfung

tokyo
24 and 26
october 1979
berlin philharmonic
wiener singverein
freni
baltsa
lima
ghiaurov

verdi messa da requiem

tokyo
25 october 1979
berlin philharmonic
wiener singverein
tomowa-sintov
baldani
schreier
van dam

mozart requiem/bruckner te deum

peking
29 october 1979
berlin philharmonic

mozart symphony 39/brahms symphony 1

peking
30 october 1979
berlin philharmonic

dvorak symphony 8/mussorgsky pictures at an exhibition

peking
1 november 1979
berlin philharmonic

beethoven programme
symphony 4/symphony 7

berlin
24 and 25
november 1979
berlin philharmonic

bach brandenburg concerto 1/beethoven symphony 3

berlin
8 and 9
december 1979
berlin philharmonic

strauss tod und verklärung/sibelius symphony 5

berlin
30 and 31
december 1979
berlin philharmonic
zeltser
mutter
ma

beethoven triple concerto/schumann symphony 4

berlin
1 january 1980
berlin philharmonic

j.strauss zigeunerbaron overture/annen polka/
künstlerleben/perpetuum mobile/an der
schönen blauen donau/fledermaus overture/
josef strauss delirienwalzer

berlin
26 and 27
january 1980
berlin philharmonic
mathis

berg lyric suite/mahler symphony 4

berlin
15 and 16
february 1980
berlin philharmonic
mutter

beethoven violin concerto/prokofiev symphony 5

berlin
17 february 1980
berlin philharmonic

berg lyric suite/prokofiev symphony 5

salzburg
30 march and
7 april 1980
berlin philharmonic
vienna opera chorus

wagner parsifal
vejzovic/hofmann/moll/halem/hornik/van dam

salzburg
31 march and
5 april 1980
berlin philharmonic
mutter

beethoven violin concerto/tchaikovsky
symphony 4

salzburg mozart requiem/verdi te deum
1 and 4
april 1980
berlin philharmonic
wiener singverein
tomowa-sintov
baltsa
araiza
halem/moll

salzburg bach brandenburg concerto 1/mahler symphony 4
2 and 6
april 1980
berlin philharmonic
mathis

vienna verdi don carlo
11, 15 and 19 *freni/baltsa/carreras/raimondi/cappuccilli*
may 1980 *karajan's final appearances in vienna staatsoper*
vienna philharmonic
vienna opera chorus

vienna stravinsky apollon musagete/mahler symphony 4
17 may 1980
berlin philharmonic
mathis

vienna beethoven violin concerto/strauss also sprach
18 may 1980 zarathustra
berlin philharmonic
mutter

salzburg mozart divertimento 17/berlioz symphonie
23 may 1980 fantastique
berlin philharmonic

salzburg berg lyric suite/prokofiev symphony 5
24 may 1980
berlin philharmonic

salzburg chopin piano concerto 2/schumann symphony 4
25 may 1980
berlin philharmonic
zimerman

tour of hannover, braunschweig, brussels, amsterdam and paris by berlin philharmonic orchestra

hannover
17 june 1980
berlin philharmonic

stravinsky apollon musagete/tchaikovsky symphony 6

braunschweig
18 june 1980
berlin philharmonic
mutter

beethoven violin concerto/prokofiev symphony 5

brussels
20 june 1980
berlin philharmonic
mathis

stravinsky apollon musagete/mahler symphony 4

amsterdam
21 june 1980
berlin philharmonic
mathis

stravinsky apollon musagete/mahler symphony 4

paris
22 june 1980
berlin philharmonic
mutter

beethoven violin concerto/tchaikovsky symphony 6

salzburg
30 july and
2, 13, 16, 25 and
29 august 1980
vienna philharmonic
vienna opera chorus

verdi aida
freni/baldani/carreras/raimondi/cappuccilli

salzburg
12 august 1980
european youth
orchestra
mutter

beethoven violin concerto/mozart symphony 41

salzburg
15 august 1980
vienna philharmonic

bruckner symphony 7

salzburg   mozart le nozze di figaro
26 august 1980   tomowa-sintov/stratas/schmidt/van dam/
vienna philharmonic   krause; additional performances of figaro at
vienna opera chorus   1980 salzburg festival conducted by gustav kuhn

salzburg   verdi messa da requiem
27 august 1980
berlin philharmonic
vienna opera chorus
freni
baltsa
carreras
raimondi

salzburg   bach brandenburg concerto 2/mahler
28 august 1980   symphony 4
berlin philharmonic
mathis

lucerne   penderecki polymorphia/mahler symphony 4
31 august 1980
berlin philharmonic
mathis

lucerne   chopin piano concerto 2/prokofiev symphony 5
1 september 1980
berlin philharmonic
zimerman

berlin   bach brandenburg concerto 3/stravinsky
26 and 27   symphony of psalms/strauss metamorphosen
september 1980
berlin philharmonic
deutsche oper chorus

tour of switzerland and west germany by berlin philharmonic orchestra
zürich   bach brandenburg concerto 2/bruckner
19 october 1980   symphony 7
berlin philharmonic

bern   stravinsky apollon musagete/mahler symphony 4
20 october 1980
berlin philharmonic
mathis

geneva   mozart divertimento 15/tchaikovsky symphony 4
21 october 1980
berlin philharmonic

mainz   schubert symphony 8/dvorak symphony 8
24 october 1980
berlin philharmonic

hoechst   brahms haydn variations/dvorak symphony 9
25 october 1980
berlin philharmonic

mannheim   stravinsky apollon musagete/mahler symphony 4
26 october 1980
berlin philharmonic
mathis

stuttgart   beethoven violin concerto/schumann symphony 4
27 october 1980
berlin philharmonic
mutter

munich   bach brandenburg concerto 2/bruckner
28 october 1980   symphony 7
berlin philharmonic

nürnberg   stravinsky apollon musagete/dvorak symphony 8
29 october 1980
berlin philharmonic

berlin   bruckner symphony 5
22 and 23
november 1980
berlin philharmonic

berlin
6 and 7
december 1980
berlin philharmonic

stravinsky apollon musagete/berlioz symphonie fantastique

berlin
27 december 1980
berlin philharmonic
pollini

beethoven piano concerto 3/tchaikovsky symphony 6

berlin
30 and 31
december 1980
berlin philharmonic
tomowa-sintov
rostropovich

strauss programme
4 letzte lieder/don quixote

berlin
1 january 1981
berlin philharmonic
mutter

bruch violin concerto 1/tchaikovsky symphony 6

berlin
25 and 31
january and
1 february 1981
berlin philharmonic

schoenberg verklärte nacht/beethoven symphony 7

berlin
19 february 1981
berlin philharmonic

penderecki polymorphia/shostakovich symphony 10

berlin
28 february and
1 march 1981
berlin philharmonic
wiener singverein
hendricks
perry
schreier
luxon

mozart mass in c minor/verdi te deum

salzburg
11 and 20
april 1981
berlin philharmonic
vienna opera chorus

wagner parsifal
vejzovic/hofmann/moll/van dam/hornik

salzburg
12 and 17
april 1981
berlin philharmonic
wiener singverein
mathis
araiza
van dam

haydn die schöpfung

salzburg
13 and 18
april 1981
berlin philharmonic

schoenberg verklärte nacht/beethoven symphony 7

salzburg
14 and 19
april 1981
berlin philharmonic
zimerman

schumann piano concerto/strauss ein heldenleben

vienna
9, 10 and 11
may 1981
vienna philharmonic

bruckner symphony 5

london
27 may 1981
berlin philharmonic

bruckner symphony 5

oxford
28 may 1981
berlin philharmonic
mutter

bach brandenburg concerto 2/mozart violin concerto 3/strauss metamorphosen
concert given in sheldonian theatre

paris
31 may and
1 june 1981
berlin philharmonic
paris opéra chorus

wagner parsifal, act three
ringart/hofmann/moll/van dam; this was a concert performance

salzburg
5 june 1981
berlin philharmonic

haydn symphony 103/beethoven symphony 5

salzburg
6 june 1981
berlin philharmonic
ma

haydn symphony 101/strauss don quixote

salzburg
7 june 1981
berlin philharmonic

haydn symphony 104/brahms symphony 1

düsseldorf
11 june 1981
berlin philharmonic

salzburg
26 and 30
july and
13, 17, 25 and 29
august 1981
vienna philharmonic
vienna opera chorus

verdi falstaff
kabaiwanska/perry/barbaux (13 and 17 august)/
schmidt/ludwig/araiza/taddei/panerai

salzburg
16 august 1981
vienna philharmonic
mutter

mozart mauerische trauermusik/brahms
violin concerto/dvorak symphony 8
mozart work played in memory of karl böhm

salzburg
27 august 1981
berlin philharmonic

bach brandenburg concerto 3/stravinsky
symphony of psalms/strauss metamorphosen

salzburg
28 august 1981
berlin philharmonic
duchable

bartok piano concerto 3/tchaikovsky symphony 6

lucerne
31 august 1981
berlin philharmonic
duchable

bartok piano concerto 3/tchaikovsky symphony 6

lucerne   bruckner symphony 5
1 september 1981
berlin philharmonic

berlin   *bartok programme*
25 and 26   piano concerto 3/concerto for orchestra
september 1981
berlin philharmonic
duchable

tour to tokyo by berlin philharmonic orchestra
tokyo   *beethoven programme*
28 october 1981   symphony 1/symphony 3
berlin philharmonic

tokyo   *beethoven programme*
29 october 1981   violin concerto/symphony 5
berlin philharmonic
mutter

tokyo   *brahms cycle*
30 october 1981   symphony 3/symphony 1
berlin philharmonic

tokyo   *brahms cycle*
31 october 1981   symphony 4/symphony 2
berlin philharmonic

tokyo   debussy la mer/debussy prélude a l'apres-midi/
2 november 1981   ravel boléro/ravel rapsodie espagnole
berlin philharmonic

tokyo   *beethoven programme*
4 november 1981   symphony 1/symphony 3
berlin philharmonic

tokyo   *beethoven programme*
5 november 1981   violin concerto/symphony 5
berlin philharmonic
mutter

tokyo
6 november 1981
berlin philharmonic

brahms cycle
symphony 3/symphony 1

tokyo
7 november 1981
berlin philharmonic

brahms cycle
symphony 4/symphony 2

tokyo
8 november 1981
berlin philharmonic

beethoven symphony 6/tchaikovsky symphony 6

berlin
21 and 22
november 1981
berlin philharmonic
brandis

bach violin concerto 2/bruckner symphony 9

leipzig
1 december 1981
berlin philharmonic

schumann symphony 4/strauss also sprach zarathustra

berlin
5 and 6
december 1981
berlin philharmonic
zimerman

schumann piano concerto/strauss eine alpensinfonie

berlin
30 and 31
december 1981
berlin philharmonic
mutter

bruch violin concerto/strauss eine alpensinfonie

berlin
24 january 1982
berlin philharmonic
duchable

bartok programme
piano concerto 3/concerto for orchestra

berlin   mahler symphony 9
30 and 31
january 1982
berlin philharmonic

visit to sofia by berlin philharmonic orchestra on 12-15 february 1982 was cancelled

berlin   puccini tosca
22 february 1982   *ricciarelli/carreras/raimondi; this was a*
berlin philharmonic   *concert performance of the opera*
rias choir

salzburg   wagner der fliegende holländer
3 and 12   *vejzovic/borris/goldberg/moser/van dam/moll*
april 1982
berlin philharmonic
vienna opera chorus

salzburg   mozart mass in c minor/bruckner te deum
4 and 9
april 1982
berlin philharmonic
wiener singverein
perry
borris
araiza
van dam

salzburg   mahler symphony 9
5 and 10
april 1982
berlin philharmonic

salzburg   *strauss programme*
6 and 11   *vier letzte lieder/eine alpensinfonie*
april 1982
berlin philharmonic
tomowa-sintov

four berlin philharmonic orchestra centenary concerts
berlin　　　　　　　　　　mozart symphony 41/beethoven symphony 3
30 april 1982
berlin philharmonic

berlin　　　　　　　　　　mahler symphony 9
1 may 1982
berlin philharmonic

vienna　　　　　　　　　　mahler symphony 9
3 may 1982
berlin philharmonic

vienna　　　　　　　　　　beethoven symphony 9
4 may 1982
berlin philharmonic
wiener singverein
tomowa-sintov
baltsa
goldberg
moll

salzburg　　　　　　　　　bruch violin concerto 1/brahms symphony 2
28 may 1982
berlin philharmonic
mutter

salzburg　　　　　　　　　bruckner symphony 8
29 may 1982
berlin philharmonic

salzburg　　　　　　　　　mozart symphony 29/shostakovich symphony 10
30 may 1982
berlin philharmonic

visit to hamburg and paris by berlin philharmonic orchestra
hamburg　　　　　　　　　*brahms cycle*
11 june 1982　　　　　　　symphony 3/symphony 1
berlin philharmonic

hamburg　　　　　　　　　*brahms cycle*
12 june 1982　　　　　　　symphony 4/symphony 2
berlin philharmonic

paris
14 june 1982
berlin philharmonic

schoenberg verklärte nacht/tchaikovsky symphony 5

paris
15 june 1982
berlin philharmonic

stravinsky apollon musagete/strauss eine alpensinfonie

salzburg
30 july and
2, 14, 17, 26 and
30 august 1982
vienna philharmonic
vienna opera chorus

verdi falstaff
kabaiwanska/perry/schmidt/ludwig/araiza/taddei/panerai

salzburg
18 august 1982
vienna philharmonic
wiener singverein
mathis
araiza
van dam

haydn die schöpfung

salzburg
27 august 1982
berlin philharmonic

mahler symphony 9

salzburg
28 august 1982
berlin philharmonic

stravinsky apollon musagete/strauss eine alpensinfonie

lucerne
31 august 1982
berlin philharmonie

haydn symphony 104/beethoven symphony 7

lucerne
1 september 1982
berlin philharmonic

stravinsky apollon musagete/bruckner symphony 7

berlin
17 september 1982
berlin philharmonic

mahler symphony 6

berlin
30 september 1982
berlin philharmonic

mahler symphony 9

tour of usa by berlin philharmonic orchestra

new york
19 october 1982
berlin philharmonic

stravinsky apollon musagete/strauss eine alpensinfonie

new york
20 october 1982
berlin philharmonic

brahms cycle
symphony 4/symphony 2

new york
22 october 1982
berlin philharmonic

brahms cycle
symphony 3/symphony 1

new york
23 october 1982
berlin philharmonic

mahler symphony 9

los angeles
27 october 1982
berlin philharmonic

brahms programme
symphony 4/symphony 2

los angeles
28 october 1982
berlin philharmonic

beethoven programme
symphony 4/symphony 7

pasadena
30 october 1982
berlin philharmonic

mozart symphony 39/tchaikovsky symphony 5

pasadena
3 november 1982
berlin philharmonic

brahms programme
symphony 3/symphony 1

berlin
20 and 21 november 1982
berlin philharmonic

beethoven programme
symphony 6/symphony 5

berlin
30 and 31
december 1982
berlin philharmonic
tomowa-sintov

strauss programme
vier letzte lieder/eine alpensinfonie

berlin
29 and 30
january 1983
berlin philharmonic
ashkenazy

beethoven piano concerto 4/saint-saens
symphony 3

berlin
31 january 1983
berlin philharmonic

beethoven programme
symphony 4/symphony 7

berlin
19 and 20
february 1983
berlin philharmonic
mutter
meneses

brahms 150th anniversary concert
double concerto/symphony 1

vienna
26 and 27
february 1983
vienna philharmonic

haydn symphony 104/tchaikovsky symphony 5

moscow
8 march 1983
vienna philharmonic
mutter

brahms 150th anniversary concert
violin concerto/symphony 1

moscow
9 march 1983
vienna philharmonic

haydn symphony 104/tchaikovsky symphony 5

salzburg
26 and 30
march and
4 april 1983
berlin philharmonic
vienna opera chorus

wagner der fliegende holländer
ligendza/borris/goldberg/winbergh/van dam/moll

salzburg
27 march and
2 april 1983
berlin philharmonic

brahms 150th anniversary cycle
symphony 4/symphony 2

salzburg
28 march and
3 april 1983
berlin philharmonic

brahms 150th anniversary cycle
symphony 3/symphony 1

salzburg
29 march and
1 april 1983
berlin philharmonic
wiener singverein
tomowa-sintov
van dam

brahms 150th anniversary cycle
ein deutsches requiem

vienna
2 may 1983
berlin philharmonic

brahms 150th anniversary cycle
symphony 4/symphony 2

vienna
3 may 1983
berlin philharmonic

brahms 150th anniversary cycle
symphony 3/symphony 1

vienna
7 and 8
may 1983
vienna philharmonic
wiener singverein
hendricks
van dam

brahms 150th anniversary cycle
ein deutsches requiem

salzburg
26 and 30
july and
12, 16, 25 and 29
august 1983
vienna philharmonic
vienna opera chorus

strauss der rosenkavalier
tomowa-sintov/perry/baltsa/cole/hornik/moll

salzburg　　　　　　　　*brahms 150th anniversary cycle*
14 and 15　　　　　　　ein deutsches requiem
august 1983
vienna philharmonic
wiener singverein
hendricks
van dam

salzburg　　　　　　　　*brahms 150th anniversary cycle*
27 august 1983　　　　　symphony 4/symphony 2
berlin philharmonic

salzburg　　　　　　　　*brahms 150th anniversary cycle*
28 august 1983　　　　　symphony 3/symphony 1
berlin philharmonic

lucerne　　　　　　　　*brahms 150th anniversary concert*
31 august 1983　　　　　symphony 3/symphony 1
berlin philharmonic

lucerne　　　　　　　　bruckner symphony 8
1 september 1983
berlin philharmonic

berlin　　　　　　　　　beethoven symphony 9
23 and 24
september 1983
berlin philharmonic
wiener singverein
perry
baltsa
cole
van dam

tour of west germany planned for october 1983 had to be cancelled

berlin　　　　　　　　　mozart divertimento 17/strauss eine
19 and 20　　　　　　　alpensinfonie
november 1983
berlin philharmonic

berlin
3 and 4
december 1983
berlin philharmonic

beethoven programme
symphony 4/symphony 7

berlin
30 and 31
december 1983
berlin philharmonic

schubert symphony 8/rossini guillaume tell overture/sibelius valse triste/smetana moldau/ josef strauss delirienwalzer/j.strauss zigeunerbaron overture

vienna
14 and 15
january 1984
vienna philharmonic

tchaikovsky programme
romeo and juliet/symphony 6

berlin
28 and 29
january 1984
berlin philharmonic

beethoven symphony 3
programme also included mozart concerto for two pianos with soloists eschenbach and frantz and conducted by eschenbach

berlin
25 and 26
february 1984
berlin philharmonic

beethoven programme
symphony 8/symphony 2

vienna
18 march 1984
vienna philharmonic

tchaikovsky programme
symphony 6/symphony 5

salzburg
14 and 23
april 1984
berlin philharmonic
vienna opera chorus

wagner lohengrin
tomowa-sintov/vejzovic/hofmann/büchner (23)/ nimsgern/moll

salzburg
15 and 21
april 1984
berlin philharmonic

tchaikovsky symphony 6
programme also included mozart concerto for two pianos with soloists eschenbach and frantz and conducted by eschenbach

salzburg
16 and 22
april 1984
berlin philharmonic
mutter
meneses

brahms double concerto/strauss also sprach zarathustra

salzburg   beethoven symphony 9
17 and 20
april 1984
berlin philharmonic
wiener singverein
perry
müller-molinari
büchner
van dam

tour of west germany by berlin philharmonic orchestra
mannheim   mozart divertimento 17/tchaikovsky symphony 6
4 may 1984
berlin philharmonic

frankfurt   beethoven symphony 4/strauss eine
5 may 1984   alpensinfonie
berlin philharmonic

frankfurt   mozart divertimento 17/tchaikovsky symphony 6
6 may 1984
berlin philharmonic

stuttgart   beethoven symphony 4/strauss eine
7 may 1984   alpensinfonie
berlin philharmonic

vienna   verdi messa da requiem
10 june 1984
vienna philharmonic
wiener singverein
tomowa-sintov
baltsa
carreras
van dam

salzburg   bach violin concerto 2/brahms symphony 1
11 june 1984
vienna philharmonic
mutter

vienna philharmonic concert also planned in sofia in june 1984 but did not take place

salzburg
31 july and
3, 11, 16, 25 and
29 august 1984
vienna philharmonic
vienna opera chorus

strauss der rosenkavalier
tomowa-sintov/perry/baltsa/cole/hornik/moll

salzburg
15 august 1984
vienna philharmonic
vienna opera chorus
tomowa-sintov
baltsa
carreras
van dam

verdi messa da requiem

salzburg
27 august 1984
vienna philharmonic
mutter

vivaldi le 4 stagioni/tchaikovsky symphony 6

salzburg
28 august 1984
vienna philharmonic
zimerman

schumann piano concerto/brahms symphony 1

lucerne
31 august 1984
vienna philharmonic
zimerman

schumann piano concerto/brahms symphony 1

lucerne
1 september 1984
vienna philharmonic
mutter

vivaldi le 4 stagioni/tchaikovsky symphony 6

vienna
23 september 1984
vienna philharmonic

haydn symphony 104/tchaikovsky symphony 4

tour of asia by berlin philharmonic orchestra

osaka mozart divertimento 15/strauss don juan/
18 october 1984 respighi pini di roma
berlin philharmonic

osaka debussy la mer/debussy prélude a l'apres-midi/
19 october 1984 ravel daphnis et chloé second suite
berlin philharmonic

tokyo mozart divertimento 15/strauss don juan/
21 october 1984 respighi pini di roma
berlin philharmonic

tokyo *beethoven programme*
22 october 1984 symphony 6/symphony 5
berlin philharmonic

tokyo *brahms programme*
23 october 1984 symphony 3/symphony 1
berlin philharmonic

tokyo debussy la mer/debussy prélude a l'apres-midi/
24 october 1984 ravel daphnis et chloé second suite
berlin philharmonic

seoul *beethoven programme*
27 october 1984 symphony 6/symphony 5
berlin philharmonic *first appearance in korea by orchestra and conductor*

seoul mozart divertimento 15/brahms symphony 1
28 october 1984
berlin philharmonic

berlin brahms symphony 4/strauss tod und
24 and 25 verklärung/strauss metamorphosen
november 1984
berlin philharmonic

berlin honegger symphony 3/brahms symphony 1
12 and 13
december 1984
berlin philharmonic

berlin
30 and 31
december 1984
berlin philharmonic
rias choir
mutter
blegen
müller-molinari
araiza
holl

bach programme
violin concerto 2/magnificat

vienna
12 and 13
january 1985
vienna philharmonic

mozart symphony 39/dvorak symphony 8

berlin
26 and 27
january 1985
berlin philharmonic
amoyal

berg violin concerto/brahms symphony 2

vienna
10 february 1985
vienna philharmonic
zimerman

schumann piano concerto/dvorak symphony 9

berlin
23 and 23
february 1985
berlin philharmonic

brahms symphony 3/strauss ein heldenleben

berlin
13 march 1985
berlin philharmonic
paris opéra chorus

bizet carmen
baltsa/perry/carreras/van dam; this was a concert performance of the opera

salzburg
30 march and
8 april 1985
berlin philharmonic
vienna opera chorus

bizet carmen
baltsa/perry/carreras/van dam

salzburg			beethoven symphony 4/strauss ein heldenleben
31 march and
6 april 1985
berlin philharmonic

salzburg			debussy la mer/debussy prélude a l'apres-midi/
1 and 7			ravel boléro
april 1985
berlin philharmonic

additional choral concert at 1985 salzburg osterfestspiele conducted by klaus tennstedt

tour to brussels, amsterdam, london, paris and gütersloh by berlin philharmonic orchestra
amsterdam		*brahms programme*
23 april 1985		symphony 3/symphony 2
berlin philharmonic

brussels			*beethoven programme*
25 april 1985		symphony 4/symphony 7
berlin philharmonic

london			beethoven symphony 4/strauss ein heldenleben
27 april 1985
berlin philharmonic

paris			mozart divertimento 15/strauss ein heldenleben
28 april 1985
berlin philharmonic

paris			*brahms programme*
30 april 1985		symphony 3/symphony 2
berlin philharmonic

gütersloh			mozart divertimento 15/brahms symphony 2
1 may 1985
berlin philharmonic

vienna			brahms ein deutsches requiem
26 may 1985
vienna philharmonic
wiener singverein
battle
van dam

salzburg
27 may 1985
berlin philharmonic

mozart divertimento 17/strauss also sprach zarathustra

rome
29 june 1985
vienna philharmonic
wiener singverein
battle
schmidt
winbergh
furlanetto

mozart coronation mass
performed as part of service for holy mass in the vatican led by pope john paul II

salzburg
26 and 30
july and
12, 16, 24 and 29
august 1985
vienna philharmonic
vienna opera chorus

bizet carmen
baltsa/perry/carreras/van dam

salzburg
15 august 1985
vienna philharmonic
mutter

tchaikovsky programme
violin concerto/symphony 4

salzburg
27 august 1985
berlin philharmonic
wiener singverein
battle
baltsa
winbergh
van dam

bach mass in b minor

salzburg
28 august 1985
berlin philharmonic

debussy la mer/debussy prélude a l'apres-midi/ravel boléro

lucerne
31 august 1985
berlin philharmonic

bruckner symphony 9

lucerne debussy la mer/debusy prélude a l'apres-midi/
1 september 1985 ravel boléro
berlin philharmonic

berlin beethoven missa solemnis
28 and 29
september 1985
berlin philharmonic
wiener singverein
cuberli
schmidt
cole
van dam

tour of west germany and switzerland by berlin philharmonic orchestra
hamburg debussy la mer/debussy prélude a l'apres-midi/
15 october 1985 ravel boléro
berlin philharmonic

hannover mozart divertimento 17/berlioz symphonie
16 october 1985 fantastique
berlin philharmonic

frankfurt *brahms programme*
17 october 1985 symphony 3/symphony 2
berlin philharmonic

stuttgart mozart divertimento 17/berlioz symphonie
18 october 1985 fantastique
berlin philharmonic

zürich *brahms programme*
20 october 1985 symphony 3/symphony 2
berlin philharmonic

geneva debussy la mer/debussy prélude a l'apres-midi/
21 october 1985 ravel boléro
berlin philharmonic

berlin
23 and 24
november 1985
berlin philharmonic

bruckner symphony 9
*programme also included bach jesu meine freude
with rias choir conducted by uwe gronostay*

berlin
7 and 8
december 1985
berlin philharmonic

debussy la mer/debussy prélude a l'apres-midi/
ravel daphnis et chloé second suite

berlin
30 and 31
december 1985
berlin philharmonic

weber freischütz overture/liszt hungarian
rhapsody 5/leoncavallo i pagliacci intermezzo/
puccini manon lescaut intermezzo/josef
strauss sphärenklänge/ravel boléro

berlin
25 and 26
january 1986
*berlin philharmonic
meneses*

furtwängler centenary concerts
schubert symphony 8/strauss don quixote

berlin
22 and 23
february 1986
berlin philharmonic

haydn symphony 104/raval pour une infante
défunte/mussorgsky pictures at an exhibition

salzburg
22 and 31
march 1986
*berlin philharmonic
vienna opera chorus*

verdi don carlo
*izzo d'amico/baltsa/carreras/cappuccilli/
van dam*

salzburg
24 and 30
march 1986
*berlin philharmonic
mutter*

bach violin concerto 2/bruckner symphony 9

salzburg mozart coronation mass/bruckner te deum
25 and 29
march 1986
berlin philharmonic
wiener singverein
bandelli
schmidt
winbergh
furlanetto

additional orchestral concert at 1986 salzburg osterfestspiele conducted by riccardo chailly

salzburg mozart divertimento 17/berlioz symphonie
18 may 1986 fantastique
berlin philhharmonic

salzburg schubert symphony 8/strauss don quixote
19 may 1986
berlin philharmonic
meneses

vienna mozart requiem/bruckner te deum
1 june 1986
vienna philharmonic
wiener singverein
tomowa-sintov
müller-molinari
cole
burchuladze

salzburg bizet carmen
26 and 30 *müller-molinari/izzo d'amico/carreras/van dam*
july and
11, 14, 21 and 23
august 1986
vienna philharmonic
vienna opera chorus

salzburg bruckner symphony 8
17 august 1986
vienna philharmonic

salzburg beethoven missa solemnis
27 and 28
august 1986
berlin philharmonic
wiener singverein
cuberli
schmidt
cole
van dam

lucerne mozart divertimento 15/brahms symphony 2
31 august 1986
berlin philharmonic

lucerne schubert symphony 8/strauss don quixote
1 september 1986
berlin philharmonic
meneses

berlin beethoven symphony 9
27 september 1986 *second performance of this concert on 28*
berlin philharmonic *september conducted by kazajumi yamashita*
wiener singverein
cuberli
müller-molinari
cole
burchuladze

concert activity in october and november 1986 halted due to illness

vienna *strauss family programme*
30 and 31 zigeunerbaron overture/sphärenklänge/annen
december 1986 polka/delirienwalzer/fledermaus overture/
and 1 january 1987 beliebte annen polka/vergnügungszug polka/
vienna philharmonic pizzicato polka/kaiserwalzer/perpetuum mobile/
unter donner und blitz/frühlingsstimmen/
ohne sorgen/an der schönen blauen donau/
radetzky march

berlin *brahms programme*
1 february 1987 haydn variations/symphony 1
berlin philharmonic

berlin
1 march 1987
berlin philharmonic

mozart symphony 29/berlioz symphonie fantastique

salzburg
11 and 20
april 1987
berlin philharmonic
vienna opera chorus

mozart don giovanni
varady/tomowa-sintov/battle/winbergh/ramey/ furlanetto/burchuladze

salzburg
13 and 17
april 1987
berlin philharmonic

beethoven symphony 6/mussorgsky pictures at an exhibition

salzburg
14 and 19
april 1987
berlin philharmonic

schubert symphony 8/strauss don quixote

additional concert at 1987 salzburg osterfestspiele conducted by carlo maria giulini

berlin
30 april and
1 may 1987
berlin philharmonic

mozart divertimento 17/strauss also sprach zarathustra

bern
5 may 1987
berlin philharmonic

mozart divertimento 17/strauss also sprach zarathustra

vienna
24 may 1987
vienna philharmonic

mozart symphony 41/schumann symphony 4

salzburg
7 june 1987
berlin philharmonic
mutter

vivaldi le 4 stagioni/tchaikovsky symphony 6

salzburg
8 june 1987
berlin philharmonic

beethoven symphony 4/mussorgsky pictures at an exhibition

HAROLD HOLT LIMITED
presents

The Berlin Philharmonic Orchestra

Herbert von Karajan

Brahms
Symphony No. 4 in E minor, Op. 98

Symphony No. 2 in D, Op. 73

Wednesday 10th June 1987

Royal Festival Hall   Programme £1

Festival of German Arts, London 1987
On the occasion of the 750th Anniversary of Berlin.
Promoted by The European Arts Foundation.
The Festival gratefully acknowledges the generous support of the Foreign Office and Embassy of the Federal Republic of Germany, the Senate of Berlin (West), and the Goethe-Institut London.
The sponsorship of the Festival of German Arts, London 1987 by Mercedes-Benz has been recognised by an award under the Government's Business Sponsorship Incentive Scheme, which is administered by the Association for Business Sponsorship of the Arts.

london
10 june 1987
berlin philharmonic

brahms programme
symphony 4/symphony 2

brussels
12 june 1987
berlin philharmonic

beethoven symphony 6/mussorgsky pictures at an exhibition

paris
13 june 1987
berlin philharmonic

mozart divertimento 17/berlioz symphonie fantastique

paris
14 june 1987
berlin philharmonic

brahms programme
symphony 4/symphony 2

salzburg
26 and 29
july and
1, 12, 17 and 25
august 1987
vienna philharmonic
vienna opera chorus

mozart don giovanni
varady/tomowa-sintov/battle/winbergh/ramey/furlanetto/burchuladze

salzburg
15 august 1987
vienna philharmonic
norman

wagner programme
tannhäuser overture/siegfried idyll/tristan prelude and liebestod

salzburg
27 august 1987
berlin philharmonic

schubert symphony 8/berlioz symphonie fantastique

salzburg
28 august 1987
berlin philharmonic

beethoven symphony 4/mussorgsky pictures at an exhibition

lucerne
31 august 1987
berlin philharmonic

mozart divertimento 17/berlioz symphonie fantastique

lucerne
1 september 1987
berlin philharmonic

beethoven symphony 4/mussorgsky pictures at an exhibition

berlin brahms ein deutsches requiem
26 and 27
september 1987
berlin philharmonic
wiener singverein
cuberli
grundheber

berlin vivaldi le 4 stagioni
28 october 1987 *opening concert of kammermusiksaal in the*
berlin philharmonic *philharmonie*
mutter

berlin mozart symphony 39/strauss ein heldenleben
1 november 1987
berlin philharmonic

tour of west germany by berlin philharmonic orchestra
hamburg beethoven symphony 6/mussorgsky pictures
2 november 1987 at an exhibition
berlin philharmonic

hannover *brahms programme*
3 november 1987 symphony 4/symphony 2
berlin philharmonic

düsseldorf schubert symphony 8/berlioz symphonie
4 november 1987 fantastique
berlin philharmonic

cologne beethoven symphony 6/mussorgsky pictures
5 november 1987 at an exhibition
berlin philharmonic

frankfurt schubert symphony 8/berlioz symphonie
6 november 1987 fantastique
berlin philharmonic

munich vivaldi le 4 stagioni/strauss eine alpensinfonie
8 november 1987
berlin philharmonic
mutter
concert on 7 november in stuttgart had to be cancelled at short notice

berlin   *wagner programme*
30 and 31   tannhäuser overture/siegfried idyll/tristan
december 1987   prelude and liebestod
berlin philharmonic
norman

vienna   mozart symphony 39/dvorak symphony 8
17 january 1988
vienna philharmonic

salzburg   puccini tosca
26 march and   *izzo d'amico/lima/grundheber*
4 april 1988
berlin philharmonic
vienna opera chorus

salzburg   mozart symphony 39/strauss eine alpensinfonie
28 march and
3 april 1988
berlin philharmonic

salzburg   brahms ein deutsches requiem
29 march and
1 april 1988
berlin philharmonic
wiener singverein
cuberli
grundheber/van dam

additional concert at 1988 salzburg osterfestspiele conducted by kurt masur

tour of japan by berlin philharmonic orchestra
osaka   mozart symphony 29/tchaikovsky symphony 6
29 april 1988
berlin philharmonic

osaka   beethoven symphony 4/mussorgsky pictures
30 april 1988   at an exhibition
berlin philharmonic

tokyo   mozart symphony 29/tchaikovsky symphony 6
2 may 1988
berlin philharmonic

tokyo
3 may 1988
berlin philharmonic

beethoven symphony 4/mussorgsky pictures at an exhibition

tokyo
5 may 1988
berlin philharmonic

mozart symphony 39/brahms symphony 1
karajan's final appearance in japan

salzburg
23 may 1988
berlin philharmonic

mozart symphony 29/strauss ein heldenleben

vienna
25 may 1988
berlin philharmonic

mozart symphony 29/strauss ein heldenleben

salzburg
6, 10 and 16
august 1988
vienna philharmonic
vienna opera chorus

mozart don giovanni
varady/tomowa-sintov/battle/aler/ramey/
furlanetto/burchuladze; additional
performances of don giovanni at 1988 salzburg
festival conducted by bruno weil

salzburg
15 august 1988
vienna philharmonic
mutter

tchaikovsky violin concerto/schumann symphony 4

salzburg
27 and 28
august 1988
berlin philharmonic
wiener singverein
cuberli/reese
grundheber

brahms ein deutsches requiem
karajan's final appearances at salzburg festival

lucerne
31 august 1988
berlin philharmonic

schoenberg verklärte nacht/brahms symphony 1
karajan's final appearance at lucerne festival

berlin
25 and 26
september 1988
berlin philharmonic

schoenberg verklärte nacht/brahms symphony 1

berlin   verdi messa da requiem
30 september and
2 october 1988
berlin philharmonic
wiener singverein
varady
quivar
cole
tomlinson

tour to vienna, paris and london by berlin philharmonic orchestra
vienna   schoenberg verklärte nacht/brahms symphony 2
3 october 1988
berlin philharmonic

paris   schoenberg verklärte nacht/brahms symphony 1
5 october 1988   *karajan's final appearance in paris*
berlin philharmonic

london   schoenberg verklärte nacht/brahms symphony 1
6 october 1988   *karajan's final appearance in london*
berlin philharmonic

berlin   *brahms programme*
22 and 23   symphony 3/symphony 4
october 1988
berlin philharmonic

vienna   bruckner symphony 8
20 november 1988
vienna philharmonic

berlin   prokofiev symphony 1/beethoven symphony 5
3 and 4
december 1988
berlin philharmonic

berlin   prokofiev symphony 1/tchaikovsky piano
30 and 31   concerto 1
december 1988   *karajan's final appearances in berlin*
berlin philharmonic
kissin

CARNEGIE HALL

1988-89 SEASON

FRIENDS OF THE VIENNA PHILHARMONIC ORCHESTRA
presents

Vienna Philharmonic Orchestra

Saturday Evening, February 25, and
Tuesday Evening, February 28, 1989, at 8:00

Herbert von Karajan, *Conductor*

SCHUBERT	Symphony No. 8 in B minor, D. 759 ("Unfinished")	
	Allegro moderato	
	Andante con moto	

Intermission

JOHANN STRAUSS	Overture to "Der Zigeunerbaron"
JOSEF STRAUSS	Sphären-Klänge Waltz, Op. 235
JOHANN STRAUSS	Annen-Polka, Op. 117
JOHANN STRAUSS	Perpetuum mobile: musicalischer Scherz, Op. 257
JOHANN STRAUSS	~~Unter Donner und Blitz Polka, Op. 324~~
JOHANN STRAUSS	Kaiser-Walzer, Op. 437

Tour Direction:
COLUMBIA ARTISTS MANAGEMENT INC.
165 West 57th Street, New York, NY 10019

The photographing or sound recording of any performance or the possession of any device for such photographing or sound recording inside this theater, without the written permission of the management, is prohibited by law. Offenders may be ejected and liable for damages and other lawful remedies.

new york
25 and 28
february 1989
vienna philharmonic

schubert symphony 8/j.strauss zigeunerbaron overture/annen polka/perpetuum mobile/radetzky march/josef strauss delirienwalzer/sphärenklänge
28 february concert was karajan's final appearance in the united states

new york
26 february 1989
vienna philharmonic

bruckner symphony 8

salzburg
18 and 24
march 1989
berlin philharmonic
vienna opera chorus

puccini tosca
barstow/pavarotti/fondary; 24 march performance was karajan's final operatic conducting appearance

salzburg
20 and 26
march 1989
berlin philharmonic
kissin

prokofiev symphony 1/tchaikovsky piano concerto 1

salzburg
21 and 27
march 1989
berlin philharmonic
wiener singverein
tomowa-sintov
baltsa
cole
burchuladze

verdi messa da requiem
27 march concert was karajan's final appearance with berlin philharmonic orchestra

vienna
23 april 1989
vienna philharmonic

bruckner symphony 7
karajan's final public conducting appearance before his death on 16 july 1989

appendix a
stage works conducted by herbert von karajan

aida verdi
arabella strauss
assassino nella cattedrale pizzetti
boris godunov mussorgsky
carmen bizet
carmina burana orff
catulli carmina orff
cavalleria rusticana mascagni
cosi fan tutte mozart
das rheingold wagner
de temporum fine comoedia orff
der fliegende holländer wagner
der rosenkavalier strauss
der waffenschmied lortzing
der wildschütz lortzing
die bürger von calais wagner-regeny
die entführung aus dem serail mozart
die fledermaus j.strauss
die frau ohne schatten strauss
die lustigen weiber von windsor nicolai
die meistersinger von nürnberg wagner
die walküre wagner
die zauberflöte mozart
don carlo verdi
don giovanni mozart
don pasquale donizetti
elektra mozart
falstaff verdi
fidelio beethoven
friedenstag strauss
giulio cesare handel
götterdämmerung wagner
hänsel und gretel humperdinck
il barbiere di siviglia rossini
il trionfo di afrodite orff
il trovatore verdi
la boheme puccini
la traviata verdi

stage works conducted by herbert von karajan/concluded

le nozze di figaro mozart
l'incoronazione di poppea monteverdi
lohengrin wagner
lucia di lammermoor donizetti
madama butterfly puccini
martha flotow
oedipus rex stravinsky
orfeo ed euridice gluck
otello verdi
parsifal wagner
pelléas et mélisande debussy
rigoletto verdi
salome strauss
schwanda der dudelsackpfeifer weinberger
siegfried wagner
tannhäuser wagner
tiefland d'albert
tosca puccini
tristan und isolde wagner
un ballo in maschera verdi
undine lortzing

appendix b
choral works conducted by herbert von karajan

a child of our time tippett
belshazzar's feast walton
cantata 50 bach
cantata profana bartok
canticum sacrum stravinsky
choral symphony beethoven
coronation mass mozart
die jahreszeiten haydn
die schöpfung haydn
ein deutsches requiem brahms
feier der neuen front trunk
great mass in c minor mozart
gurrelieder schoenberg
magnificat bach
mass in b minor bach
mass in e minor bruckner
matthäus-passion bach
messa da requiem sutermeister
messa da requiem verdi
missa papae marcelli palestrina
missa solemnis beethoven
nelson mass haydn
psalm 47 schmitt
psalmus hungaricus kodaly
requiem mozart
sinfonische friedensmesse philipp
symphony of psalms stravinsky
te deum bruckner
te deum verdi
von deutscher seele pfitzner
war requiem britten

appendix c
major pianists who appeared with herbert von karajan

aeschbacher adrian
arrau claudio
badura-skoda paul
baumgartner paul
casadesus robert
cortot alfred
demus jörg
erdman eduard
fischer annie
frantz justus
gilels emil
gulda friedrich
haskil clara
kallir lilian
kempff wilhelm
kolessa lubka
lipatti dinu
lupu radu
michelangeli arturo benedetti
pollini maurizio
richter sviatoslav
schuchter gilbert
uninsky alexander
wührer friedrich
zimerman kristian

anda geza
ashkenazy vladimir
backhaus wilhelm
brendel alfred
cherkassky shura
curzon clifford
duchable francois-rené
eschenbach christoph
fischer edwin
gieseking walter
gould glenn
hansen conrad
herzog gerty
kann hans
kissin evgeny
leimer kurt
loriod yvonne
meyer marcelle
ney elly
pommier jean-bernard
richter-haaser hans
then-bergh erik
weissenberg alexis
zeltser mark

appendix d
major violinists who appeared with herbert von karajan

amoyal pierre
brandis thomas
de vito gioconda
francescatti zino
gerle robert
grümmer detlef
kim yong uck
kremer gidon
menuhin yehudi
mutter anne-sophie
oistrakh david
parikian manoug
schneiderhan wolfgang
shiokawa yuko
szeryng henryk

borries siegfried
bustabo giulia
ferras christian
friedman eric
grumiaux arthur
hirschhorn philipp
kolberg hugo
kulenkampff georg
milstein nathan
neveu ginette
oistrakh igor
prihoda vasa
schwalbé michel
spierer leon
telmanyi emil von

appendix e
major cellists who appeared with herbert von karajan

borwitzky ottomar von
finke eberhard
hoelscher ludwig
machula tibor de
mainardi enrico
starker janos

cassado gaspar
fournier pierre
ma yo yo
meneses antonio
rostropovich mstislav
tortelier paul

appendix f
major sopranos who appeared with herbert von karajan

angeles victoria de los
arroyo martina
barbaux christine
battle kathleen
berger erna
borkh inge
brivkalne pauline
caballé montserrat
caniglia maria
casa lisa della
collier marie
crespin régine
cunitz maud
davy gloria
donath helen
fahrni helene
felbermayer anny
fuchs marta
galli gianna
gayer catherine
ginster ria
grob-prandl gertrud
grümmer elisabeth
hallstein ingeborg
heidersbach käthe
hillebrecht hildegard
ilitsch daniza
janowitz gundula
kabaiwanska raina
kittel hermine
konetzni anni
köth erika

angelici marthe
bandelli antonella
barstow josephine
behrens hildegard
bernard anabelle
briem tilla
brouwenstijn gré
callas maria
carteri rosanna
cebotari maria
cotrubas ileana
cuberli lella
danco suzanne
dernesch helga
duval denise
favero mafalda
freni mirella
fusco elisabetta
gatta dora
gencer leyla
grist reri
gruberova edita
güden hilde
harwood elizabeth
hendricks barbara
holm renate
izzo d'amico fiamma
jurinac sena
kanawa kiri te
kniplova nadezna
konetzni hilde
kuchta gladys

major sopranos who appeared with herbert von karajan/concluded

laszlo magda
lebrun louise
ligabue ilva
lipp wilma
mack hanni
martinis carla
micheau janine
miltschewa alexandrina
müller maria
noni alda
paruto mirella
pilou jeanette
price leontyne
reese sarah
rothenberger anneliese
rysanek leonie
scheppan hilde
schlüter erna
sciutti graziella
seefried irmgard
spletter carla
steffek hanny
stich-randall teresa
tebaldi renata
trötschel elfriede
ursuleac viorica
varnay astrid
vicenzi edda
zadek hilde
zeumer gerty

lazzarini adriana
lemnitz tiana
ligendza caterina
lubin germaine
martino adriane
mathis edith
miljakovic oliviera
moffo anna
nilsson birgit
nordmo-lövberg aase
perry janet
popp lucia
ratti eugenia
rethy esther
rünger gertrud
schech marianne
scheyrer gerda
schwarzkopf elisabeth
scotto renata
sighele metta
stader maria
stella antonietta
stratas teresa
tomowa-sintov anna
tucci gabriella
varady julia
vejzovic dunja
watson claire
zeani virginia
zylis-gara teresa

beilke irma
loose emmy
welitsch ljuba

goltz christel
roberti margherita

appendix g
major mezzos and contraltos who appeared with herbert von karajan

anderson sylvia
baldani ruza
barbieri fedora
berglund ruth
brice carol
canali anna maria
cervena sona
cossotto fiorenza
dominguez oralia
ewing maria
fassbänder brigitte
finnilä birgit
gorr rita
höffgen marga
hoffman grace
kenney margareta
lilowa margarita
ludwig hanna
malagu stefania
meyer kerstin
müller-molinari helga
pitzinger gertrud
radev marianne
rankin nell
reynolds anna
schiml marga
schröder-feinen ursula
simionato giulietta
stade frederica von
tegethoff else von
troyanos tatyana
verrett shirley
wagner sieglinde

angervö helga
baltsa agnes
berganza teresa
borris kaja
bumbry grace
cavelti elsa
chookasian lily
cvejic biserka
dow dorothy
forrester maureen
ferrier kathleen
fischer lore
hermann dagmar
höngen elisabeth
horne marilyn
klose margarete
ludwig christa
madeira jean
malaniuk ira
mödl martha
obraztsowa elena
quivar florence
randova eva
resnik regina
rössl-majdan hilde
schmidt trudeliese
siewert ruth
smith carol
szantho enid
töpper hertha
veasey josephine
villa luisa
watson jean

appendix h
major tenors who have appeared with herbert von karajan

albanese francesco
aldenhoff bernd
alva luigi
aragall giacomo
argyrus basso
bergonzi carlo
bonisolli franco
büchner eberhard
carreras josé
cioni renato
corelli franco
dermota anton
domingo placido
fernandi eugenio
gedda nicolai
grahl hans
gui henri
haefliger ernst
hollweg werner
kesteren john van
klein peter
kollo rené
kraus alfredo
kuen paul
lima luis
lorenz max
majkut erich
mccracken james
moser thomas
ochman wieslav
patzak julius
pistor gotthelf
poggi gianni

aler john
anders peter
araiza francisco
beirer hans
böhm karl-walter
brilioth helge
burrows stuart
cecchele gianfranco
cole vinson
craig charles
dickie murray
fehenberger lorenz
friedrich karl
goldberg reiner
grobe donald
guichandut carlo
hofmann peter
kalenberg josef von
king james
kmennt waldemar
konya sandor
krenn werner
laubenthal horst
limarilli gastone
ludwig walther
maslennikov aleksei
monaco mario del
noort henk
parly ticho
pavarotti luciano
prandelli giacinto
prevedi bruno

major tenors who appeared with herbert von karajan/concluded

raimondi gianni
rosvaenge helge
simoneau léopold
stefano giuseppe di
suthaus ludwig
tappy eric
tear robert
treptow günther
unger gerhard
vickers jon
winbergh gösta
winkler hermann
wittrisch marcel
wunderlich fritz
zednik heinz

rendall david
schreier peter
spiess ludovic
stolze gerhard
svanholm set
taubmann horst
thomas jess
uhl fritz
usunow dimiter
vinay ramon
windgassen wolfgang
witt josef
wohlers rüdiger
zampieri giuseppe
zimmermann erich

appendix i
major baritones and basses who appeared with herbert von karajan

adam theo	**bastianini** ettore
berry walter	**björling** sigurd
blanc ernest	**bockelmann** rudolf
borg kim	**braun** hans
bruscantini sesto	**burchuladze** paata
cappuccilli piero	**calabrese** franco
cava carlo	**christoff** boris
colzani anselmo	**crass** franz
czerwenka oskar	**dalberg** friedrich
dam josé van	**diaz** justino
domgraf-fassbänder willi	**dönch** karl
dooley william	**drissen** fred
duhan hans	**edelmann** otto
engen kieth	**evans** geraint
filacuridi mario	**fischer-dieskau** dietrich
fondary alain	**franc** tugomir
frantz ferdinand	**frick** gottlob
fuchs eugen	**furlanetto** ferruccio
ghiaurov nicolai	**ghiuselev** nicolai
glossop peter	**gobbi** tito
greindl josef	**grossmann** walter
grundheber franz	**guelfi** gian-giacomo
guthrie frederick	**halem** victor von
hendrix louis	**herlea** nikolai
höfermayer walter	**hoffman** ludwig
holl robert	**hornik** gottfried
hotter hans	**hüsch** gerhard
imdahl heinz	**kelemen** zoltan
kerns robert	**kipnis** alexander
krause tom	**krenn** fritz
kreppel walter	**kunz** erich
lagger peter	**leib** günther
london george	**luxon** benjamin
manowarda josef von	**metternich** joseph
meven peter	**mill** arnold van
milnes sherrill	**modesti** giuseppe
moll kurt	**neidlinger** gustav

major baritones and basses who appeared with herbert von karajan/concluded

neralic tomislav
nienstedt gerd
nimsgern siegmund
palombini mario
pasero tancredo
petri mario
petrov ivan
plishka paul
prey hermann
protti aldo
ramey samuel
rödin gustav
roux michel
salminen matti
schirp wilhelm
schöffler paul
sereni mario
sordello enzo
souzay gérard
taddei giuseppe
tadeo giorgio
talvela martti
uhde hermann
wächter eberhard
watzke rudolf
welter ludwig
zaccaria nicola

nicolai claudio
nilsson sven
palma piero da
panerai rolando
pernerstorfer alois

pflanzl heinrich
poell alfred
prohaska jaro
raimondi ruggiero
ridderbusch karl
roth-ehrang peter
rydl kurt
savarese ugo
schmitt-walter karl
scott norman
siepi cesare
sotin hans
stabile mariano

tajo italo
tomlinson john
vinco ivo
washington paolo
weber ludwig
wiener otto

Music and Books published by Travis & Emery Music Bookshop:

Anon.: Hymnarium Sarisburiense, cum Rubricis et Notis Musicis.
Agricola, Johann Friedrich from Tosi: Anleitung zur Singkunst.
Bach, C.P.E.: edited W. Emery: Nekrolog or Obituary Notice of J.S. Bach.
Bateson, Naomi Judith: Alcock of Salisbury
Bathe, William: A Briefe Introduction to the Skill of Song (c.1587)
Bax, Arnold: Symphony #5, Arranged for Piano Four Hands by Walter Emery
Burney, Charles: The Present State of Music in France and Italy (1771)
Burney, Charles: The Present State of Music in Germany, Netherlands... (1773)
Burney, Charles: An Account of the Musical Performances ... Handel (1784)
Burney, Karl: Nachricht von Georg Friedrich Handel's Lebensumstanden (1784)
Burns, Robert: The Caledonian Musical Museum ... Best Scotch Songs (1810)
Cobbett, W.W.: Cobbett's Cyclopedic Survey of Chamber Music. (2 vols.)
Corrette, Michel: Le Maitre de Clavecin (1753)
Crimp, Bryan: Dear Mr. Rosenthal ... Dear Mr. Gaisberg ...
Crimp, Bryan: Solo: The Biography of Solomon
d'Indy, Vincent: Beethoven: Biographie Critique (in French, 1911)
d'Indy, Vincent: Beethoven: A Critical Biography (in English, 1912)
d'Indy, Vincent: César Franck (in French, 1910)
Fischhof, Joseph: Versuch einer Geschichte des Clavierbaues (1853).
Frescobaldi, Girolamo: D'Arie Musicali per Cantarsi. Primo & Secondo Libro.
Geminiani, Francesco: The Art of Playing the Violin (1751)
Handel; Purcell; Boyce et al: Calliope or English Harmony: Vol. First. (1746)
Häuser: Musikalisches Lexikon. 2 vols in one.
Hawkins, John: General History of the Science & Practice of Music (5 vols. 1776)
Herbert-Caesari, Edgar: The Science and Sensations of Vocal Tone
Herbert-Caesari, Edgar: Vocal Truth
Hopkins and Rimboult: The Organ. Its History and Construction.
Hunt, John: Adam to Webern: the recordings of von Karajan
Hunt, John: several discographies – see separate list.
Isaacs, Lewis: Hänsel and Gretel. A Guide to Humperdinck's Opera.
Isaacs, Lewis: Königskinder (Royal Children) A Guide to Humperdinck's Opera.
Kastner: Manuel Général de Musique Militaire
Lacassagne, M. l'Abbé Joseph : Traité Général des élémens du Chant.
Lascelles (née Catley), Anne: The Life of Miss Anne Catley.
Mainwaring, John: Memoirs of the Life of the Late George Frederic Handel
Malcolm, Alexander: A Treaty of Music: Speculative, Practical and Historical
Marx, Adolph Bernhard: Die Kunst des Gesanges, Theoretisch-Practisch (1826)
May, Florence: The Life of Brahms (2nd edition)
May, Florence: The Girlhood Of Clara Schumann: Clara Wieck And Her Time.
Mellers, Wilfrid: Angels of the Night: Popular Female Singers of Our Time
Mellers, Wilfrid: Bach and the Dance of God
Mellers, Wilfrid: Beethoven and the Voice of God
Mellers, Wilfrid: Caliban Reborn - Renewal in Twentieth Century Music

Music and Books published by Travis & Emery Music Bookshop:

Mellers, Wilfrid: François Couperin and the French Classical Tradition
Mellers, Wilfrid: Harmonious Meeting
Mellers, Wilfrid: Le Jardin Retrouvé, The Music of Frederic Mompou
Mellers, Wilfrid: Music and Society, England and the European Tradition
Mellers, Wilfrid: Music in a New Found Land: ... ... American Music
Mellers, Wilfrid: Romanticism and the Twentieth Century (from 1800)
Mellers, Wilfrid: The Masks of Orpheus: ...... the Story of European Music.
Mellers, Wilfrid: The Sonata Principle (from c. 1750)
Mellers, Wilfrid: Vaughan Williams and the Vision of Albion
Panchianio, Cattuffio: Rutzvanscad Il Giovine (1737)
Pearce, Charles: Sims Reeves, Fifty Years of Music in England.
Pettitt, Stephen: Philharmonia Orchestra: Complete Discography (1987)
Playford, John: An Introduction to the Skill of Musick (1674)
Purcell, Henry et al: Harmonia Sacra ... The First Book, (1726)
Purcell, Henry et al: Harmonia Sacra ... Book II (1726)
Quantz, Johann: Versuch einer Anweisung die Flöte traversiere zu spielen.
Rameau, Jean-Philippe: Code de Musique Pratique, ou Methodes (1760)
Rastall, Richard: The Notation of Western Music.
Rimbault, Edward: The Pianoforte, Its Origins, Progress, and Construction.
Rousseau, Jean Jacques: Dictionnaire de Musique
Rubinstein, Anton : Guide to the proper use of the Pianoforte Pedals.
Sainsbury, John S.: Dictionary of Musicians. Vol. 1. (1825). 2 vols.
Serré de Rieux, Jean de : Les dons des Enfans de Latone
Simpson, Christopher: A Compendium of Practical Musick in Five Parts
Spohr, Louis: Autobiography
Spohr, Louis: Grand Violin School
Tans'ur, William: A New Musical Grammar: or The Harmonical Spectator
Terry, Charles Sanford: John Christian Bach (Johann Christian Bach) (1929)
Terry, Charles Sanford: J.S. Bach's Original Hymn-Tunes for Congregational Use
Terry, Charles Sanford: Four-Part Chorals of J.S. Bach. (German & English)
Terry, Charles Sanford: Joh. Seb. Bach, Cantata Texts, Sacred and Secular.
Terry, Charles Sanford: The Origins of the Family of Bach Musicians.
Tosi, Pierfrancesco: Opinioni de' Cantori Antichi, e Moderni (1723)
Van der Straeten, Edmund: History of the Violoncello, The Viol da Gamba ...
Van der Straeten, Edmund: History of the Violin, Its Ancestors... (2 vols.)
Waltern: Musikalisches Lexicon
Walther, J. G.: Musicalisches Lexikon ober Musicalische Bibliothec

Travis & Emery Music Bookshop
17 Cecil Court, London, WC2N 4EZ, United Kingdom.
Tel. (+44) 20 7240 2129

© Travis & Emery 2009

Discographies by Travis & Emery:
Discographies by John Hunt.

1987: 978-1-906857-14-1: From Adam to Webern: the Recordings of von Karajan.
1991: 978-0-951026-83-0: 3 Italian Conductors and 7 Viennese Sopranos: 10 Discographies: Arturo Toscanini, Guido Cantelli, Carlo Maria Giulini, Elisabeth Schwarzkopf, Irmgard Seefried, Elisabeth Gruemmer, Sena Jurinac, Hilde Gueden, Lisa Della Casa, Rita Streich.
1992: 978-0-951026-85-4: Mid-Century Conductors and More Viennese Singers: 10 Discographies: Karl Boehm, Victor De Sabata, Hans Knappertsbusch, Tullio Serafin, Clemens Krauss, Anton Dermota, Leonie Rysanek, Eberhard Waechter, Maria Reining, Erich Kunz.
1993: 978-0-951026-87-8: More 20th Century Conductors: 7 Discographies: Eugen Jochum, Ferenc Fricsay, Carl Schuricht, Felix Weingartner, Josef Krips, Otto Klemperer, Erich Kleiber.
1994: 978-0-951026-88-5: Giants of the Keyboard: 6 Discographies: Wilhelm Kempff, Walter Gieseking, Edwin Fischer, Clara Haskil, Wilhelm Backhaus, Artur Schnabel.
1994: 978-0-951026-89-2: Six Wagnerian Sopranos: 6 Discographies: Frieda Leider, Kirsten Flagstad, Astrid Varnay, Martha Moedl, Birgit Nilsson, Gwyneth Jones.
1995: 978-0-952582-70-0: Musical Knights: 6 Discographies: Henry Wood, Thomas Beecham, Adrian Boult, John Barbirolli, Reginald Goodall, Malcolm Sargent.
1995: 978-0-952582-71-7: A Notable Quartet: 4 Discographies: Gundula Janowitz, Christa Ludwig, Nicolai Gedda, Dietrich Fischer-Dieskau.
1996: 978-0-952582-72-4: The Post-War German Tradition: 5 Discographies: Rudolf Kempe, Joseph Keilberth, Wolfgang Sawallisch, Rafael Kubelik, Andre Cluytens.
1996: 978-0-952582-73-1: Teachers and Pupils: 7 Discographies: Elisabeth Schwarzkopf, Maria Ivoguen, Maria Cebotari, Meta Seinemeyer, Ljuba Welitsch, Rita Streich, Erna Berger.
1996: 978-0-952582-77-9: Tenors in a Lyric Tradition: 3 Discographies: Peter Anders, Walther Ludwig, Fritz Wunderlich.
1997: 978-0-952582-78-6: The Lyric Baritone: 5 Discographies: Hans Reinmar, Gerhard Huesch, Josef Metternich, Hermann Uhde, Eberhard Waechter.
1997: 978-0-952582-79-3: Hungarians in Exile: 3 Discographies: Fritz Reiner, Antal Dorati, George Szell.
1997: 978-1-901395-00-6: The Art of the Diva: 3 Discographies: Claudia Muzio, Maria Callas, Magda Olivero.
1997: 978-1-901395-01-3: Metropolitan Sopranos: 4 Discographies: Rosa Ponselle, Eleanor Steber, Zinka Milanov, Leontyne Price.
1997: 978-1-901395-02-0: Back From The Shadows: 4 Discographies: Willem Mengelberg, Dimitri Mitropoulos, Hermann Abendroth, Eduard Van Beinum.
1997: 978-1-901395-03-7: More Musical Knights: 4 Discographies: Hamilton Harty, Charles Mackerras, Simon Rattle, John Pritchard.
1998: 978-1-901395-94-5: Conductors On The Yellow Label: 8 Discographies: Fritz Lehmann, Ferdinand Leitner, Ferenc Fricsay, Eugen Jochum, Leopold Ludwig, Artur Rother, Franz Konwitschny, Igor Markevitch.
1998: 978-1-901395-95-2: More Giants of the Keyboard: 5 Discographies: Claudio Arrau, Gyorgy Cziffra, Vladimir Horowitz, Dinu Lipatti, Artur Rubinstein.
1998: 978-1-901395-96-9: Mezzo and Contraltos: 5 Discographies: Janet Baker, Margarete Klose, Kathleen Ferrier, Giulietta Simionato, Elisabeth Hoengen.

1999: 978-1-901395-97-6: The Furtwaengler Sound Sixth Edition: Discography and Concert Listing.
1999: 978-1-901395-98-3: The Great Dictators: 3 Discographies: Evgeny Mravinsky, Artur Rodzinski, Sergiu Celibidache.
1999: 978-1-901395-99-0: Sviatoslav Richter: Pianist of the Century: Discography.
2000: 978-1-901395-04-4: Philharmonic Autocrat 1: Discography of: Herbert Von Karajan [Third Edition].
2000: 978-1-901395-05-1: Wiener Philharmoniker 1 - Vienna Philharmonic and Vienna State Opera Orchestras: Discography Part 1 1905-1954.
2000: 978-1-901395-06-8: Wiener Philharmoniker 2 - Vienna Philharmonic and Vienna State Opera Orchestras: Discography Part 2 1954-1989.
2001: 978-1-901395-07-5: Gramophone Stalwarts: 3 Separate Discographies: Bruno Walter, Erich Leinsdorf, Georg Solti.
2001: 978-1-901395-08-2: Singers of the Third Reich: 5 Discographies: Helge Roswaenge, Tiana Lemnitz, Franz Voelker, Maria Mueller, Max Lorenz.
2001: 978-1-901395-09-9: Philharmonic Autocrat 2: Concert Register of Herbert Von Karajan Second Edition.
2002: 978-1-901395-10-5: Sächsische Staatskapelle Dresden: Complete Discography.
2002: 978-1-901395-11-2: Carlo Maria Giulini: Discography and Concert Register.
2002: 978-1-901395-12-9: Pianists For The Connoisseur: 6 Discographies: Arturo Benedetti Michelangeli, Alfred Cortot, Alexis Weissenberg, Clifford Curzon, Solomon, Elly Ney.
2003: 978-1-901395-14-3: Singers on the Yellow Label: 7 Discographies: Maria Stader, Elfriede Troetschel, Annelies Kupper, Wolfgang Windgassen, Ernst Haefliger, Josef Greindl, Kim Borg.
2003: 978-1-901395-15-0: A Gallic Trio: 3 Discographies: Charles Muench, Paul Paray, Pierre Monteux.
2004: 978-1-901395-16-7: Antal Dorati 1906-1988: Discography and Concert Register.
2004: 978-1-901395-17-4: Columbia 33CX Label Discography.
2004: 978-1-901395-18-1: Great Violinists: 3 Discographies: David Oistrakh, Wolfgang Schneiderhan, Arthur Grumiaux.
2006: 978-1-901395-19-8: Leopold Stokowski: Second Edition of the Discography.
2006: 978-1-901395-20-4: Wagner Im Festspielhaus: Discography of the Bayreuth Festival.
2006: 978-1-901395-21-1: Her Master's Voice: Concert Register and Discography of Dame Elisabeth Schwarzkopf [Third Edition].
2007: 978-1-901395-22-8: Hans Knappertsbusch: Kna: Concert Register and Discography of Hans Knappertsbusch, 1888-1965. Second Edition.
2008: 978-1-901395-23-5: Philips Minigroove: Second Extended Version of the European Discography.
2009: 978-1-901395--24-2: American Classics: The Discographies of Leonard Bernstein and Eugene Ormandy.

Discography by Stephen J. Pettitt, edited by John Hunt:
1987: 978-1-906857-16-5: Philharmonia Orchestra: Complete Discography 1945-1987

Available from: Travis & Emery at 17 Cecil Court, London, UK. (+44) 20 7 240 2129. email on sales@travis-and-emery.com .

© Travis & Emery 2009

www.ingramcontent.com/pod-product-compliance
Lightning Source LLC
Chambersburg PA
CBHW070823250426
43671CB00036B/1842